CHRISTIANITY

A new approach

Kevin O'Donnell

Acknowledgements

The publishers would like to thank the following for their permission to reproduce copyright material: The Bible Society for scripture quotations from the Good News Bible © American Bible Society 1966, 1971, 1976, published by the Bible Societies and Collins; Eyre and Spottiswoode (Publishers) Limited, Her Majesty's Printers London for extracts from the Book of Common Prayer 1662, which is Crown Copyright in the United Kingdom; The General Synod of the Church of England for material from The Alternative Service Book 1980. The Nunc Dimittis and the Apostles' Creed are copyright © the International Consultation on English Texts and other extracts and prayers are copyright © the Central Board of Finance of the Church of England.

Orders: please contact Bookpoint Ltd, 130 Milton Park, Abingdon, Oxon OX14 4SB. Telephone (44) 01235 827720, Fax: (44) 01235 400454. Lines are open from 9.00–6.00, Monday to Saturday, with a 24 hour message answering service.

You can also order through our website www.hodderheadline .co.uk

British Library Cataloguing in Publication Data

A catalogue record for this book is available from the British Library

ISBN 0 340 69777 6

First published 1998
Impression number   11   10   9   8   7   6   5
Year   2005   2004   2003

© 1998 Kevin O'Donnell

Typeset by Wearset, Boldon, Tyne and Wear.
Printed in Dubai for Hodder & Stoughton Educational, a division of Hodder Headline, 338 Euston Road, London NW1 3BH.

Photo Acknowledgements

The publishers would like to thank the following for permission to reproduce copyright photographs: AKG Photo pp15, 108, 109, 151, 165, 172, 173, 174; Andes Press Agency pp133, 135, 144, 186, 187r, 189, 190; British Library p70; CIRCA Photo Library pp3t, 4, 10, 19, 21, 34l, 35l, 43, 45, 51, 53, 55, 56, 58, 59, 60t, 76, 87l, 120t, 126, 127, 140t, 154, 144, 170, 175, 176; Donald Cooper (Photostage) p23; Corbis (Patsy Lynch) p102; Corbis (Corbis-Bettmann) p104; Daily Mirror p182; Phil and Val Emmett pp7, 8t, 30, 31, 38, 39, 50, 61, 65, 119, 129, 183; Life File pp35tr, 48, 107, 116, 145t, 152, 187t; Dr A A Mason/Weidenfeld (Publishers) Ltd p18; Popperfoto pp3b, 146; Religious Society of Friends p9; D Rose pp 8b, 42, 44 (both), 87r, 101, 120r, 123, 124, 139, 140b, 177; John Rylands Library, University of Manchester p27; Alison Stewart/Jan Thompson p32; Jan Thompson p46 (both); Mel Thompson pp5, 35br, 60b; Kim Till (Catholic Pictorial) p37; Topham Picturepoint pp12t, 34r, 141, 142t, 142r, 145b; Travel Ink/Jeremy Phillips p143; USPG p49; Paul Yates p147.

Every effort has been made to trace and acknowledge ownership of copyright. The publishers will be glad to make suitable arrangements with any copyright holders whom it has not been possible to contact.

The artwork for this book has been supplied by Jim Eldridge, Peter Hudspith and David Hancock.

Contents

CONTENTS

Preface

It is hoped that this book will provide a solid foundation and guide for the GCSE and KS4 courses on Christianity as a contemporary, world religion. It covers most of the syllabus content offered by the different boards, with only a few omissions to keep the book to a reasonable size.

This book adopts a variety of approaches in both visual and written material and in the different types of questions it sets. This is to cater for a wide ability range. The pupils are presented with a considerable amount of factual information on Christianity; they are helped to understand its meaning for practising Christians today; and they are encouraged to think about and discuss what they have studied and to offer their own opinions.

Teachers are advised to use the questions selectively, according to the abilities and interests of their pupils. There is an extensive Word List at the back of the book, giving definitions of much of the important Christian vocabulary in the book. When such a word appears for the first time, it is printed in heavy type to alert the reader to its use. Teachers may wish to set exercises on the meanings of these words as they appear in each chapter. The Word List can also be used for revision word-games at the end of the course; or simply for easy reference. Teachers will want to supplement the book with a variety of other resources and activities, such as field-trips, visiting speakers, videos and worksheets. There are some suggestions for activity-based learning throughout the book.

Setting out to study Christianity as a world religion can seem a formidable undertaking but I hope that pupils will find it stimulating and enjoyable.

K.O'D.

To the Heathfield girls

1

The Church for Beginners

The Christian **Church** today is divided into a number of different groups or denominations, but when Christianity first began there was only one Church. Local groups were led by **elders** or 'presbyters', later called **priests**, and had overseers called **bishops**. In the large cities there were senior bishops, and the bishop of Rome was given special respect.

After a while, however, various groups started separating from the main Church. A major split came in the eleventh century when the Western and Eastern sections of the Church separated from each other. Some Eastern Churches had separated earlier in the fifth century CE, over different ways of understanding Jesus.

Five hundred years later there was a major split in the Western Church. A movement known as the **Reformation** questioned many of the traditional teachings. These Reformed Churches, also known as **Protestant** Churches, would no longer accept the **Pope** (the bishop of Rome) as leader. Some of them kept bishops but some did not, looking mainly to the **Bible** for their guidance.

The Orthodox Churches and the Roman Catholic Church believe that the bishops are a living link with the first Church, descended in a long line from the Twelve Apostles. They also help to keep the right teachings. The Church of England, and some of the Lutheran Churches, kept a number of ancient traditions and also bishops. Though these are Churches influenced by the Reformation, they also have much in common with the Roman Catholics and the Orthodox.

This chapter will introduce the following Churches, or **denominations**:

* The Roman Catholic Church
* The Orthodox Churches
* The **Anglican** Church (which includes the Church of England)

ALL HAVE BISHOPS

* The Lutheran Churches

SOME HAVE BISHOPS

* The Methodist Church
* The Baptist Church
* The United Reformed Church
* The Pentecostal Church
* The House Churches
* The Society of Friends (Quakers)

FREE CHURCHES OR **NON-CONFORMIST** CHURCHES

The Roman Catholic Church

The Roman Catholic Church has the Pope as its leader. The Pope is the Bishop of Rome, and hence the Roman part of the name. The word **catholic** means 'worldwide' and all the churches in the world that are in union with the Pope are Roman Catholic churches. About half of all the Christians in the world are Roman Catholics.

We believe that Jesus made Peter the leader of the Church after his death, and that Peter took charge of the Church in Rome, and therefore that the bishops of Rome are his successors. The Pope lives in the Vatican, an independent state in Rome. The chief bishops help to advise him and they are called **cardinals**. Each local area has a bishop to look after it, with parish priests under him.

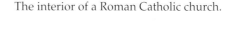

The interior of a Roman Catholic church.

The Pope, as the Bishop of Rome, is the leader of the Roman Catholic Church. Here he is blessing the crowd in Rome.

Activities

Key Elements

1 Who is the leader of the Roman Catholic Church and where does he live?
2 Why do Catholics think this person should be the leader of their Church?
3 What is a cardinal?
4 What is kept in the Tabernacle in a Catholic Church?

The Orthodox Churches

We call ourselves Orthodox *Christians because we believe that our Church has guarded the right belief since the time of Jesus (orthodox = 'right belief' and 'right worship'). The Pope in Rome separated from us in 1054. This was over a question of authority. We were happy to respect the Pope and treat him as an elder to come to for advice, but not as our ruler.*

Orthodox Churches are federations of Churches in different areas. Some areas have **patriarchs** over them and some have archbishops. Some patriarchs are given more honour than others, such as the Patriarch of Constantinople, who is known as the Ecumenical Patriarch. There are five patriarchs: of Constantinople (Istanbul), Antioch, Alexandria, Jerusalem and Moscow. Most Orthodox Christians live in Greece, Cyprus, Eastern Europe and the USSR. In Britain, Orthodox Christians are in the minority. The Russian Orthodox arrived here first, though the Greeks are now the largest community, and there are also many Serbians (from Yugoslavia). They, or their families, settled here either because of business or to escape troubles in their homeland. (There have also been some English converts.)

Activities

Key Elements

1   What are the leaders of the Orthodox Churches called?
2   What does 'Orthodox' mean?
3   When did the Orthodox Church and the Pope separate? What was the main reason for this?
4   Most Orthodox believers in Britain originally came from abroad; from which countries in the main?
5   What is an iconostasis?

In an Orthodox church there is an altar, but there is a screen in front of it that is decorated with paintings of Jesus, Mary and the saints (holy Christians from the past). This screen is called an **iconostasis**. There may be other paintings on the walls, and the ceiling is usually in the shape of a dome. This helps sound to carry, but it is also a symbol of God and Heaven (circles have no end, and so they stand for eternity, for everlasting life). Find out if there is an Orthodox church near you that you can visit.

The Anglican Church

The Church of England is a part of the world-wide Anglican Church, which includes, for example, the Church in Wales and the Church of South Africa, as well as many other national Churches.
*All Anglican Churches have the Archbishop of Canterbury as their figurehead. A number of bishops run the Church below him, with the help of the priests (also called **vicars**) and the people in each **parish**. A parish is an area under the care of a priest. There has been Christianity in England since Roman times, but the Church of England was separated from the Pope in 1534 when King Henry VIII ruled that the Pope had no authority in the English Church. The British monarch is still governor of the Church, but most decisions are taken by the Church leaders themselves. The monarch is now seen as a guardian or protector of the Church of England.*

A typical Church of England church. It has a tower, but others might have a pointed steeple. The churchyard is consecrated ground. This means that a bishop has blessed it and that people can be buried there. Why do some people want to be buried in a churchyard?

The Anglican Church is a mixture of Catholic and Protestant. You can find different styles in different parish churches. Some are more Protestant ('Low Church'), some are in between (Middle Church), and some are more Catholic ('High Church'). The Anglican Church is a 'bridge' church between extremes; it is Catholic and Reformed. Anglican Churches spread overseas when British explorers started colonising different parts of the world. British rule might have gone from those places, but the Churches remain.

Inside a typical Anglican church. The **altar** is where bread and wine are blessed. The priest preaches from the **pulpit**. The Bible is read from the **lectern**. Pews are wooden benches. The **font** is a container for water that is sprinkled on children when they are baptised.

KEY
A ALTAR   D CROSS
B PULPIT   E PEWS
C LECTERN   F FONT

SANCTUARY

CHANCEL

NAVE

The Lutheran Churches

The Lutheran Church began when some Christians separated from the Pope in the sixteenth century. We followed the teachings of a priest called Martin Luther. He wanted us to go back more to the Bible and to question many of the ways of worshipping God at the time. He stressed that we could not earn our peace with God. Jesus had died for us, and we simply had to turn to him.

Some Lutheran Churches kept bishops, as in Sweden, but others had no bishops who would support them. They appointed their own leaders. Some groups rejected the idea of bishops, arguing that the role of Pastor, teaching the Bible, was all that was necessary. (The minister in charge of an individual Lutheran parish is called a Pastor.) Some Lutherans have a great deal of ceremonial, and some have simpler services. Some Lutherans are more Catholic, some more Protestant, as with the Anglican Church. Lutherans and Anglicans are working very closely together today, with many recognising each other's priests and pastors.

Lutherans are found in Germany and parts of Europe, Scandinavia, and parts of the USA.

Activities

Key Elements

1   Who is the leader of the Anglican Church?
2   What is a bishop?
3   What is a parish?
4   When and why did the Anglican Church separate from the Pope?
5   Why did Anglican Churches spread over different parts of the world?
6   What do people mean when they say that some Anglican churches are 'low' and some are 'high'?
7   When did the Lutheran Churches begin?
8   Whose teachings started the Lutheran Churches?
9   What do Lutherans call their ministers?
10 Where would most Lutheran Christians be found today?

The Methodist Church

John Wesley started the Methodist Church. He was a Church of England priest who started preaching in the open air in 1739. He carried on travelling around and preaching until shortly before his death in 1791. The followers of Wesley were eventually forced to leave the Church of England and form their own Church. The name Methodist *came from Wesley's student days at Oxford. He and some friends followed a very strict,* religious life and others made fun of this methodical approach by calling them 'Methodists'.

The interior of a Methodist church. There is no altar. Instead there is the **Lord's Table** where the bread and wine are placed. How does this church interior differ from any of the others shown so far?

Each circuit is part of a wider district, and Methodist **ministers** (their leaders are not called priests) are expected to move around the circuit. There are no bishops but there is an annual Methodist conference where policies are decided upon. Representatives are sent to it from the various circuits. A president is elected each year.

The Baptist Church

Baptists believe that people should only be baptised in water when they are old enough to understand what they are doing. They also baptise people fully in water, and do not just sprinkle them. The first Baptist church was opened in London in 1611. Baptist churches are all independent, but most of them belong to the Baptist Union, a federation which is an advisory body.

Baptist churches have a similar layout to Methodist ones. There is the pulpit and the lectern, with a simple Lord's Table in front. The main difference is that, instead of a font, there is a pool under covers near the pulpit and Table. This is the **baptistry** and it is filled with water on special occasions.

The United Reformed Church

The United Reformed Church was formed in 1972 when two Churches joined together – the Congregational Church and the Presbyterian Church in England. Each congregation (people who regularly attend a church) is independent and elects its own minister. All the churches are part of a federation with twelve **moderators** acting as overseers. Britain is divided up between them into Provinces. A moderator is elected, and can stop being one later, unlike a bishop, who, once consecrated, always remains a bishop.

Pentecostal worship.

The Pentecostal Church

Pentecostal churches began at the turn of the century. They have joyful worship, where anyone is free to take part, and lively singing. They claim to have had a special blessing from the Spirit of God. Pentecostal churches are independent, but belong to different federations, such as the Assemblies of God, or the Church of God of Prophecy.

The House Churches or New Churches

The House Church movement started in the 1960s and has grown rapidly. These Christians usually meet in houses rather than church buildings because they feel that this is more friendly. Some members were brought up in other denominations, but they wanted a freer type of worship. They do not have ceremonial and decoration. They have modern music and feel free to clap and dance.

Each House church is run by an elder who is elected, and they belong to federations. (There are five main ones, such as 'New Frontiers' or 'The Vineyard Fellowship'.) Worship is very informal, like the Pentecostal churches. Some groups of House churches have gained so many members that they meet in rented halls, sports centres or even in church buildings that they have bought, and many now call themselves 'New Churches'.

The Society of Friends

Is there any special decoration in this building? Is there an obvious leader? What does this suggest about the beliefs of the people?

The Quakers do not call themselves a Church but a 'Society of Friends'. They do not have any set beliefs, and some members would not quite believe the same things about Jesus as other Christians. They worship in silence, and people will pray or speak if they feel moved to do so by the presence of God within their minds. They are committed to working for peace and justice in society.

This movement began in the seventeenth century when George Fox went around preaching. He warned some people to 'tremble at the Word of the Lord' and his followers were then given the nickname of Quakers.

Activities

Key Elements

1   Who started the Methodist Church? Did he intend to start a new Church?
2   What is a Methodist circuit?
3   When was the first Baptist church opened in Britain?
4   What is the main difference in the beliefs of a Baptist from those of other Christians?
5   When was the United Reformed Church founded, and which two Churches joined together to form it?
6   Which people are in charge of the national United Reformed Church? How many of them are there?
7   What would seem to be very different about a Pentecostal service compared to other services?
8   Find out why there are many Black Pentecostal churches in Britain. Do you think it was better for them to form their own churches?
9   What is meant by a House Church? Why do some people prefer it?
10 How did Quakers get their name?
11 What happens during their meetings? What do you think of this?

So, the Christian faith is found in many countries of the world and includes people of many different races. And there are a variety of Christian groups, denominations or 'Churches', all with slightly different beliefs or customs. Many Christians – one Christ; many styles of worshipping God – one basic faith. Think of soap powder. There are many different brands which perform in slightly different ways, and might be suited to particular machines, but they are all soap powder for washing clothes!

Assignments

1 Draw a map of your town or village and mark in as many churches of different denominations as you can find.
2 Visit three different church buildings in your area and write a description of each of them. Use photographs or diagrams to help you.
3 Write a paragraph listing the denominations that you know of and stating your views on whether it is wrong or right to have all these different denominations.

4 Write an essay on bishops: (i) say which Churches have bishops, and why, (ii) say what other Churches have instead, (iii) conclude with whether you think it is better to have bishops or not.
5 Look at this photograph of a church service:
   a) Can you identify which denomination it is? Say why you think this.
   b) Can you name three items in the picture and say what they are for?

2

Jesus

When and Where Did He Live?

Jesus of Nazareth lived from about 4 BCE to 30 CE. (BCE used to be called BC = Before Christ; CE was AD = In the year of the Lord, or after Christ's birth.) It is surprising to hear that he was born in the years BC, but a monk made a mistake when the BC/AD scheme was being worked out. Jesus died in 30 or 33 CE.

He was born in the land of Judaea, where Israel and Palestine are today, and brought up in Galilee in the north. He was a Jew by birth and by religion. (He was not a Christian; his followers were called that later on.) Jesus might not have intended to start a new religion, but rather to renew and enrich Judaism, and to bring blessings to all people through it. How Christianity developed as a new faith, separate from Judaism, is described later in this book.

Galilee and Judaea were under the control of the Romans during the lifetime of Jesus. Galilee was ruled by Herod Antipas, a son of Herod the Great, who had to be careful to stay in favour with Rome. Judaea was ruled directly by Rome (since 6 CE) through a prefect (a governor of a province). Pontius Pilate was governor from 26–36 CE. Tiberius was the Emperor of Rome for most of that time (14–37 CE).

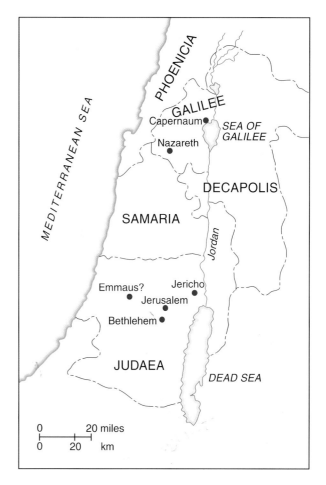

Bethlehem – Jesus was born here, in a stable that was probably a cave.
Nazareth – Jesus was brought up here and worked as a carpenter, joiner or builder.
Jerusalem – Jesus visited the Temple here several times, and spent the last week of his life teaching here.
River Jordan – Jesus was baptised here by John.
Capernaum – Jesus stayed here often during the first part of his ministry. Mary Magdalene came here to hear him teach.

The Messiah

The Jews longed for the coming of a special man, the **Messiah** (= the Anointed One, or the Chosen One). There were many different ideas current about the Messiah, but most people hoped that he would be like one of the old kings of Israel, whom God would help to fight and destroy the Romans. Some thought that there would be a final battle that would shake the earth, and that God would re-create everything. A time of peace and joy would follow, as described in the Book of Isaiah in the Hebrew Bible (which Christians call the Old Testament):

Wolves and sheep will live together in peace,
and leopards will lie down with young goats. . . .
On Zion, God's sacred hill,
there will be nothing harmful or evil.
The land will be as full of knowledge of the
    LORD
as the seas are full of water.   (Isaiah 11:6, 9)

The atmosphere was electric at the time. Some people were known as **Zealots**. They were planning to rise up against the Romans and throw them out by force. Others withdrew to the desert and joined monastic groups such as the Qumran Community near the Dead Sea. These people prayed and studied, and waited for the Messiah. Their writings (known to us as the Dead Sea Scrolls) were preserved in caves near the Dead Sea, and have now been translated and studied by scholars.

The Qumran Community was probably run by a religious group known as the **Essenes**, who also had a number of followers who lived on the outskirts of towns. Some were full members who donated all their wealth into a common treasury, and some were lay members, who worshipped with the others. The Essenes practised **baptism** – their members would have frequent ritual baths to purify themselves.

There might have been a number of different baptist movements in the country then, all having slightly different rituals, but all hoping for the coming of the Messiah. Baptism was probably practised to make a special point: new converts to Judaism were baptised to show that they had turned away from their old way and started a new life. Jews were baptised into the new movements to show that they were turning away from their sins and preparing for the coming of the Messiah.

The Dead Sea Scrolls were written in Hebrew and Aramaic and stored in jars in caves near the Dead Sea, probably to protect them from the Romans. They contain a number of commentaries on books of the Bible, including the earliest complete copy of Isaiah. These photographs show the caves where the scrolls were discovered and part of the Psalms scroll.

One holy man at the time, John the Baptist, taught that the Messiah was about to arrive and (according to the stories of Jesus in the **Gospels** in the New Testament) he baptised Jesus in the River Jordan, and came to believe that Jesus was the Messiah.

John spoke of the Messiah as a coming judge who would shake up the nation:

'I baptise you with water to show that you have repented, but the one who will come after me will baptise you with the Holy Spirit and fire. He is much greater than I am; and I am not good enough even to carry his sandals. He has his winnowing shovel with him to thresh out all the grain. He will gather his wheat into his barn, but he will burn the chaff in a fire that never goes out.'

(Matthew 3:11–12)

Besides these Messianic groups, there were the **Pharisees** and the **Sadducees**. The Pharisees were careful to keep all the laws of Moses and, although Jesus in the Gospels sometimes attacks them as hypocrites (people who were pretending to be good and making a show of their religion), most of them were faithful and holy people.

The Sadducees controlled the Temple in Jerusalem, and had a majority in the Sanhedrin, the Jewish Parliament. Many of them were rich landowners, and they were eager to please the Romans and compromise wherever they could. They wanted to keep the peace, and suspected any new movement of being dangerous.

Jesus was a holy man with a group of disciples. In some ways he would have been close to the Pharisees, preaching a holy lifestyle. In other ways his followers can best be seen as part of the widespread Messianic movement of the time. Some have even suggested that he might have had links with the Essenes (though some of his ideas were very different). His preaching ministry began when he was baptised by John in the Jordan. Jesus must have identified himself with the baptist movements. The four Gospels all mention a religious experience that Jesus had at this time:

As soon as Jesus came up out of the water, he saw heaven opening and the Spirit coming down on him like a dove. And a voice came from heaven, 'You are my own dear Son. I am pleased with you.' (Mark 1:10–11)

Activities

Key Elements

1 When did Jesus live?
2 Was Jesus a Jew or a Christian?
3 What did Jesus hope would happen to the Jewish faith?
4 Why are the following places connected with the life of Jesus: Bethlehem, Nazareth, Capernaum, the River Jordan, Jerusalem?
5 What does the word 'Messiah' mean?

Think about it

6 Why do you think many people joined baptising groups at this time?

We are probably meant to understand that Jesus had a vision, like a waking dream, of God's Spirit resting upon him like a dove, representing peace. The voice was calling him to be the Messiah, God's Man on earth.

'Jesus Christ' was not Jesus' proper name. **Christ** was a title, the Greek word for 'Messiah'. 'Jesus Christ' means 'Jesus the Messiah'. Jesus' proper name would have been something like Jesus Bar Joseph (Jesus, son of Joseph). Jesus meant 'God is Saviour'.

A number of details in Jesus' life were seen as fulfilling prophecies about the coming of the Messiah in the Hebrew Bible:

- He was born in Bethlehem.

> The LORD says, 'Bethlehem Ephrathah, you are one of the smallest towns in Judah, but out of you I will bring a ruler for Israel, whose family line goes back to ancient times.'
> (Micah 5:2)

- He worked many signs and wonders, healing the sick.

> The blind will be able to see, and the deaf will hear.
> The lame will leap and dance . . .
> (Isaiah 35:5–6)

- He came riding into Jerusalem on a donkey towards the end of his ministry.

> Look, your king is coming to you!
> He comes triumphant and victorious, but humble and riding on a donkey . . .
> (Zechariah 9:9)

However, he did not fight the Romans; he was eventually crucified by them, and to many people he was a failure. There were no earth-shaking changes. That is why some people mocked him on the cross: 'Come down from the cross and save yourself!' Even John the Baptist seems to have doubted whether Jesus was the Messiah at one point (read Matthew 11:2–6). This was the main reason for the eventual split between Christianity and Judaism – many Jews could not, and cannot, see how Jesus could have been the Messiah if he did not change everything and bring peace on earth.

Christians believe that Jesus was a very unexpected type of Messiah. He was a man of peace and not a mighty warrior. He came to show people the way to live, quietly, not forcing his way upon anyone. If people follow his teaching, then there will be peace, they believe. He showed people the way; it is up to them to work to bring it about. Christians believe that Jesus was raised from the dead to prove that he was the Messiah. The cross was not the final word.

Activities

Key Elements

1. What was Jesus' actual name? What does 'Jesus Christ' mean?
2. Name three religious groups that existed at the time of Jesus. Describe each of them briefly.
3. Mention three Old Testament prophecies that Jesus was thought to have fulfilled. Why did some of the Jews refuse to accept him as the Messiah, even so?

Assignments

1. Write a paragraph describing what happened when Jesus was baptised in the River Jordan. What did it mean for Jesus? What did the symbols of water and the dove represent?
2. Write an imaginary debate between a Jew and a Christian about Jesus being the Messiah. Have each of them make a strong case, and be sure to include their feelings.

What Did Jesus Look Like?

There is no description of Jesus in the New Testament. It is only tradition that shows him with long hair and a beard. There could be some truth in this, since some Jewish holy men did grow their hair and beards long as a sign of being dedicated to God. Jesus would have had black hair and a coloured skin.

Many pictures of Jesus do show him with brown hair, brown beard and blue eyes. This is just to make Jesus look European. How do you think Jesus would be portrayed in Chinese or Indian art? People want to imagine Jesus as one of their own race.

Jesus' father, Joseph, worked as either a carpenter, a joiner or a builder (the Greek word used in the Gospels could mean any of the three). Presumably Jesus learned his father's trade and worked in Nazareth until his baptism in the Jordan. This would place Jesus among the lower middle classes, with their own small family businesses. He spoke Aramaic, which was the common language of the day, and he would have had a Northern accent as he came from Galilee. The distance of Nazareth from Jerusalem is roughly that of Birmingham from London.

Questions

- What trade did Jesus follow before he became a preacher?
- What language did he speak?

Although we do not know what Jesus looked like, Christian artists have created many images of him. This seventh or eighth century fresco is on the wall of a catacombe in Rome, a place used for Christian worship since the third century.

Jesus' Ministry

The New Testament hardly tells you anything about the childhood of Jesus. Most of the stories are about the last three years of his life, and then, mainly about his last week!

The Gospels present a series of sayings and stories strung together in a loose framework. This framework traces his ministry from his baptism, when he was about thirty, until his death about three years later. The framework is summed up by Peter in a speech in Acts 10:37–41:

'You know of the great event that took place throughout the land of Israel, beginning in Galilee after John preached his message of baptism. You know about Jesus of Nazareth and how God poured out on him the Holy Spirit and power. He went everywhere, doing good and healing all who were under the power of the Devil, for God was with him. . . . Then they put him to death by nailing him to a cross. But God raised him from death three days later and caused him to appear, not to everyone, but only to the witnesses that God had already chosen.'

- His preaching started in Galilee.
- News spread about him because of his healings.
- He was put to death in Jerusalem.
- The disciples believed that he had risen three days later and appeared to them.

There are many details that we are not told in the Gospels – they are not like biographies. They give us only an outline of the career of Jesus, and an impression of him.

A Miracle Worker?

The Gospels contain many miracle stories. These can be divided into four types: healing, nature, raising and exorcism. Most of the miracles that Jesus is supposed to have worked are of *healing*. The story of the paralysed man is one example: read it in Mark 2:1–12. Here, Jesus performed a cure because of the faith of the paralysed man's friends. The Gospel writer was trying to show the authority of Jesus – an authority to forgive and to heal, as the Messiah.

Nature miracles are when Jesus affects the laws of nature, such as the story of him walking on water in Mark 6:45–52:

'[Jesus] saw that his disciples were straining at the oars, because they were rowing against the wind, so some time between three and six o'clock in the morning he came to them, walking on the water . . . "It's a ghost!" they thought, and screamed. They were all terrified when they saw him.'

(Mark 6:48–50)

Here, Jesus seems to perform something more supernatural, and the Gospel writer probably intended his readers to recognise the power of God he saw to be at work in Jesus. There are only five nature miracles recorded in the Gospels, as against the many healing stories.

There are also a few *raising the dead miracles*. Read about Jairus's daughter in Mark 5:21–4, 35–43. The Gospel writer saw this story as showing that Jesus had power over death, and it prefigured his own **resurrection**. The difference was that the little girl was revived by Jesus but then she lived out her life and died later on. In the story of the resurrection of Jesus, he is supposed to live for ever, in a spiritual way.

Another type of miracle story is that of *exorcism*. Read Mark 5:1–20. Exorcism – driving evil spirits out of someone – was a sign of having God's blessing and power. Many of the Jews then believed that the air was filled with evil spirits that were trying to control people, given half a chance. Mentally ill people, and sufferers from epilepsy, were thought to be demon-possessed because people knew so little about the human brain and mind then. Jesus, as the Messiah, cured a deeply disturbed person, and this was seen as a victory over the forces of evil.

Activities

Key Elements

1 Describe one example of a healing miracle from the Gospels. What was the writer trying to tell his readers about Jesus?

2 Describe one example of a nature miracle from the Gospels. What was the point of this story?

3 Describe one example of a raising from the dead story in the Gospels. What was the story trying to tell people about Jesus?

4 Describe one example of an exorcism from the Gospels. What was this trying to say about Jesus?

Did Jesus Really Work Miracles?

- Some people think that all the miracle stories are legends, and that they were added to the story of Jesus as it was handed down. They made him seem more special in a time when many more people believed in magic and the supernatural than today. There were many stories of gods appearing and performing cures in the Roman Empire, such as among the worshippers of the god Asclepius. His temples were full of people who hoped to be healed through their prayers and their sacrifices. According to this point of view, Jesus was a good and holy preacher, whose words helped and changed many people for the better, but there were no actual miracles. They were exaggerations added to the story later.

However, many people do think that Jesus worked miracles. There are two points of view here, and it all depends on what is meant by a 'miracle':

- Some understand 'miracle' as an event contrary to the laws of nature: God suspends the laws of nature that he has created, to intervene in the world in a special way. So, a cure or the ability to walk on water are direct actions of God breaking into our lives. They are beyond nature (hence 'supernatural') and beyond our understanding, but these people believe that God is all-powerful and can work such miracles.

- The other way of understanding 'miracle' is as the operation of laws of nature that we do not understand yet. So, a few centuries ago an electric light would have seemed like magic, or a miracle, to the people then, and science might discover many new things that seem to be impossible to us now. Jesus, therefore, might have been using forces that we do not know of yet, like some kind of mind-over-matter ability. The power of the mind is just being discovered by scientists. The way we feel can affect our bodies and our health. If we are very nervous we might be physically ill. If we feel very guilty about something, then it might affect us in a number of ways. In extreme cases it might cause paralysis (the medical term is catatonic schizophrenia). Perhaps then, one day, we shall be able to explain Jesus' miracles and find them more easy to accept.

Healing Miracles

Can some of the healing miracles be explained in this second way? In the story of the paralysed man, Jesus told him his sins were forgiven before he told him to get up and walk. Did Jesus do this because he realised that the man's problem was mental and not physical? Once he felt free of guilt the man could walk again.

The power of **faith** or belief might explain some of the cures. Jesus often told people that their faith had cured them, and, in fact, he could not perform any cures in his home town, Nazareth, because the people had no faith in him (see Mark 6:5–6). If a person believes hard enough that they are going to get well, then they might do. The power of suggestion has been used in hypnotism. A famous case is when a cold iron bar was placed on a hypnotised person's arm and he was told that it was red hot. The person's skin blistered!

There is no evidence that Jesus ever used hypnotism, but his presence and his words might have given people a deep sense of forgiveness and peace. This would give the strength to believe deeply enough that they could be made well. Jesus might have triggered off forces in people's minds that we are only just starting to understand.

Fact Box

Another interesting case involved a sixteen-year-old boy who had a disfiguring skin disease that looked like a black, reptilian, scaly layer over his body. A doctor hypnotised the boy and suggested that the scaly layer on the left arm should fall away, and it did shortly afterwards. Gradually, after a series of hypnotic sessions, the boy had received a cure that was 50 to 90 per cent successful on different parts of his body. This is recorded in the British Medical Journal of 23 August 1952.

Some people might object: 'But where is God in all of this?' Those who argue that Jesus cured by the power of faith feel that he did so because God was with him, and hence his sensitivity to people's problems and the effect his presence had on them: God worked through him, through natural forces. Furthermore, the difference between one of Jesus' healings and one done through hypnosis is that the person seemed to feel spiritually healed also – they felt refreshed within, and morally changed. They had met with God.

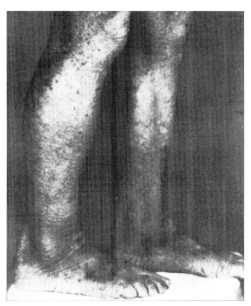

Before the course of hypnotism and afterwards. Do you think there is a striking difference?

One reason why many Christians believe that Jesus did work some kind of healing miracles is that there are so many stories of Jesus healing people in the Gospels. He emerges from them as a Teacher and as a Healer. The cures seem to be a central part of his story; they do not seem to have been added later. (Usually when this happens to a great teacher, there are a few miracle stories that circulate about him at least a hundred years or more after his death, and they are absent from any earlier writings about him. With the case of Jesus, there are so many stories and they were written down between about 35 to 60 years after his death. The earliest writings say he was a healer.)

Nature Miracles

The nature miracles are slightly different. There are far fewer of them. Some Christians who believe that Jesus cured people doubt that he walked on water, turned water into wine or fed 5,000 people with a few loaves and fishes, for example. These stories seem to them more fantastic and far-fetched. They are the type of thing that might have been exaggerated and added on to the story.

Many others do think they happened – either by a direct intervention of God, or by some force that we do not understand yet. If we take the walking on the water story as an example, these are the different ways of understanding nature miracles:

- It was a supernatural event. God acted through Jesus to break the law of gravity.
- It was a real event, and Jesus used some kind of mind over matter that he had developed through his closeness to God.

Those who doubt that the nature miracles happened at all might suggest two other possibilities:

- Jesus was walking by the edge of the lake, telling his disciples to have courage. In their panic, the disciples mistook this for actually walking on the

water. The story in the Gospels is therefore an exaggeration.
- It is a made-up story with a meaning, using picture-language, or symbols. The wind and the waves suggest the forces of evil, and Jesus walking over them suggests that he is stronger than evil. He is above it, and has it 'under his feet'.

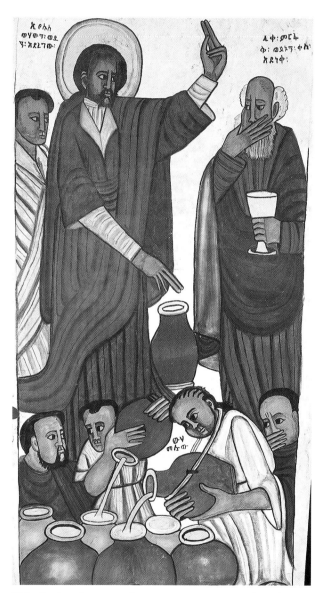

This depicts Jesus turning water into wine. What alternative explanations could there be for this miracle?

The Raising the Dead Miracles

- Some Christians say Jesus used a supernatural or paranormal power to revive the dead, and that as the Messiah, or God's Man, he could do this.
- Some say the 'dead' people were not really dead but were in a coma and that Jesus revived them. (Note that he said that Jairus's daughter was only sleeping.)
- Some think that as there are only a few raising miracles, they might have been invented and added to the story later, after the belief in Jesus' resurrection.

Exorcisms

- Some Christians think that all the exorcism stories in the Gospels were really cures of mentally disturbed people, or of epilepsy victims, and that evil spirits were only superstitions dreamed up by people who did not understand much about the human body and mind. The cures of these people therefore show the incredible peace of mind that Jesus was able to bring to some.
- Others say that evil spirits might exist; that there are mysterious things in life that we do not fully understand. Films, novels and scary newspaper articles play on this fear. Some of the people

Jesus helped might have been mentally ill, but some might have been possessed and these stories show the power of Jesus over the devil.

Outcasts

The authorities found Jesus hard to figure out. He was a holy man and a preacher of God's Kingdom, and yet he spent time with the undesirables of their society. They often criticised him for this, and one passage in the Gospels shows what was in his mind:

'People who are well do not need a doctor, but only those who are sick. I have not come to call respectable people, but outcasts'.
(Mark 2:17)

- Jesus talked to and helped people with a dreaded skin-disease (not always the same as modern-day leprosy). To cure some of them he actually touched them. This must have seemed shocking then, as people avoided any contact with them in case they caught the disease (see Mark 1:40–5).
- Jesus called a tax collector to be one of his disciples (Mark 2:13–17) and ate a meal with another (Luke 19:1–10). Tax collectors were hated by the rest of the Jews because not only did they work for

Activities

Think About It

1 If it is believed that Jesus did cure people, what two ways might there be to try to explain this?
2 How might the case of the boy cured of a skin disease by hypnotism help us to understand the healing miracle stories in the Gospels?

3 a) How do those Christians who believe that the nature miracles actually happened explain them?
 b) How do other Christians make sense of these stories, if they are not taken as real events? (Use the walking on the water story as an example.)

the Romans, but they usually cheated people out of extra money.

- Jesus forgave a prostitute and allowed her to weep at his feet, washing them with her tears, and drying them with her hair, much to the amazement and shock of the Pharisee he was eating a meal with (Luke 7:36–50).

From these actions we can learn something of Jesus' attitude to the **Kingdom of God**: it was open for anyone to enter if they turned from their sins. It was not just for one race, nor the wealthy nor the respectable. All people, no matter how insignificant in society, were seen by Jesus as being precious to God.

Being homeless can make you feel that you are an outcast.

Activities

Think About It

1 People with a skin disease, tax collectors and prostitutes – why were each of these groups treated as social outcasts at the time of Jesus? What was Jesus' attitude to these people?

2 What does Jesus' reaction to the outcasts tell us about his beliefs about the Kingdom of God?

3 Read the story of the call of Matthew (Matthew 9:9–13):
  a) How do you think Matthew would have felt?
  b) How do you think the people watching this felt?

The Disciples

A **disciple** means a follower of a master or a teacher. Jesus had numerous disciples during his lifetime, and these were as follows:

- 12 main disciples.
- 70 close disciples and helpers.
- The women – a group of women who were committed to Jesus and offered the others hospitality.
- Ordinary people – varying in commitment. Some might come to hear Jesus once or twice; others would follow him wherever he went.

Jesus probably chose 12 main disciples to represent the 12 tribes of Israel in the Old Testament. He was trying to start a renewed Israel that would spread the Kingdom to all people. A verse in the Old Testament said that the Jews were to be a light to the nations. Mark's Gospel gives the names of the Twelve as follows (3:13–19):

1 Simon (whom Jesus called Peter)
2 & 3 James and his brother John, the sons of Zebedee
4 Andrew
5 Philip
6 Bartholomew
7 Matthew
8 Thomas
9 James, son of Alphaeus
10 Thaddaeus
11 Simon the Patriot (or Zealot)
12 Judas Iscariot

Some of these names vary in the other Gospels (see Luke 6:12–16, for example). Some lists might use forenames or surnames, Jewish or Greek names (some people had both) or even nicknames ('Peter' means 'rock'). Peter and the two sons of Zebedee seem to have been the three closest male disciples to Jesus.

The disciples do not seem to have always understood their master. Once, Jesus warned them that he was going to be arrested and put to death if he went to Jerusalem again. Peter tried to talk him out of this and Jesus gave him a sharp telling off! (See Mark 8:31–3.) All the male disciples, with the possible exception of John, deserted Jesus when he was crucified. Peter even denied he had ever known him in order to save his own life (see Mark 14:66–72).

The 12 disciples were called the **apostles** after the death and resurrection of Jesus. An 'apostle' means 'one sent out with a message' – a missionary.

The women did not desert their master. When Mark describes the crucifixion and death of Jesus he adds:

Some women were there, looking on from a distance. Among them were Mary Magdalene, Mary the mother of the younger James and of Joseph, and Salome. They had followed Jesus while he was in Galilee and had helped him. Many other women who had come to Jerusalem with him were there also.

(Mark 15:40–1)

Mary Magdalene (meaning 'from Magdala' – a village in Galilee) seems to have been very close to Jesus. According to John's Gospel, the risen Jesus appeared to Mary first, before Peter and the others. There might have been a special love between them, and some people have wondered whether in different circumstances they might have married. That we shall never know, and it is likely that Jesus had taken a vow of celibacy – to remain unmarried.

Some people think that the only reason why Jesus did not include her among the Twelve, along with other women, was because of the kind of society they lived in. Women were expected to be married and to look after the home. If they wandered about from town to town preaching then people would think such women were probably prostitutes. They would not have been listened to. Others think Jesus chose 12 men to represent him in a special way, and so women cannot be priests today.

Many Free Churches have women ministers, Lutherans have women pastors, and the Anglican Churches have women priests. (The Church of England voted in favour of this in 1992.)

Question
• Do you think it is right to have women ministers or priests? Find out why some people think it is wrong.

There is a tradition that Mary was an ex-prostitute whom Jesus had converted. There is no evidence that she was. Luke's Gospel says that Jesus had cast seven devils out of her. Mental illness used to be thought to be caused by demons, and so Mary might have been severely disturbed emotionally, or she might have had epilepsy.

The musical 'Jesus Christ, Superstar' brought out the relationship between Jesus and Mary Magdalene very well in Mary's song, 'I don't know how to love him. He's a man; he's just a man and I've had so many men before, and in so very many ways, he's just one more ... but he scares me so ...'. (This was much to the shock of some Christians who did not believe that Jesus had anyone that came close to being a girlfriend.)

Activities

Key Elements

1 What were the four groups of disciples that Jesus had?

2 Why did he have 12 main disciples? List them.

Think About It

3 Which women were named in the Gospels as his disciples? Why would it have been strange to have had women disciples at that time?

4 Why do some think that Jesus only chose men for his 12 disciples, and did not include any women among them? Give more than one reason if you can.

Jesus' Teaching

> How would you sum up what Jesus had to say? What was his message, in a nutshell?

> Well, why not look at the Lord's Prayer? I think you'll find all you want in there!...

The **Lord's Prayer** was taught by Jesus to his disciples when they asked him how to pray. It contains all the essentials of his teaching – God as Father; the Kingdom; and forgiveness. This is one version of it (Matthew 6:9–13):

> *Our Father in heaven*:
> May your holy name be honoured;
> *may your Kingdom come;*
> may your will be done on earth as it is in heaven.
> Give us today the food we need.
> *Forgive us the wrongs we have done,*
> *as we forgive the wrongs that others have done to us*
> Do not bring us to hard testing,
> but keep us safe from the Evil One.

Father

Some people were afraid of God, thinking of him as a stern judge or as a cosmic king who could order their life or death. The Old Testa-

ment, particularly in its later writings, taught that God was a God of love and like a Father. Jesus stressed this, and tried to stop people being afraid of God. He used a special word in Aramaic when he prayed to God: *Abba*, as did a few other Jewish holymen. This word was used by little children when talking to their fathers. It was intimate. Jesus was not trying to say that God is male, though. He taught that God is spirit, not human (see John 4:24). God was like a human father in his care for people, and wanted people to have a close relationship with him.

The Aramaic term abba, written in modern Hebrew.

Kingdom

The phrase 'the Kingdom of God' means 'the rule of God'. Many Jews thought this would come crashing in as a supernatural event when the Messiah came, and that they would be in charge of the world as a race. Jesus seems to have taught that the Kingdom was open for all people, although news of it had come to the Jews first.

Sometimes in the Gospels Jesus teaches that the Kingdom will come crashing in (see Mark 13). However, there are many things in his teaching which suggest that the Kingdom was to come *inside people's hearts* as they turned from sin and opened themselves up to God. Luke 17:21 has Jesus saying: 'The Kingdom of God is within you.' For Christians, the Kingdom is both an inner change of heart and a symbol of peace on earth.

Forgiveness

Jesus often taught in **parables** (stories with a meaning) and the parable that best illustrates his teaching on forgiveness is that of the Lost

Son (or the Prodigal Son in some Bibles) in Luke 15:11–32. The characters in the story are a father and his two sons. One runs off and wastes his inheritance from his father, but hits hard times. He returns home in disgrace, thinking that his father might hire him as a servant, but would never take him back as a son. He is mistaken, and the father runs out to greet him. Note, though, that this is not 'soft', for the son had to come to his senses and be sorry for what he had done, though his father was always willing to forgive him. The father in the story stands for God, and the lost son for the sinner.

The word 'radical' means 'to get to the root'. Imagine that you are trying to remove weeds from a garden; it is no use unless they are pulled out by the roots. To be radical is to hit the nail on the head, to turn things upside down, to go against traditional expectations. Jesus was radical in his teaching about forgiveness. God did not hold people's wrongs against them; they could turn round and receive his blessing. It was costly for they had to be prepared for a change of heart, but God was welcoming them with open arms and would come to them where they were. They did not have to reach a standard before they were acceptable.

The Lost Son welcomed by his father.

Jesus followed in the footsteps of the great **prophets** of the Old Testament in preaching that God wanted a change of heart and not sacrifices or special rituals of washing (such as the bathing practised at Qumran, or the hand washing by the Pharisees before they said a blessing over a meal).

Activities

Key Elements

1 What does the word 'Abba' mean? What did Jesus think God was like when he used this word?

2 Jesus spoke about the Kingdom of God in two ways – how?

3 Describe the parable of the Lost Son. What point was Jesus trying to make in this story?

Think About It

4 What does the idea 'God is love' suggest to you? What idea of God was Jesus trying to change when he taught this?

5 What do you think forgiveness means? Can you think of a situation where it would be very hard to forgive someone, and one where an argument was solved by forgiving someone?

6 What do you think Jesus meant when he said, 'The Kingdom of God is within you'?

Why do Christians Think Jesus was Important?

Firstly, Christians see Jesus as a *Revealer*. They think he showed humanity what God was like: a forgiving, loving God who got involved with humankind in a special way when he came to people in Jesus. In John's Gospel there is a story of Thomas falling at Jesus' feet after his resurrection: 'My Lord and my God' was his response. In meeting Christ he felt that he had met God.

Secondly, Christians follow Jesus as a *Teacher*. He has shown them a way of life and a set of values. The central points of his teaching are of the Fatherhood of God and the family of humankind: 'Love the Lord your God with all your heart ... and your neighbour as yourself.'

Thirdly, Christians follow Jesus as the *Risen Lord*. They do not think he was just a great man in the past, but that he is now alive in God, and a living presence with them. This gives them the hope that there is a life after death for them too. They see Jesus as a living Saviour, and his words and his example of a loving life and death on earth can help people to change their way of life today.

Activities

- Write an imaginary interview with the elder brother in the story of the Lost Son; ask him how he feels about his brother's behaviour and his return.
- Draw or paint a picture, or write a poem, with the title, 'May your Kingdom come!'
- Write an imaginary scene where representatives of each of the religious groups at the time of Jesus are invited to give their teaching in a nutshell to a reporter. Jesus is interviewed last of all.

Did Jesus Exist?

There are a number of pieces of evidence that prove that Jesus existed, as well as the existence of any person in history can be proved.

Evidence from Non-Christian Writers

Some Roman writers mentioned Jesus, such as Tacitus, a Roman historian. He wrote at the end of the first century CE and early in the second century. When he was writing about the lives of previous emperors he mentioned the Christians:

> They got their names from Christ, who was executed by Pontius Pilate in the reign of Tiberius.

Josephus was a Jewish historian born in 37 CE, who wrote a history of his own people to try to convince the Romans that they were a learned and civilised race. He mentioned Jesus as a 'doer of wonderful works' who had disciples and was put to death by the leaders of the people.

Neither Tacitus nor Josephus had any sympathy for the Christians. If Jesus had been a **myth**, intelligent writers like these would have been quick to point this out; they had no doubt he existed.

Pliny and Suetonius, both Roman writers, referred to Jesus early in the second century CE. Pliny wrote that the Christians worshipped him as though he were a god. Suetonius mentioned a disturbance that happened involving the Jews in Rome in the reign of the Emperor Claudius. He says it was over 'Chrestus', which is though to have been a reference to Jews and Christians arguing about Christ.

The Talmud, a book of ancient teachings and sayings of Jewish rabbis, many from the time of Jesus, mentions Jesus as having five disciples and that he was crucified. It also accuses him of sorcery, a charge that sounds like the one brought against him in Matthew

12:22–4. This might even prove that he did work some kind of miracles – the Jewish leaders could not deny that he did, so they claimed he did so by an evil power.

These writers do not give us much information but they do date the life of Jesus – when Pilate was governor, and when Tiberius was emperor – as well as confirming the fact of his execution.

Evidence from Christian Writers

The fullest accounts in the New Testament of the life of Jesus are the four Gospels. These are not meant to be read as biographies, though, for they only deal with highlights from the life of Jesus.

The Gospels are thought to have been written at these times:

Mark *c.* 65–70 CE
Matthew *c.* 85 CE
Luke *c.* 80–90 CE
John *c.* 100 CE

These dates are not certain, but they are good and reasonable guesses from all kinds of clues (e.g. parts of the first three Gospels were quoted by Christian writers by the end of the first century CE, and the earliest known fragment of John's Gospel was found in Egypt and has been dated to 110–150 CE).

The earliest fragment of John's Gospel, written in Greek on a piece of papyrus. It is in the John Rylands Library in Manchester.

Activities

Key Elements

1 What are the two different types of written evidence about Jesus?
2 What did the Roman writer, Tacitus, say about Jesus?
3 What did the Jewish writer, Josephus, say about Jesus?
4 Why is it likely that Jesus did live if the two above writers mentioned him?
5 When were the four Gospels probably written?
6 How old is the earliest known fragment of John's Gospel, and where is it kept today?

Think About It

7 How does the story of Thomas meeting the risen Jesus show what Christians believe about Jesus?
8 What were the central points of Jesus' teaching?
9 Do Christians think Jesus was just a great man in the past, and nothing more?
10 Make a summary of what the non-Christian writers had to say about Jesus. How do you react to this?

Can the Gospels Be Used as Evidence?

There was a period of about 30 to 50 years between the death of Jesus and the writing of the first three Gospels. This is a fairly short length of time: some religious leaders only had their stories committed to writing about 100 to 300 years after their deaths, such as the Buddha. It is possible that some things were added and exaggerated, but not as much as people might think. People in the past were trained to use their minds and remember much more than we do, for many people could not read or write.

It has also been found that if some of the sayings of Jesus are translated back into Aramaic, the language he spoke, they have particular rhythms and rhymes. Most people in the East taught in this way. This suggests that these sayings are probably genuine, from Jesus.

However, it must also be remembered that ancient writers did not write history as modern people do. They would include anything that seemed good and reliable, but they would sometimes include legends or invent speeches and put these into the story to bring out the meaning of the events as they saw them.

Some New Testament scholars feel that certain stories and sayings in the Gospels are unreliable legends or were the invention of the Gospel writers to put across their point of view. Some of the things Jesus said are therefore the views of the early Church, rather than of Jesus himself. This is especially seen to be the case with John's Gospel. Here, Jesus teaches his disciples through long, theological speeches. In the other Gospels he speaks in parables or short sayings. Jesus is far more like a god on earth in John, too: he knows what people are thinking before they tell him, and is conscious of having lived with the Father before his birth on earth. This might suggest a later interpretation of the Jesus story, at the end of the first century CE.

The Jesus shown in the other Gospels is far more human and he has limitations: he does

Question

- Do biographies tell us everything we need to know about famous people? Imagine someone was going to write about you. Who would know the most about you? What different things would different people be able to tell about you?

not always know what people are thinking, and he only gradually seems to become aware of God's plan. He seems to have only realised that the cross was a part of this plan towards the end of his ministry. Before this he seemed to expect the Kingdom to come in power.

Perhaps the strong and clear belief that Jesus was God come in human flesh took time to develop. Such a faith in Jesus is clearly presented in John's Gospel, written later, but all the writings about Jesus, from the earliest times, present a figure who is striking, unique and has an authority like no one else. They all feel that Jesus showed so powerfully what God was like, that God was in him in some special way.

Not all Christians agree with these conclusions; some think the Gospels present us with a very reliable picture of everything Jesus said and did, but others think they are less reliable as history, though the basic story is true.

If some stories and sayings *were* invented, though, the writers did not mean to tell lies. They were reinterpreting the story of Jesus after their belief in his resurrection, which they thought had made many puzzling things click into place; they might have needed new symbolic stories about him to put these ideas across. They needed to put words on to his lips to make it clear who they thought he was. Some of these words might even have come from prophets in the churches speaking in the name of the Risen Jesus.

Activities

Think About It

1 Why do Christians feel that the writings in the Gospels are very reliable even though there was a gap of time between the death of Jesus and their writings?

2 How did the ancient way of writing history differ from that of today?

3 Why do some people think that certain sayings of Jesus in the Gospels were invented (refer especially to John's Gospel)?

4 Why are the Gospels not biographies of Jesus? What do they try to tell people about him?

Assignments

1 Explain what Jesus really looked like, and how we know this. Then explain why different races imagine him in different ways. How do Western, Indian, African and Chinese Christians sometimes imagine him?

2 Organise a debate between two ministers. One holds traditional views about miracles and the other is more critical.

3 What social outcasts are there today? Find out about the work of one voluntary organisation that helps such people, and write an account of your findings.

4 Make a file on the life of Jesus, entering details of all the highlights.

3

Worship

Worship: to say 'thanks' to God for the gift of life; to spend time on something you feel is worthwhile; to appreciate something that means a great deal to you. People can worship a hobby, a football team or a pop group. It isn't only religious people who worship! You appreciate and spend time with people and things that are really important to you. Christians worship God in church, or on their own, to give thanks for the gift of life, for what Jesus did, and to feel spiritually refreshed inside.

Christians use a number of things to help them to worship. In a service you will find a combination of some or all of these: actions, words, music and singing, silence, clothes and symbolic objects.

Actions

The way we move our bodies can express feelings that we have. A person who is happy might jump up and down and clap her hands, or a nervous person might twitch his fingers. In a church service, people might kneel down or bow their heads when they say prayers. This is to show respect for God – they are showing that God is greater than them and it helps them to stop feeling proud.

Some people might bow to the cross on the altar at the front of the church, or kneel down on one knee (**genuflection**) for the same reasons. Some Christians make the sign of the

Why do some people bow their heads and close their eyes when they pray silently?

Words

Most services will be full of words, spoken or sung. Prayers will be said, and these will either be made up by the people on the spot or read from a Service Book where everyone will join in. Sections from the Bible will always be read out before the whole congregation: usually one passage from the Old Testament, one from the letters in the New Testament and one from the Gospels. The Bible is important to Christians as a source of ideas and teachings. They believe they hear God speaking through it in some way: it contains God's Word.

The minister will preach a **sermon**, which will vary in length, but will average about fifteen minutes. He, or she, might base this on the Bible passages that were read out, or upon some event in the news, or in the life of the congregation. Christians also hope to hear God's word to them through the sermon.

cross over their bodies to remember that Jesus died for them. Other Christians might prefer to raise their hands when praying or singing. This suggests joy, surrender to God ('Put your hands up!' idea) and openness to him. (Opening your arms out suggests that you are welcoming someone.)

Actions can also involve touch. In many services, people shake hands at one point and say, 'Peace be with you!' This is to express friendship, and to show that all Christians should think of one another as brothers and sisters – even if they do not always live up to that! This action is called the **Peace**.

Worship can involve action in many other ways too, outside an actual church service. Helping other people is a form of worship, of cherishing the gift of their lives, whether it is visiting an elderly person, helping with an employment scheme, campaigning for human rights, or whatever.

What is happening in this service? Why do all Christians think this is important?

Music and Singing

Music can express deep feelings, and can raise our spirits if we are feeling sad or worried in some way. Also, songs can be a way of showing and of sharing happiness. Music and songs help Christians to praise God. The instruments used may vary from church to church. Many churches have an organ, which can play rich, deep tones, or a piano. Sometimes guitars, flutes or tambourines are used if the songs are more modern and lively.

Many of the hymns sung in churches contain deep meanings and are sung happily by older people who understand them. However, the words of some hymns might be difficult, and the tunes seem slow. For this reason, shorter songs have been written which are being introduced into many churches. The words are often based on passages from the Bible, such as this song:

> *He is Lord, he is Lord;*
> *He is risen from the dead, and he is Lord.*
> *Every knee shall bow, every tongue confess,*
> *that Jesus Christ is Lord.*

(This is based on some words of St Paul in his letter to the Philippians 2:10–11.)

Some churches have choirs or music groups that lead the singing or sing parts of the service themselves. Orthodox Christians sing their services without musical instruments and they have specially trained **cantors** to help with this. Ethiopian Orthodox priests use a gold-coloured instrument which has metal washers threaded on to a metal frame. This is held in the hand and shaken, as the priests sing and move from side to side.

Music has an important part to play in worship.

Silence

It is wrong to think that Christians have to do things all through a service. Sitting quietly in silence can also be a very important part of it. It helps all the words and teachings to sink into their minds. It is also a form of **meditation**, of calming the mind and feeling at peace. Many Christians say that they feel the presence of God with them in these times. This sitting quietly, thinking, praying, or just being still, is called **contemplation**.

Clothes

Some ministers might just wear ordinary clothes, like a smart suit. This would be the case in many of the Free Churches. This is to emphasise that all believers are equal; the minister leads the services because he or she is specially trained, that is all. However, other Churches have ministers who dress in special robes to take a service. It might be a long white robe called an **alb**, or a shorter one called a **surplice**. The whiteness suggests purity and life – the goodness of God. In Roman Catholic, Orthodox and some Anglican churches the minister will wear a series of colourful robes. These give a sense of grandeur and beauty to a service, as an offering to God. The main robes would be the alb;

the **stole**, like a colourful scarf; and the **chasuble**, which slips over the head. The colours of the stole and chasuble will vary throughout the year. The colours will vary from purple, white (or gold), red and green. The chasuble may have designs on it, such as stylised doves or crosses. Priests are thought to represent Christ to the people, as well as representing the people to God.

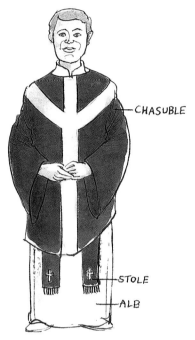

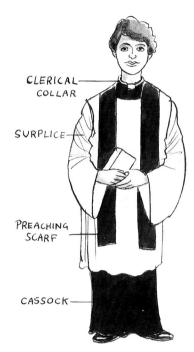

Left: an Anglican or Roman Catholic priest, dressed to celebrate a Eucharist. Right: an Anglican priest in choir dress ready to take Morning or Evening Prayer.

Activities

Key Elements

1 What is meant by the word 'worship'
   a) in a general sense, and
   b) in a religious sense?
2 Mention any four actions used in Christian worship. Why are these done?
3 What do Christians hope to hear when the Bible is read out, besides just spoken words?
4 What sort of things might the sermon contain?
5 What changes have taken place in the type of songs and musical instruments used in churches today? Why is this?

Think About It

6 Why do you think silence is an important part of Christian worship? Are there any times when you sit alone in silence? What benefit do you receive from this?

Symbolic Objects

There are many pictures and objects that might be found in churches and which help people to worship. They are often symbolic as well. A **symbol** represents something else, such as a feeling or a truth that is difficult to put into words.

Holy-water Stoup

Water suggests life and purity. Roman Catholic and some Anglican churches have small containers of holy water by the entrance that people will dip their fingers into and then make the sign of the cross with. Holy water is water that has been blessed by a priest.

Making the sign of the cross with the holy water.

Incense

Roman Catholic, Orthodox and some Anglican churches use incense. This is a sweet-smelling spice which is burned with charcoal in a censer or thurible and wafted around during a service by a person called a thurifer. It produces a pleasant, rich atmosphere and suggests prayers going up to God.

Candles and Flowers

Some churches light candles on the altar. The flickering lights add to the beauty of the church, and light also suggests life and truth, and the presence of God.

Flower arrangements in various parts of the church add to the beauty and atmosphere. The colours can remind people of the glory of God and flowers suggest life.

Worshippers have lit candles and set them in front of this shrine.

Rosary Beads

Some Roman Catholic, Anglican, Orthodox and Methodist Christians use sets of prayer beads. These are called **rosaries** (though, strictly speaking, 'The Rosary' means the prayers that are said). The beads are arranged into five groups of ten, with extra beads marking the divisions between these. A short prayer or phrase is said as each bead is slipped through the fingers. This type of prayer can be said in times of silence, when the words can be concentrated on more easily. This prayer is often said in the Western Church:

> Hail Mary, full of grace,
> the Lord is with you.
> Blessed are you among women,
> and blessed is the fruit of your womb, Jesus.
> Holy Mary, Mother of God,
> pray for us sinners,
> now and at the hour of our death.

In the Eastern Church the Jesus prayer is used.

An icon is a special painting of Jesus, Mary or one of the saints, often in vivid colours with light shining from their bodies or having a gold background. Orthodox Christians pray before them and light candles in front of them. This one is from Russia.

Besides pictures and statues there will be crosses and crucifixes. An empty cross not only reminds people of the death of Jesus, but also of his resurrection. A **crucifix** has a carving of the dead Jesus upon it. This helps people to remember his suffering. Some Christians say that they find praying in front of a crucifix to be very moving. The initials, INRI, are often seen above Jesus' head. These stand for 'Jesus of Nazareth, King of the Jews', in Latin (Iesus Nazarenus Rex Iudaeorum).

Saying the rosary. How do you think this type of prayer can help people?

Pictures and Statues

Some churches have pictures or statues of Jesus, Mary and the saints to remind people of the founder of their religion and the great people who have belonged to the Church in the past. These people set an example to follow, and they are honoured for their closeness to God.

Sometimes there will be various designs hanging on the walls, or on the pulpit or altar. They often stand for something to do with Jesus:

These are the first three letters of the Greek word for Jesus: IHSOYS.

These are the first two letters of the Greek word for Christ (ΧΡΙΣΤΟΣ). It is called the chi-rho.

The word ΙΧΘΥΣ (pronounced 'ichthos') is Greek for 'fish'. Each letter of this word is the first letter of the words 'Jesus Christ, Son of God, Saviour' in Greek. A simple drawing of a fish was used as a secret sign by the early Christians to avoid being arrested by the Romans. The fish symbolised three things about Jesus and the faith:

1 He was the Saviour of people, the fisher of souls.
2 It suggested the washing of baptism and the new life that this brought.
3 The fish suggested sharing. Jesus had shared out fish at the feeding of the 5,000, and had cooked fish for the disciples in John 21. It came to signify the **Holy Communion**, the meal of bread and wine that was shared in services.

The dove is a symbol of God's Spirit. It suggests the peace and tranquillity Christians say they feel in the presence of God.

Prayer Umbrellas and Crosses

Ethiopian Orthodox Christians hold highly decorative umbrellas over their priests during special festivals. Besides giving shade from the sun in a hot country, these give a sense of colour and celebration. There is a suggestion of the protection and shelter of God, bringing peace. Crosses are carried in the processions too, of varying and ornate design. Worship, for the Ethiopian Orthodox, is to be visually beautiful.

Part of an Ethiopian prayer for peace:
'O King of Peace, give us your peace, for you have given us all things . . . we make mention of your holy name, and call upon it, that we may live in peace through the Holy Spirit . . .'

Activities

- Draw one of the symbols for Jesus and explain it.
- Design a symbol for God, Jesus or the Spirit that could be used on a poster or banner in a church and explain it.
- Design a class 'prayer umbrella', decorating an old umbrella with Christian symbols which have been mentioned in this chapter.

Buildings

The opening service of the Roman Catholic Cathedral in Liverpool in 1967. What things in the design suggest togetherness as well as the greatness of God?

The design of a church building is also symbolic. The traditional style of English parish churches was intended to give the worshipper the sense of being on a journey through life. You stepped through the door, walked along to take a seat, listened to the service, and then went forward to take the bread and wine at the altar, the holy place where only the priest and his helpers would stand, which represented the goal of life – moving forwards and joining God after death. The service was like a symbol, or a rehearsal for life's journey through the outside world.

Modern churches tend to be designed in different ways. The problem with the old style of building was that it was like being on a train journey, with the driver at the front, and you did not see much of the people in front of you, except the backs of their heads. One idea has been to bring the altar, or Lord's Table, further forward, so seats can be arranged to the sides of it. Then the minister stands in amongst the people.

Some new churches are circular, so that the people can see each other more easily. This tries to create a more friendly atmosphere. The Roman Catholic **Cathedral** in Liverpool (the Metropolitan Cathedral of Christ the King) is a good example of this: the seats are in a circle with the altar in the middle and there are side **chapels** around the perimeter. This new style emphasises that God is close to people and with them in everyday life. People sit round the altar, looking at each other, and feeling that God is at the centre.

The old style buildings stressed the idea that God is very different from people, and gave the idea that God is very great by making him seem far away, with the altar right at the other end of the church from the people.

Modern churches do not always lose a sense of God's greatness, though, as in Liverpool Catholic Cathedral where the tower that sweeps up above the altar gives an idea of height and distance.

This is a Free church chapel. Notice how plain and simple it is.

Many Free churches are, however, very simple in design and have very few symbolic objects inside – perhaps only a cross and a hanging showing a dove or the IHS symbol. This is because some Christians feel that too many objects are a distraction. God is invisible and should be felt inside the mind and listened to in the words of the Bible. They might also fear that some more superstitious people might start to worship pictures and statues instead of God. (They think of the second commandment, see Exodus 20:4–5.)

There seem to be two different types of character amongst Christians, therefore: those who like simple worship with few decorations, and those who prefer to worship with an abundance of colourful sights, smells and sounds.

The Service: Order or Freedom?

Liturgy is an order of service with words and actions. Some Christians enjoy worshipping by using a Service Book that follows a set service. They read it through during the service and repeat some of the prayers. They feel that they know where they are and what to expect next. Also, once many of the words become familiar, people can think about them more as they are saying them, or quietly meditate upon them.

Other Christians find this very restricting. They like to be freer in their worship, with no set prayers, but with times when anyone in church can start a song, or say a prayer out loud, or even stand up and share some thoughts or ideas from the Bible. The minister will keep overall charge, and will start and close the meeting and make sure nothing goes wrong during it. There is usually lively singing, hand-clapping and even joyful dancing. The Churches that have services like this are the Pentecostal and New Churches. (The Quakers have open meetings where anyone can speak or pray, but they tend to be much quieter, spending long periods of time in silence.)

This freedom is also entering other Churches, as a result of the influence of the **charismatic** movement. Charismatic Christians believe in freer and livelier worship, and they feel that God's Spirit makes them joyful. They will adapt set services so that there are times of open prayer and times when people can suggest different songs to sing. The charismatic movement is quite strong in the Anglican and Roman Catholic Churches.

Even among Christians who prefer set services there are sometimes disagreements. If a new style of service is introduced, with more up-to-date words, some people will love it and some will hate it. In the Anglican Church, for example, the traditional Service Book until 1980 was the Book of Common Prayer. It was written in 1666 and has much fine poetry in it. It is known off by heart by many older members, and they have a deep affection for it. In 1980, however, the Alternative Service Book was introduced and many churches switched to that. Its language is more modern and the services are easier to understand for younger people and for newcomers to the Church. However, people who knew and loved the older services were angry and frustrated. Many old people felt insulted for they thought they were being told that the way they had worshipped for so many years was no longer good enough.

An example of the change of style can be seen by comparing the Song of Simeon (or Nunc Dimittis) from the two Service Books:

Book of Common Prayer

Lord, now lettest thou thy servant depart in peace: according to thy word.
For mine eyes have seen: thy salvation,
Which thou hast prepared: before the face of all people;
To be a light to lighten the Gentiles: and to be the glory of thy people Israel.
Glory be to the Father, and to the Son: and to the Holy Ghost;
As it was in the beginning, is now, and ever shall be: world without end. Amen.

Alternative Service Book

Lord now you let your servant go in peace: your word has been fulfilled.
My own eyes have seen the salvation: which you have prepared in the sight of every people;
a light to reveal you to the nations: and the glory of your people Israel.
Glory to the Father and to the Son: and to the Holy Spirit;
as it was in the beginning is now: and shall be for ever. Amen.

Roman Catholics use an order of service written in a book called a **missal**; there is a Weekday Missal for weekday **Masses** (the service where the bread and wine is shared), and a Sunday Missal for Sunday Masses. These have been put into modern English but Mass used to be said in Latin before the 1960s. Many older Catholics miss the old service, but many younger people welcome the new ones.

Orthodox Christians have Service Books in Greek or Russian, sometimes with English translations in them. The main service is written in the 'Liturgy of St John Chrysostom'.

Charismatic worshippers. Is there any difference in the attitude of the people compared with the photographs of other services?

Why Pray?

There are four types of prayer:

Adoration

This is when people simply adore God and think about his greatness. God is thought to be vast and endless and the creator of all life. Christians say that adoring God gives them a sense of perspective on life. For all their brains and abilities, people are really quite insignificant and there is much more to life and the universe than them. So, a prayer of adoration would be something like: 'O God, how great and marvellous you are!' Or a person might spend time adoring God in silence.

Confession

When people feel that they have done something wrong, or have hurt someone in some way, it is healthy to admit this and face up to it. Confessing to God can help Christians face up to their wrongs. It can also help them to put things right again. Christians believe that God is forgiving and can be turned to for help. The person has to be sincere, though; a prayer of confession is not like just saying 'Sorry' and not meaning it.

Thanksgiving

When Christians want to thank God for something, this is a prayer of thanksgiving. It might be for some good news they have heard, or for getting better after an illness, or simply for the gift of life itself. It can help people to feel grateful, and it helps to stop them taking things for granted.

Supplication

Supplication means asking for help. A person might pray for one of their own needs, such as for the strength to do a difficult job, or to have the courage to stand up and be counted over some issue. Or it could be that they pray for the needs of others, for a family that has little money or for a sick friend. It could be a prayer for the whole world, such as one against famine or war.

They might also pray for things that are necessary – it gives them a sense of priorities and what is important in life, i.e. it gives them a sense of perspective. But Christians feel that it is no use praying for things selfishly, like for a new TV or to pass an examination when no revision has been done.

Christians' views about whether prayers of supplication are answered depend on their ideas of God. If they think of God as some kind of force 'up there' or 'out there', above them, then if a prayer is not answered it is either because the message did not get through – maybe they were not praying hard enough – or it was because it was not God's will to change things.

However, if Christians see God as being deep within themselves, rather than floating about above them, then they will see prayer as a way of opening up channels between people's minds and various situations in order to let new hope and strength flow through. For example, praying for sick people might give them the strength to get better more quickly. Praying for people with problems might help these people emotionally because they know someone cares. Or it might give the person praying more insight, and the strength or inspiration to do something or help someone. They can then start to answer the prayer themselves.

In whatever way prayers of supplication are understood, all Christians are agreed that saying them helps them to feel good and to face life better.

Keeping a sense of perspective on life, not bottling up guilt but facing up to it, not taking things for granted, are all important if people are going to have a healthy emotional life. And realising that you are not always able to cope on your own, but need the help of others at times, is also essential.

The idea that prayer gives a person a sense of perspective is a very important one for Christians. People cannot spend all their time praying; they have a life to lead; although some monks and nuns do spend long hours in prayer. Christians feel that prayer helps them to live their lives by providing an opportunity to step aside from the hustle and bustle of everyday life, by seeking quietness, peace of mind and guidance. It helps them to feel refreshed within. One Christian poet summed this up when he wrote: 'There lives the dearest freshness deep down things.'

Activities

Key Elements

1 What is a rosary, and how is it used?
2 What is the difference between a crucifix and a cross? Why do some Christians find it helpful to pray in front of a crucifix?
3 Why is God's Spirit often pictured as a dove?
4 Why do Ethiopian Orthodox Christians use decorative umbrellas?
5 What are the different types of prayer that Christians use? Write a sentence to explain each type.
6 Make up a prayer for each of the types mentioned.

Assignments

1 How to Meditate
Find a quiet place. Sit comfortably, so you won't feel like moving for a while. Start to breath deeper and count your breaths to yourself, up to 20. Listen, for a few moments, to all the sounds around you. Focus on one for a while, and then another. Start to say a word or phrase to yourself, over and over again, such as 'Peace', while imagining a calm place. Finish by counting 20 more breaths.

2 Prepare a questionnaire to find out what type of church service people prefer and why. It could be done across your year at school. First find out if they go to church. *Or* find out about preferences for school assemblies – do people prefer a set assembly or a freer one?

Holy Communion

There is one action that is very important in most Christian worship: Holy Communion. This is where bread and wine are shared out. This is done because of the last supper that Jesus had with his disciples. On the night before his arrest he gathered his disciples into an upper room in Jerusalem, and ate a special meal with them. This was probably the Passover meal that the Jews eat once a year. It is a meal that remembers the time when the ancestors of the Jews were slaves in Egypt, nearly thirteen hundred years before the time of Jesus. Jews believe that God sent Moses to set their ancestors free and they remember this event each year with this special meal. It consists of bread and wine and other symbolic items. At the Last Supper Jesus took the bread and wine and shared them with his disciples, giving them a new meaning. The earliest account of this is in one of St Paul's letters, 1 Corinthians 11:23–6, and it is in the first three Gospels. Here is Mark's version:

> *While they were eating, Jesus took a piece of bread, gave a prayer of thanks, broke it, and gave it to his disciples. 'Take it,' he said, 'this is my body.' Then he took a cup, gave thanks to God, and handed it to them; and they all drank from it. Jesus said, 'This is my blood which is poured out for many . . .'*

> *(Mark 14:22–4)*

Jesus took the bread and the wine in the Passover meal and made it refer to himself: the bread was his body, and the wine was his blood. Christians have shared out bread and wine ever since. The early Church used to share it as part of a full meal that everyone had. This was called the **agape** feast (*agape* is a Greek word for love). This is not always practical now that there are many more people in churches. Some Churches share the bread and the wine at least each week, such as Roman Catholics, Orthodox and Anglicans (with some having daily Holy Communions). Free Churches, however, tend to share it once or twice a month.

The bread suggests the body of Jesus, the wine his blood. Christians remember his death, but celebrate his risen presence. Death and new life are present.

Activities

Key Elements

1 Tell the story of what Jesus did at the Last Supper.
2 Which Jewish festival was this probably based on? What event in Jewish history was remembered at this time?
3 What new meaning did Jesus give to the bread and wine that was a part of the meal?

The Meaning of Holy Communion

The bread and wine remind Christians of the death of Jesus, but also of his resurrection. Bread can stand for life (it is the basic foodstuff) and wine can stand for joy (it makes people feel warm inside).

Different Churches call this meal by different names, such as: Holy Communion; the **Eucharist**; the Mass; the **Lord's Supper**; and the **Breaking of the Bread**. There are also different ways that Christians understand the meal:

- Some see it as just a *symbol*, where the bread and wine stand for the body and blood.
- Others think that *Jesus is spiritually present* in the bread and wine, and that, in some sense, it becomes his body and blood.

Whether Christians see the Holy Communion as bringing Jesus' presence to them, or simply as a visual aid to remember the death and resurrection of Jesus, they all agree that it is a *eucharist*, a 'thanksgiving' meal, to translate the Greek. It is a way of sharing with one another. Eating is a basic human activity and sharing food can break down barriers between people and strengthen friendships. Besides this, they can celebrate the centre of their faith – the love of God shown in the story of the death and resurrection of Jesus.

The following photographs show how different Churches celebrate Holy Communion, and suggest their different beliefs about it. What do you think these different Churches believe about the Eucharist they are celebrating?

A Roman Catholic Mass, showing the elevation of the host. When in service does this happen?

A Greek Orthodox Eucharist. What makes this seem a little more mysterious than the Roman Catholic Mass?

(Note: the priest faces the people behind the iconostasis while the deacon brings up the bread for the Eucharist.)

The Roman Catholic, Orthodox and Anglican Churches

These Churches believe that the Eucharist becomes a special vehicle for the presence of Christ, and that by eating and drinking it they can draw closer to God. The bread is called the **host** (Latin for 'victim'), as this represents Jesus. They have more ceremonial in their Holy Communions than other Christians. The priests have special robes (albs and chasubles) and there will be special containers for the bread and wine (**patens** and **chalices** – a paten is a shallow dish; a chalice is a special wine-cup). There will be decorative cloths over the altar as well.

After the priest has prayed over the bread and wine (this is called the **consecration**) and asked the **Holy Spirit** to come upon them, he will raise the bread up high so that all the people can see it, and bells might be rung.

These Churches have altars rather than tables at the front because they believe that they are offering a **sacrifice** when they consecrate the bread and wine. It is an offering of the sacrifice Jesus made of his own life on the cross, represented in the form of bread and

Orthodox Christians receive the bread and wine together on a spoon.

wine. They do not think that they are re-sacrificing Jesus, but that they are representing his one sacrifice made 2,000 years ago (i.e. 're-presenting' it, bringing it out of the past into the present). The Anglican services stress that the sacrifice of Jesus is complete, on the cross, 'a full oblation, once offered'.

They see the Holy Communion as a **sacrament**. A sacrament is more than a symbol that just reminds people of something; it is a special action that Christians believe is a vehicle or channel for God's presence, and by taking part in it they feel closer to him.

How do these Churches think the bread and wine become the body and blood of Christ?

- Roman Catholics believe in **transubstantiation**. This means that they think a change takes place in the bread and wine to make it Christ's body and blood. By this argument, an object is made up of two aspects: *substance* and *accidents*. Accidents are the physical characteristics and the appearance of an object. The underlying, invisible essence that somehow makes it what it is is the substance. So, when a priest consecrates the bread and wine, their substance changes into Christ's body and blood, but their accidents remain the same.

- Many Anglicans and Orthodox Christians just believe that Christ is somehow specially present in the bread and wine, and that the bread and wine are changed spiritually. It is a mystery. Anglican theology teaches the **real presence** – meaning that the Holy Communion is more than a symbol, but does not define it any further.

- Some modern Roman Catholic theologians are not happy with the doctrine of transubstantiation as it stands, and have proposed that of **transignification**. This stresses that the significance of the bread and wine changes once it has been consecrated, just as coloured inks on paper take on a special meaning when a five-pound note is printed. Here, there is the idea that the bread and wine become a special focus for the presence of Christ in the minds of the worshippers. Other Roman Catholics say that this is not enough – Christ has to be present in the bread and wine regardless of the worshippers. His presence does not depend upon their belief.

Receiving Communion in an Anglican church.

The Lutheran Churches

Martin Luther believed that Jesus was really present in the bread and the wine, but he taught **consubstantiation**. The substance of the bread and wine remained unchanged, but the substance of the Body and Blood of Jesus was added. This meant that the reality of bread and wine remained after they were blessed, but the reality of the risen Jesus was also joined to them. Lutherans today treat the communion with great respect and some have a great deal of ceremonial.

Lutherans are wary of calling the Eucharist a sacrifice. They want to stress that Christ's sacrifice was on the cross, and is finished.

A Communion service in a Methodist church. Notice the pieces of bread in the upper photograph and the individual glasses in the lower. Which would you prefer, to have individual glasses or share a single cup?

The Free Churches

These Churches do not regard the Eucharist in the same way. They think a sacrament is a special symbol that Jesus told people to use in worship. The bread and wine is a powerful reminder of what Jesus once did and of how he lives within the believers now. It is not a reoffering of his sacrifice, and it is put on a plain table. The bread and wine are symbols.

These Churches do stress that Jesus is present in a special way during the whole Eucharist, in the prayers, the blessings and in the sharing of the bread and wine. He is not specially present in the bread and wine, though.

Activities

Key Elements

1 a) What does the word 'Eucharist' mean?
  b) Why is Holy Communion called this?
  c) What other names might it be called?

Think About It

2 Why does bread and wine represent the death of Jesus whenever Christians meet together for Holy Communion?

3 What are the different ways Christians have of understanding Holy Communion? Make sure you explain what is meant by 'transubstantiation' and the 'real presence'.

4 Why do some Christians think Holy Communion is a sacrifice?

Assignments

1 Write an essay on how the senses of smell, touch, taste, hearing and sight are used in Christian worship.

2 Write a paragraph on:
  a) The differences between the design of modern church buildings from that of older ones.
  b) What ideas about God are the two designs stressing?
  c) How does the modern Roman Catholic Cathedral in Liverpool combine both ideas about God in its structure.

3 Design or make a model of a church building, bearing in mind what ideas about people and God you want to put across. Explain your design afterwards.

4 Write an essay on prayer, saying (i) why Christians think prayer is important, (ii) how they think it works and how it benefits people, (iii) how they explain why some prayers go unanswered and (iv) conclude with a paragraph saying whether you think their explanations are convincing.

5 Visit a Communion service and
  a) arrange with the minister for you to interview a few people afterwards to see what they believe happens when the bread and wine are shared out, or
  b) write a report about your reactions to the service and how you felt when you were there.

4

Festivals

Events like birthdays and anniversaries are special occasions when something can be celebrated. When we celebrate birthdays we are giving thanks for the life of a friend or relative. A few people decide not to keep birthdays and similar times because they say that you should be thankful for a person's life or relationship all the year round. There is a point to this, but human nature being what it is, we do tend to take things and people for granted and get caught up in the ordinary events of everyday life.

Having special days on which to remember and celebrate things makes sure that we do take time to value people or memories. It also gives a pattern to the year, so that time does not just seem to flow by, and it gives people something to look forward to and to plan for. Celebrating a birthday or an anniversary or the New Year makes us take time to think about things and take stock of where we are and what we are doing. As these are specially set dates, the celebrations usually follow a ritual, such as giving cards and eating special food that is associated with the time, such as turkey at Christmas or cake on a birthday. These things are familiar and focus your mind on what is going on.

Christianity has specially set days and times to celebrate various events in its faith. There are three main times of celebration: **Christmas**, **Easter** and **Pentecost** (also called **Whitsun**). These are the festivals of the Church, and festivities suggest joy and a party spirit. Each of these has moments like a

Celebrations are an important part of everyone's life. What might this couple be celebrating?

thanksgiving party, but there are serious moments and times of reflection, too. The three great festivals celebrate events in the life of Jesus and in the life of the Church:

- Christmas celebrates the birth of Christ.
- Easter celebrates the death and resurrection of Christ.
- Pentecost/Whitsun celebrates the gift of the Holy Spirit to the Church.

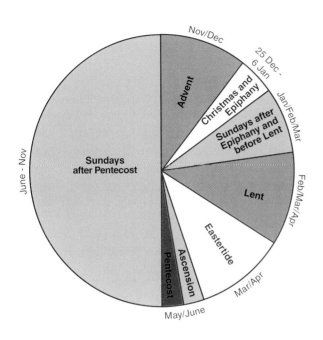

A carving of the Annunciation by an African pupil. Describe Mary's reation to the angel's message.

Christmas

The Story

The Christmas story is told in two of the Gospels: Matthew and Luke. The other two Gospels start their stories when Jesus is an adult. In both Matthew and Luke the story is that Jesus was born of a virgin mother as a result of a miracle. In Matthew's account (1:18–21) an angel appeared to Joseph in a dream:

'Do not be afraid to take Mary to be your wife. For it is by the Holy Spirit that she has conceived. She will have a son, and you will name him Jesus – because he will save his people from their sins.'

Luke tells the story from Mary's point of view. This is part of his description of Mary's encounter with an angel, an event known as the **Annunciation**:

The angel said to her, 'Don't be afraid, Mary; God has been gracious to you. You will become pregnant and give birth to a son, and you will name him Jesus. . . .' Mary said to the angel, 'I am a virgin. How, then, can this be?' The angel answered, 'The Holy Spirit

will come on you, and God's power will rest upon you. For this reason the holy child will be called the Son of God.' (1:30–1, 34–5)

Matthew saw the miraculous birth as a fulfilment of an Old Testament prophecy in Isaiah 7:14. Matthew's version of the prophecy is usually translated into English as, ' "A Virgin will become pregnant and have a son, and he will be called Immanuel" (which means, "God is with us").'

Matthew also has the story of the wise men bringing gifts to the baby Jesus (2:1–12). He does not say how many men there were, but people have assumed that there were three of them because they brought three gifts (gold, frankincense and myrrh). It is a much later tradition that calls them kings. The word used to describe them in Greek is *magoi*, meaning magicians, astrologers or wise men. They followed a star from the East to Bethlehem. (This event is celebrated by some

Churches on 6 January and is known as the **Epiphany**.)

Luke has the story of the angels appearing to the shepherds in the fields and telling them the good news that Christ had been born (2:8–20). Note that each Gospel tells one of these stories; they do not have both; they were combined together by people in artwork later on.

Mary would have been a young girl when she gave birth, some think possibly between 14 and 16 years of age. According to Luke she and Joseph had to travel to Bethlehem because of a census (a register of names) that was being taken by the Romans. There was no room to stay in any of the inns and so she had to give birth in a stable. Many eastern stables are in caves, and are not very clean!

Whatever truth there is behind all these stories, it is a fact that Jesus was born. No one knows exactly when, though. It was in or before 4 BCE, because Matthew says that King Herod the Great was still alive at the time,

and he died in 4 BCE. (If the story of the shepherds is anything to go by, he must have been born in spring, because they would only have been out at that time watching their flocks because of the lambing season.)

December 25 was the date of a Roman festival called Saturnalia, which celebrated the Sun god's victory over winter. When the Roman Empire accepted Christianity as its official religion in the fourth century CE, they stopped worshipping the Sun god and made 25 December Jesus' official birthday. It seems that Christmas was not celebrated before this time, though.

Questions

- One of the writers says that Jesus' birth fulfilled a prophecy from the Old Testament. What was the prophecy, and where is it found in the Old Testament?

- Read through the Christmas stories in Luke and Matthew:
  a) From whose point of view are each of them written?
  b) What was special about the birth of Jesus? Why do many people find this surprising and hard to believe?

The Celebrations

Christians celebrate Christmas in a number of ways. Roman Catholics and Anglicans keep the season of **Advent**. This is a time of preparation for four weeks before Christmas. Some churches light Advent wreaths that have four candles, one for each Sunday. Advent calendars will be kept in homes, each having 24 small card windows to be opened, day by day, through December until the 24th – Christmas Eve. Christmas carols, special hymns about the birth of Jesus, will be sung, and some church groups will go singing around the streets, collecting money to give to charities. Children act out the story of the birth of Jesus in church or school. Advent is a

A crib outside an Indian home at Christmas.

A children's nativity play.

time of reflection for Christians, a time to think about their lives and their faith. Although Free Churches might not follow the formal season of Advent, they will join in the general festivities.

At midnight on Christmas Eve many Christians will gather for a special service, or they may go to a family service on Christmas Day itself.

Many of the other traditions surrounding the celebration of Christmas have got nothing to do with Christianity. Holly and mistletoe were brought into the homes of people in ancient times since they thought the berries were magical because they appeared in winter when most other plants died.

Christmas trees were thought by the Vikings to contain the secret of eternal life because the trees kept their leaves in winter. They used to bring them into their homes hoping for good luck. Christmas trees were unknown in this country until the last century when Prince Albert, Queen Victoria's husband, was sent one as a present from Norway.

Activities

Key Elements

1 Why do people have special days and festivals in the year? What special times do your family keep?

2 Draw a diagram of the three main Christian festivals showing what events they remember.

3 Which of the Gospels is the Christmas story found in?

4 Which Gospel has the story of the wise men? What gifts did they bring?

5 What event does the 'Annunciation' refer to? In which Gospel will you find it?

6 In what year and in which season was Jesus possibly born? Why is his birth celebrated on 25 December?

7 What happens during Advent?

8 What happens on Christmas Eve and Christmas Day?

The Meaning

Christians believe that God came to people in a special way at Christmas. He showed his love for people through the life of Jesus, showed that he is with people and that good is stronger than evil. The birth of Jesus is seen by Christians as a turning-point for the world and a hope for a new beginning where nations can live together in peace. This is up to each person, though, and will not happen magically, but Christmas reminds Christians of this goal, this ideal. To sum up this message, Matthew quoted from another Old Testament prophecy (4:16).

*'The people who live in darkness
will see a great light.
On those who live in the dark land of death
the light will shine.'*

One carol speaks of the birth of Jesus like this: 'The hopes and fears of all the years are met in thee tonight.'

Yes, nothing unusual there. But what about Mary being a virgin, and the angels and stars appearing?

All this talk about peace is fine. OK, he was born.

Christmas makes Christians think of peace. In the First World War, in 1914, the fighting stopped in the trenches on Christmas Day and the troops played football with each other and exchanged food and drink!

Most Christians do feel that the events in the Christmas story actually happened. Some do not, though. They believe that Jesus was born, and that God was with him in a special way, but they think the Christmas story is a collection of symbolic stories with a meaning. They think it is a myth. By 'myth' they do not mean that it is not true, and that is that. They mean that it is not literally true, but has a true *message* or meaning.

It is like tinsel, or icing put on a cake to make it more attractive - the stories make people realise how special Jesus was. Their reasons are as follows:

- The Christmas stories are only in *two* of the Gospels (Matthew and Luke), and they are not mentioned anywhere else in the New Testament. This is strange if Jesus was born in such a dramatic way.
- The Gospels of Matthew and Luke were written some 15 to 20 years after Mark's Gospel (which does not mention the virgin birth). The myth may have been developed in this time and then added on to the story of Jesus.
- There were many stories of people being born in a miraculous way in the Greek and Roman world. The great philosopher Plato, for example, (fourth century BCE) was said to have been born before his father had had sex with his mother. The god Apollo had made her pregnant. If the Christians wanted to show that

Jesus was special, in such a culture, it was natural to invent a story of his miraculous birth. They were not lying; it was a poetic way of saying that God was with him in a special way. He was an outstanding person; Christians believe the most outstanding person.

An ancient coin showing the head of Alexander the Great. He was worshipped as a god by many of his subjects, and the ram's horns on the coin suggest divinity. Legends said that he was the son of Zeus, who had had intercourse with Alexander's mother. How is this story both similar to and different from that of the birth of Jesus?

- The story of the wise men could have been made up to make a point because the three gifts have a symbolic meaning: they tell us what the Gospel writer believed about Jesus. Gold suggested kingship; frankincense (incense used in worship) suggested the presence of God; myrrh was a bitter herb used in burials – it suggested that Jesus was destined to die on the cross.
- There is no evidence of a census being carried out at the time of Jesus' birth.
- The prophecy in Isaiah 7:14 can also be translated: 'a *young woman* who is pregnant will have a son...' It need not imply a virgin birth.

This might all seem negative, but it is important to stress that these Christians believe in Jesus very deeply. They just think that the Christmas story is symbolic and not actual history. They think many other things in the Gospel stories are, however, historical.

Other Christians would argue as follows:

- It is true that only two Gospels mention the story of the miraculous birth. But it is possible that this was not known about until later on because Mary kept it a secret. (It would have been very personal.)
- The story of the birth of Jesus is similar to Greek and Roman stories in some ways, but it is different from them in others. In the Greek stories a god usually had sex with a woman, and sometimes even raped her. This is not the Christmas story. It does not say that God had sex with Mary! It says a miracle was performed in her womb.

- Just because the wise men's gifts had a symbolic meaning does not mean that the story did not happen. Ancient Babylonian and Chinese records suggest that there were three unusual sightings in the sky between 7 BCE and 4 BCE (a conjunction of two planets – where they would appear on the same line of vision and so look like a bright star; a nova – an exploding star; and a comet of some kind). Any of these might have been the star.
- There might be no evidence of a census, but new evidence might come to light if more ancient records are discovered one day.

However, all Christians agree that the manner of Jesus' birth is not as important as who he was and what he did. Christians can enjoy the message of Christmas whether they treat its story as symbolic or factual.

If Christians do believe that his birth was miraculous, then they either think this happened because:

- God suspended the normal laws of nature,
  or
- Jesus' birth took place through laws of nature that we do not understand yet, and so it only seems to have been supernatural.

So, do you believe in the virgin birth?

I'm not sure, but I don't think it really matters as much as the story of his death and resurrection. They're far more important.

Question

- Some Christians think the virgin birth is symbolic only. What point do they believe it is making?

Lent, Holy Week and Easter

The Story

The oldest festival that Christians celebrate is that of Easter. It remembers the story of Christ's resurrection. Lent and Holy Week build up to this.

The story of the arrest, trial and execution of Jesus takes up most of the space in each of the Gospels. Six out of the 16 chapters in Mark describe the events at the end of Jesus' life. His arrest, trial and crucifixion are known as the **Passion**. The outline of events is as follows:

1. Jesus went to pray in the Garden of Gethsemane with his disciples on the night of his arrest.
2. Judas betrayed his whereabouts to the Jewish authorities, and led a group of guards to Gethsemane to arrest him.
3. Jesus was taken to the High Priest's house where he was questioned all night. It was in the courtyard here that Peter denied he had ever known his master.
4. The Jewish leaders took Jesus before Pilate, the Roman governor, early in the morning.
5. Pilate questioned him, but found him to be a harmless preacher. He offered to let Jesus go free, but the Jewish leaders threatened to report him to Caesar.
6. Pilate had Jesus whipped, thinking that would satisfy them. He offered to set one of two prisoners free: Jesus, or a revolutionary called Barabbas. The people chose Barabbas.

The Garden Tomb just outside Jerusalem. Jesus would have been buried in one similar to this. Some Christians believe this to be his real tomb.

7 Jesus was forced to carry his own cross, but he fell under the weight of it, and Simon of Cyrene had to help him.

8 Jesus was crucified between two thieves on a hill called Golgotha, just outside Jerusalem. He died after six hours.

Jesus was buried in a tomb that had been donated to the disciples by a rich merchant, Joseph of Arimathea. He was a sympathiser, or maybe a disciple himself. The tomb was cut out of rock in a garden nearby.

Normally, a body would be cleaned and covered with spices to help to preserve it. The Gospels say that Jesus was placed in a burial shroud and put in the tomb quickly because it was Friday evening and the Jewish Sabbath was approaching, when Jews were not allowed to work. The tomb would have been sealed by rolling a huge stone in front of the entrance. This would deter any grave robbers.

Some of the women came to the tomb early on Sunday morning (after the Jewish Sab-

A cross-section of a tomb.

bath) to prepare Jesus' body properly with the right spices. They found that the stone had been rolled away and that the tomb was empty. A young man in white, according to one Gospel, or an angel according to another, told them that Jesus had risen. Mark's version continues:

'Don't be alarmed,' he said. 'I know you are looking for Jesus of Nazareth, who was cruci-fied. He is not here – he has been raised! Look, here is the place where they put him.

An Armenian portrayal of the resurrection of Jesus. Notice the empty tomb below the figure of Jesus.

Now go and give this message to his disciples, including Peter: "He is going to Galilee ahead of you; there you will see him just as he told you." ' So they went out and ran from the tomb, distressed and terrified. They said nothing to anyone, because they were afraid. *(16:6–8)*

Mark ends there rather suddenly. Many people think that there was originally more to his Gospel, but that the ending was lost as it was copied and handed down. The other Gospels carry on the story:

1 The women tell the disciples, and they think they have gone mad.
2 Peter goes to the tomb to check, and finds it empty.
3 Jesus appears to the disciples several times, either all together or in small groups.
4 They all return to Jerusalem and meet behind locked doors for fear of the Romans.
5 Later, they find the courage to carry on preaching.

John has an account of an appearance to all the disciples at once (20:19–21):

Jesus came and stood among them. 'Peace be with you,' he said. After saying this, he showed them his hands and his side. The disciples were filled with joy at seeing the Lord. Jesus said to them again, 'Peace be with you. As the Father sent me, so I send you.'

Questions
- Describe what happens at the end of Mark's Gospel. Why does this account seem to end suddenly?

- Write a paragraph on Mark 14:32–42 and what this suggests to you about Jesus.

Luke (24:13–35) has a story of an appearance to two disciples walking along the road from Jerusalem to Emmaus. They did not recognise him at first, but they realised who it was when he shared some bread with them. Then he vanished. They said afterwards that their hearts had felt as though they had burned within them as he talked with them.

So the resurrection story involves three aspects: (1) the empty tomb, (2) appearances of the risen Christ, (3) the revived faith of the disciples, many of whom had given up. Instead they found new life and courage.

Activities

Key Elements

1 What is the Passion?
2 Where was Jesus arrested and who betrayed him?
3 Why was Pilate surprised when he met Jesus, and what happened when he offered to release Jesus?

4 Who carried Jesus' cross, and where was Jesus crucified?
5 How long did it take Jesus to die on the cross? Was this unusual?
6 How did Joseph of Arimathea help the disciples?

Assignments

• Draw a diagram of the type of tomb that Jesus was placed in and describe how it worked.

• Read through the account of Peter's denial in Mark 14:66–72. Tell the story as if you are Peter, explaining how you felt.

The Celebrations

The date of Easter varies each year because it is based on the Jewish calendar which follows the cycle of the moon, not the sun as in our calendar.

Lent and Holy Week

Anglican, Roman Catholic and Orthodox Christians keep a period of 40 days before Easter known as **Lent**. This period recalls the time Jesus spent in the desert being tempted by the Devil. It used to be a time of fasting, with only certain foods being eaten (meat, dairy produce and alcohol were not eaten, as is still the case in the Orthodox Churches). **Shrove Tuesday** is a leftover of this, when sweet pancakes are made. This was a final feast before Lent began the following day. Lent begins on **Ash Wednesday** and is a period of reflection and preparation. A special Eucharist is held on Ash Wednesday, and the sign of the cross is made upon the foreheads of worshippers with ashes. It is to show humility.

Many Christians today give up something for Lent (e.g. sweets, or sugar in drinks) or

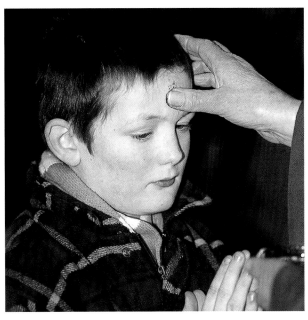

A Roman Catholic priest smears ashes on worshippers' foreheads on Ash Wednesday. What does this suggest?

might spend more time in prayer or the study of the Bible. It is a time of reflection and spiritual preparation as people think about their lives and prepare for Easter, when they are to celebrate the most important events in their faith.

Holy Week starts on **Palm Sunday** and ends on Holy Saturday, recalling the events of the last week of Jesus' life. The story of Jesus riding into Jerusalem on a donkey is remembered on Palm Sunday. (Read Mark 11:1–10.) Small crosses made from palm leaves are given out in churches and are held

by worshippers during the service. Some Churches will have a procession around the church or the local area. In Israel, Christians carry palm leaves and large wooden crosses

from Bethphage to Jerusalem, trying to follow the route that Jesus would have taken himself. The Ethiopian Orthodox Church uses decorative palms for Palm Sunday. These might be a ring of woven palm leaves worn around the finger, or a crown around the head.

The Meaning

Palm Sunday

The story of Jesus riding into Jerusalem is full of meanings that are hidden from people today unless they are explained. The people were cheering Jesus as the coming Messiah, and many were expecting a warrior Messiah who would drive the Romans out. The palm branches they waved were signs of victory, and they used to be waved after a battle was won, when people rejoiced in the streets. The people thought that the 'kingdom of King David' was to be restored. David was an ancient Jewish king who united the tribes of Israel into a mighty kingdom.

Yet Jesus came riding on a donkey. It is not exactly the way a warrior would ride to victory. Some people have compared this to the idea of the Prime Minister arriving on a scooter rather than in a Jaguar! Perhaps Jesus was deliberately showing that he was not the kind of Messiah that most people were expecting. He was a humble man of peace. A verse in the Old Testament could be taken as referring to the arrival of the Messiah, and Jesus chose to fulfil it because it suited his purposes: 'Shout for joy, you people of Jerusalem! Look, your king is coming to you! He comes triumphant and victorious, but humble and riding on a donkey – on a colt, the foal of a donkey.' (Zechariah 9:9)

The Celebrations

Maundy Thursday

Maundy Thursday is the next special day in Holy Week. The name comes from a Latin word *mandatum*, meaning commandment, and it refers to the commandment to love one another that Jesus gave on the night of the Last Supper, before he was arrested.

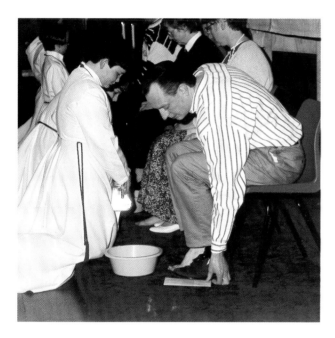

Many Churches include a foot-washing ceremony as a part of the Eucharist on this day. Some people sit at the front of the church and have their feet washed by the priest. This is because Jesus did this to the disciples in the upper room where they ate the Last Supper.

After Jesus had washed their feet, he put his outer garment back on and returned to his place at the table. 'Do you understand what I have just done to you?' he asked. 'You call me Teacher and Lord, and it is right that you do so, because that is what I am. I, your Lord and Teacher, have just washed your feet. You, then, should wash one another's feet. I have set an example for you, so that you will do just what I have done for you.'
(John 13:12–15)

The point here is that it was usually the job of the servants to wash the feet of guests. Foot washing was common in the East where the people walked in sandals on dry, dusty roads. Jesus was saying that Christians should love and serve one another.

Good Friday

The crucifixion of Jesus is remembered on **Good Friday**. This is a serious and sombre occasion.

Anglican, Roman Catholic and Orthodox churches are stripped of all colourful decorations, crosses, candles and hangings. This is to remind the worshippers of the fact that Jesus felt deserted and desolate on the cross. The story of the Passion is read, and, in some Churches, the priest will unveil a crucifix and say, 'This is the wood of the cross on which the Saviour of the world died.' The people will then walk up to the altar to kiss the feet of the carved Christ as a mark of respect.

Free Churches will not have the same ritual, but they will have a special service where the Passion story is read, and thanks will be given because Jesus went to the cross to save humanity from their sins.

All Churches teach that the death of Jesus saved the world somehow, although they have different ways of explaining that. Perhaps the easiest way is by thinking of the cross as a token of the love of God present in Christ; he was prepared to be rejected and he suffered, but he still forgives people. As a popular Easter hymn says, 'There is a green hill far away, without a city wall, where the dear Lord was crucified, who died to save us all.'

Holy Saturday

Roman Catholic, Orthodox and many Anglican churches keep an Easter **Vigil** on the Saturday evening. The congregation gather outside the church where a bonfire is burning. A large candle is brought out, called the **Paschal Candle**. It has a cross on it and the Greek letters alpha and omega. The priest places five grains of incense on it, in memory of the five wounds Jesus received on the cross

The Easter Vigil service on Saturday evening.

(both wrists, both feet and a spear wound in his side). The candle is then lit and the priest leads a procession into the church, holding the candle up high, and saying, 'Christ our Light'. The people reply, 'Thanks be to God!' They then carry small candles that are lit from the Paschal Candle and hold them during the Eucharist.

The vigil is in preparation for the celebration of the resurrection the next day. If Good Friday seemed to be about the victory of darkness, then the ceremony of the light symbolises the victory of Jesus over death.

Easter Sunday

This is the day of the resurrection, the third day after Jesus died. Anglican, Roman Catholic and Orthodox churches are full of decoration again with the priest in white robes, flowers on the altar and candles burning. Songs of victory are sung in all churches, such as, 'Thine be the glory, risen conquering Son. Endless is the victory thou over death has won . . .'

The story of the empty tomb and the appearances of the risen Jesus will be read out.

Some Customs

Eating hot cross buns began as a way of celebrating the end of Lent. The cross design, of course, remembers the death of Jesus.

The Easter egg is a symbol of new life. In Orthodox churches, hard-boiled eggs are coloured red to suggest blood, and are cracked open on Easter Day to celebrate the resurrection when Jesus burst free from the tomb.

The Easter egg might also be linked with ancient religion and the celebration of spring, when new life comes. The name 'Easter' comes from the old Saxon spring goddess, Eostre. The early Christians in Britain probably thought spring time was an appropriate time to remember the death and resurrection of Christ because it is a season of hope and new life.

The Ethiopian Orthodox Church calls Easter 'Fassika'. Tall candles ('twaf') are sold outside churches, being thin threads of cotton bound with wax. The churches are ablaze with light for the service celebrating the resurrection. People wear white robes ('yabesha libs') and the prayers go on from 8.00 p.m. until 3.00 a.m. The families will celebrate by sharing a special meal afterwards, 'injera', which is a mutton stew eaten with pancakes and cottage cheese.

Lighting candles from the Easter fire.

Questions

- a) What happens on these days in Holy Week: Palm Sunday, Maundy Thursday, Good Friday?
- b) What happened in the life of Jesus on those days?

- a) What happens at the Easter Vigil and on Easter Sunday?
- b) Explain what happened to Jesus at this time.

Activities

- Design a poster to advertise the church services during Holy Week.

- Write out recipes for typical Easter foods and explain their significance.

- Design an egg decoration.

The Meaning of Easter

The story of Jesus' passion and resurrection is a movement from tears to joy, and touches Christians very deeply when they hear it. It is about the struggle between good and evil, or light and darkness, and the final victory of good. It is about an innocent teacher of peace being persecuted by an oppressive government and put to death, and yet his message of love goes on. Even more, for the Christian, it is the story of how God showed that he was involved in human struggles and suffering, and of how God promises life after death.

Activities

Key Elements

1 What happens on Ash Wednesday and why does this take place?
2 How long does Lent last for, and what do Christians do during this period?
3 What do modern Christians do on Palm Sunday? What event in the life of Jesus does this remember?

Think About It

4 Why is Good Friday 'Good' to Churches?

Going Deeper

The Passion Narrative

New Testament scholars think that the earliest, continuous story told about Jesus was the Passion. It takes up a large proportion of space in each of the Gospels, and might have been the first narrative about Jesus to have been written down. The Gospel writers adapted earlier versions of the story to fit in with their Gospels. (Despite a few small differences they all tell the same story.)

The reason for telling the Passion story as a connected story so early may have been two-fold:

- To use it in the celebration of the Eucharist, remembering the details of the Last Supper.
- To use it to show both Jews and Romans that Jesus had not really been a criminal.

Why was Jesus Killed?

Crucifixion was a criminal's death. When the Romans heard that the Christians followed a crucified master, they would have suspected them of anti-social behaviour. Christians believe Jesus was a preacher of peace and love, challenging people to let the Kingdom of God enter their hearts. Why was he put to death? A possible answer is that the Jewish authorities were frightened that he might cause an uprising of the people because he was so unpopular (as can be seen in the story of the entry into Jerusalem). The Romans would then step in and many people might lose their lives. If the Jews handed him over to the Romans, and he was executed, then people would think he was a failure and they would stop following him.

Although Pilate found Jesus to be harmless in himself, the Romans would have been glad to have any potential trouble-maker out of the way. John's Gospel suggests that the Romans were involved in the plot to have Jesus killed, because a Roman cohort (about 480 men) accompanied the Jewish Temple guards to the Garden of Gethsemane to arrest Jesus (18:3).

Why did Judas Betray Jesus?

It has often puzzled people why Judas, one of the Twelve, should have betrayed his master. The usual explanation given is that he did it for the money. He was paid thirty silver coins by the Temple authorities. But this was not a large amount: it was the traditional price paid for the loss of a slave. Furthermore, Judas was filled with guilt and committed suicide after Jesus' death. (Matthew 27:5 says he hanged himself; Acts 1:18 suggests that he fell on a sword.) It is therefore hard to imagine that he was only in it for the money.

It is possible that Judas misunderstood Jesus. He might have really believed that Jesus was going to drive the Romans out, either by giving the people a sign to rise up in revolt or by bringing God's supernatural Kingdom crashing in. He might also have feared that the people were losing faith in Jesus after his entry into Jerusalem – many people would have been waiting for his signal then, but nothing happened. Judas might therefore have arranged the arrest in order to corner Jesus and force his hand; yet this backfired upon him and Judas could not live with himself when he realised that he had betrayed an innocent man of peace.

Facts and Symbols

Some people think that the style of writing that the Gospel writers used should not be taken as straightforward reporting of facts. The Gospel writers are always trying to interpret what Jesus said and did; and perhaps sometimes they add details to the story that are symbolic.

This might be seen in some of the details of the story of the death of Jesus. Mark says that at noon the whole country was covered in darkness, and three hours later Jesus died. Mark then adds that the curtain hanging in the Temple was torn in two, from top to bottom.

The darkness may have been some form of eclipse, but it could be a symbolic point: the time when Jesus was dying was a time of spiritual darkness; it seemed like a victory of evil over good.

The curtain in the Temple covered the entrance to the most holy part of it, the Holy of Holies, where only the High Priest could go, where it was believed he was in the presence of God. There is no evidence from any Jewish writings of anything happening to the curtain. Mark may have been writing symbolically: Jesus had died to bring God to all the earth; he could not be contained in a Temple any more; it was 'torn open'.

The Resurrection – What Happened?

Most Christians believe the stories of the resurrection in the Gospels, but some doubt the story of the empty tomb:

- They think the story of the empty tomb was a detail that was added on later to make the resurrection sound more dramatic.
- They think Jesus' body was just left to rot in the tomb; but his spirit was raised to new life in God.
- They point out that the earliest mention of the resurrection story (in Paul's first letter to the Corinthians 15:3–7 – which was written before the Gospels) does not mention the empty tomb at all. It just says that Jesus was raised and appeared to Peter, the rest of the Twelve, and to over 500 disciples, then to James, and finally to Paul.
- They feel that the empty tomb story makes the resurrection sound too physical; Jesus was not just a dead body come back to life, but a transformed spirit.

Traditional believers point out that they do not believe that Jesus was just a dead man come back to life, either:

- He was transformed and was alive in a new way, but his physical body was transformed, too. The body was not left to rot.
- The stories of the appearances of Jesus show he was different; sometimes he was not recognised at first, and sometimes he appeared and disappeared suddenly. See, for example, Luke 24:13–32; and John 20:19–21.
- If the empty tomb story was made up, it is hard to see why the women were made out to be the first witnesses, as in Jewish society the word of a woman was not valid in a court of law.

- The raising of Jesus' body shows that there is hope for the material world. This will be glorified one day.

Activities

- Write an imaginary interview with Pilate, trying to find out what he thought about Jesus and why he sentenced him to death.

- Discuss why you think Judas betrayed Jesus. Was it for money or to force Jesus to do something, or for some other reason?

- Arrange a debate: one side to argue that the tomb was empty on Easter Sunday; the other side to argue that it was just Jesus' spirit that was raised.

Pentecost (Whitsun)

The Story

Pentecost celebrates the reawakening of faith in the disciples after the resurrection. This reawakening, and sense of renewed courage, is seen as a result of the gift of the Holy Spirit.

The fullest account of it in the New Testament is in Acts 2:1–42. The disciples were gathered together in prayer, waiting for the coming of the Holy Spirit, as Jesus had told them to:

Suddenly there was a noise from the sky which sounded like a strong wind blowing, and it filled the whole house where they were sitting. Then they saw what looked like tongues of fire which spread out and touched each person there. They were all filled with the Holy Spirit and began to talk in another language, as the Spirit enabled them to speak.　　　　　　　　　　*(2:2–4)*

When people came to listen, Peter explained what had happened by quoting an Old Testament passage (from Joel 2:28):

'This is what I will do in the last days, God says:
I will pour out my Spirit on everyone.
Your sons and daughters will proclaim my message . . .'　　　　　*(Acts 2:17)*

Then Peter went on to explain:

'God has raised this very Jesus from death, and we are all witnesses to this fact. He has been raised to the right-hand side of God, his Father, and has received from him the Holy Spirit, as he had promised. What you now see and hear is his gift that he has poured out on us.'　　　　　*(Acts 2:32–3)*

This is said in Acts to have happened 50 days after the crucifixion, on the day of the Jewish feast of Pentecost, which celebrated the giving of the Law to Moses. John's Gospel, however, gives a different version of the events, where the gift of the Holy Spirit is given to the disciples in the upper room when they first see the risen Christ (20:22). There are no tongues of fire or roaring wind in this version.

The Celebrations

The main celebration is on Pentecost Sunday. Special reference is made to the gift of the Holy Spirit during the service in church, and the story from Acts is read out.

Churches are decorated in red for the fire of the Spirit. Sometimes Christians will be confirmed in the faith at this time, when a bishop lays his hands on their heads and prays for the Spirit to come into their lives (see pp. 122–3).

During Pentecost, or Whit week, some churches take part in walks of witness through a town – Christians will carry banners with simple messages or texts from the scriptures on them. Their walk ends at a short service in a church or in the open air. The

Pentecost: notice the dove and the flames.

walk recalls the boldness of the disciples when they first went out preaching.

It used to be the custom to buy children new clothes at this time: it suggests the renewing power of the Spirit and the new life the disciples felt.

The Meaning

What may have happened is that the disciples were downhearted and confused after the crucifixion, but their energy and faith revived when they came to believe that Jesus had risen from the dead. This renewal was possibly a gradual process until they felt that God was alive within them in a new, fresh way. So John has the coming of the life-giving Spirit at the same time as the first sight of the risen Christ; and the writer of Acts has the full revival coming later when things had sunk in more.

The wind and fire in the Acts story may be symbols. The writer probably does not mean his readers to think that there were physical wind and fire there. Instead it is poetry – a way of describing the disciples' revival of faith.

The Holy Spirit is often pictured as wind or fire in the Bible. Wind suggests power, an invisible force that cannot be controlled. Fire suggests the warmth of love or joy, and the light of knowledge and purity. The Acts passage is using this picture-language to show that the lives of the disciples were being shaken up; their fears disappeared (burned away) and they saw with the inner eye of faith that Christ was alive (the light of knowledge).

The result of the gift of the Spirit was that the disciples went out fearlessly, teaching the message of Jesus, even when their lives were threatened (read Acts 4:18–22, for example).

The 'other languages' (Acts 2:4) spoken by the disciples are understood in various ways:

- As a miracle, a new ability given by God to spread the Gospel.
- As a made-up story to make a point that the Gospel is for all nations and races.
- As a misunderstanding of an excited babbling and wordless praise that people overheard in the disciples who were so overjoyed.

Activity
- Design a Pentecost banner.

Activities

Key Elements

1   What did the Jews celebrate on the day of Pentecost?
2   What happened to the disciples on the day of Pentecost?
3   Why are wind and fire symbols of the Holy Spirit?
4   How were the disciples affected by their experience?
5   a) What happens on Pentecost Sunday and what special events take place at Pentecost?
    b) What meaning do these events have?

Think About It

6   What do you think Christians mean by the Holy Spirit?

Assignments

1   Write an essay on the virgin birth:
    (i) explain the arguments that some Christians put forward *against* a virgin birth, and (ii) those arguments that other Christians have *for* a virgin birth. (iii) Conclude with what you think – whose arguments do you find more convincing?
2   Write a paragraph comparing the story of the coming of the Spirit in John 20:19–23 with that in Acts 2:1–8.
3   Imagine you were in the crowd which gathered when the disciples came out into the street (Acts 2:5–42). Write a letter to a friend back home describing what happened and how you reacted.
4   Write a paragraph explaining how the story of speaking in different languages might be understood, and giving your own opinion.

5

The Bible

WHAT IS IN THE BIBLE?

The Bible is in two sections, the Old Testament and the New Testament. The Old Testament has 39 books in some versions, and 54 in others. The New Testament has 27 books. The Bible is like a library between two covers, with books that were written at different times by different people. The Old Testament is about the Jews, their history and beliefs, and the New Testament is about Jesus and the first Christians.

What's so special about this book, anyway?

What's it all about?

THE BIBLE IN CHRISTIAN LIFE AND WORSHIP

The Bible is studied to get ideas about God and how we should live.

Ministers preach from the Bible to inspire other Christians.

The Bible is read quietly and meditated upon, prayerfully, to seek God's guidance.

MAKING SENSE OF THE BIBLE

All Christians think that the Bible is the Word of God, in some sense, but there are different ideas about its inspiration by God:

The Bible is the Word of God, word for word.

The Bible is the Word of God, through the words of the authors who interpret it.

The Bible contains or carries the Word of God, but it is also the word of human beings who sometimes got things wrong.

But what's it all about?

THE BIBLE STORY

While there are many different things in the Bible, it has a central story which is about God's plans for humanity and his attempts to help them.

The story starts with the creation of the world. The book of Genesis suggests that it was made in six days, but most Christians think this is poetry, not scientific fact. The world came about in stages, over millions of years, but they think God has been guiding and planning it.

Human beings appeared with minds of their own. They could choose God or turn away from him; it was up to them. God did not want a race of robots. God wanted a race that could love him and obey him.

Moses was sent by God to rescue the Hebrews, a group of slaves, from Egypt. They escaped across the Sea of Reeds, a marshy area north of the Red Sea, which dried up when a strong wind blew.

Moses gave the people commandments to follow. He believed these came from God who wanted the Hebrews to be his special people.

Other prophets were sent to teach the people, and it was hoped that they would set an example for the other nations, so that all would worship one God again. But the people did not always listen!

So, God decided to come himself, in Jesus, to make things clear, and to try to set things right. He came as one of the special race, the Hebrews.

IESVS NAZARENVS REX IVDEORVM

Some of the people still did not listen, and they crucified Jesus. God still forgave people, and wanted them to turn round and start again.

Christians believe that God raised Jesus from the dead, and he is still calling people to himself.

The Bible (also known as Scripture or the Scriptures) is the holy book of Christians. It has been translated into many different languages. John Wycliffe was the first person to translate the Bible into English, in the fourteenth century. (Though St Bede had written an Anglo-Saxon version earlier.) The first approved translation was the 'Great Bible' in 1539. Before this, Bibles were written in Latin in England.

Some Bibles look very sombre, in black bindings and with old English words. But there are also many more modern translations, such as the *New English Bible*, the *Good News Bible* or the *Jerusalem Bible* (the Roman Catholic version). All of these try to put the Bible words into modern English so that it is easier to understand. Compare these two passages, for example, from John 6:47–51. Jesus is the speaker:

Authorised Version (King James Version) of 1611:

'Verily, verily, I say unto you, He that believeth on me hath everlasting life. I am that bread of life. Your fathers did eat manna in the wilderness, and are dead. This is the bread which cometh down from heaven, that a man may eat thereof, and not die. I am the living bread which came down from heaven: if any man eat of this bread, he shall live for ever.'

Good News Bible of 1976:

'I am telling you the truth; he who believes has eternal life. I am the bread of life. Your ancestors ate manna in the desert, but they died. But the bread that comes down from heaven is of such a kind that whoever eats it will not die. I am the living bread that came down from heaven. If anyone eats this bread, he will live for ever.'

The Bible was written originally in a number of languages long before it was translated into English. The languages were Hebrew, Aramaic and Greek. Most of the Old Testament was in Hebrew, with a few sections in Aramaic, a similar language, and the New Testament was written in Greek.

Part of the New Testament written in Greek, from the fourth-century Codex Sinaiticus.

Activities

Key Elements

1 What are the two sections in the Christian Bible? Why are there two sections?
2 What do Christians use the Bible for?
3 What do Christians think God has got to do with the writing of the Bible?
4 Do all Christians think the world was made in six days? What do most think?
5 Why do Christians think that God came himself in the end?

Think About It

6 If God created people, why do Christians think people cause so much suffering in the world?
7 Discuss whether you think the Bible story could help people make sense of life. Is it a sad or happy story? Is it a success story, or a story of failure?

The Old Testament
(The Hebrew Bible)

Christians value the Old Testament because it was the book of the Jewish ancestors of Jesus and they interpret many of the prophecies about a coming deliverer – the Messiah – as being about Jesus. (Jewish people do not accept this of course.)

Most English versions have 39 separate books:

- 5 law books
- 12 history books
- 5 poetry books
- 17 prophetic books (though these also contain much poetry)

The Jews divide these books up into three sections: the Law, the Prophets and the Writings.

The Law

The Law (*Torah* in Hebrew) is the most important section for the Jews; it contains 613 laws. The first five books of the Bible form the Torah (Genesis, Exodus, Leviticus, Numbers and Deuteronomy). They contain many different types of laws, as well as stories about the ancestors of the Jews, like Abraham. There are laws for punishments, rights of slaves, repaying debts, protecting the poor, religious worship and sacrifice, for example, and even for which animals can and cannot be eaten (see Leviticus 11 and Exodus 34:26). Orthodox Jews believe that the whole of the Law came from God, being dictated to Moses on Mt Sinai, and they try to keep as many of the laws as possible. Reform Jews think parts of the Law came from Moses and other laws were added on later. They believe that some of the laws were relevant for their time but are now outdated, though there are general laws, such as love for neighbour and the worship of one God only, which are true for all ages.

Christians believe that Jesus has given new laws, in the New Testament, and that these complete the Law that God gave to Moses.

The Prophets

The prophets rarely foretold the future. They were *forthtellers* rather than *foretellers*. They believed they had a message from God for their times, challenging or encouraging the world they lived in. Amos, for example, in the eighth century BCE, reminded people of God's justice and challenged them to turn from their **sins**. He criticised the false, hypocritical religion of his day because it kept the rich rich and the poor poor.

The words of the prophets contained great insights and morals that Christians believe all ages can learn from. In a general way they did speak of the future: they spoke of the coming Messiah and of an age of peace when all would know God:

The prophet Amos.

Wolves and sheep will live together in peace,
and leopards will lie down with young goats.
Calves and lion cubs will feed together,
and little children will take care of them...
there will be nothing harmful or evil.
The land will be as full of knowledge of the
   LORD
as the seas are full of water.   (Isaiah 11:6, 9)

Isaiah also contains a moving passage about the Servant of God who is rejected by the people and suffers for their sins. For Christians, Jesus is the supreme example of the Servant since he went to his death on the cross after speaking out for what he believed in. Jewish people, however, think the Servant is anyone who tries to do what is right and who is badly treated by other people. They see their own race in the Servant, often persecuted and slandered in history:

'All of us were like sheep that were lost,
each of us going his own way.
But the LORD made the punishment fall on
   him,
the punishment all of us deserved.
He was treated harshly, but endured it
   humbly;
he never said a word.
Like a lamb about to be slaughtered,
like a sheep about to be sheared,
he never said a word.
He was arrested and sentenced and led off to
   die,
and no one cared about his fate.
He was put to death for the sins of our
   people.'   (Isaiah 53:6–8)

The prophets also predicted more local events. For example, Jeremiah predicted that Babylon, 'a foe from the north', would descend upon Judah and exile the people unless they turned from their sins. But the bulk of their teaching was forthtelling rather than foretelling.

The Writings

There are various types of poetry books in this section, such as the **Psalms**. These are prayers and hymns of praise, some by King David, with moving imagery such as these lines from Psalm 42:1–2: 'As a deer longs for a stream of cool water, so I long for you, O God. I thirst for you, the living God: when can I go and worship in your presence?'

The Book of Job is about an innocent man who suffers, and Proverbs is a series of wise sayings. There is even a collection of love songs, the 'Song of Songs', and a book about an ancient prophet, Daniel, which has vivid poetry that tells of the coming Kingdom of God.

Christians value these books for their insights about God. The Psalms are recited in Christian worship regularly.

Activities

Key Elements

1 Give two reasons why Christians use and respect the Old Testament.
2 What did the prophet Amos think was wrong with the religion of his day? Do you think he might say the same about religious people today?
3 Write a paragraph about the teaching of the prophets.
4 How do Jews and Christians understand the identity of the Servant of God in Isaiah 53? Write a paragraph on this.

The New Testament

The New Testament contains the writings of the early Christians, and once these had been written, the Church placed them alongside the Old Testament writings to form the complete Christian Bible that is known today. The New Testament contains 27 different books:

- 5 books about Jesus and his followers
- 21 letters
- 1 prophetic book

The Books about Jesus and his Followers

Four of the books about Jesus are called Gospels. They tell the story of the main events in the life of Jesus, and contain his teaching. They are named after their traditional authors: Matthew, Mark, Luke and John. The word *gospel* means 'good news' and the idea is that the books are about the good news of the coming of Jesus and of his resurrection from the dead. The Gospels largely ignore the childhood of Jesus and are mainly concerned with the last few years of his life when he became a public preacher. They are

even more interested in the last week of his life – Holy Week and his journey to the cross. (See also pp. 54–60 and 91–3.)

The fifth book, The Acts of the Apostles, is about the beginning of the Church, when the apostles rallied together after Jesus' death and spread the belief in his resurrection. It concentrates mainly on the exploits of Peter and Paul and finishes when Paul is awaiting trial in Rome.

The Letters

Most of the New Testament is composed of **epistles**, or letters. This sounds strange at first, but there is a good reason. Most of these letters were written by Paul and his disciples, with two said to have been written by Peter, three by John (but which John? – the apostle,

or a later disciple?), one by James and one by Jude. These Christian leaders wrote to gatherings of believers to give them advice and encouragement. Usually, they wrote to churches that they had founded and for which they felt a special responsibility. 1 Corinthians, for example, thus means 'The first letter that Paul wrote to the Christians in Corinth'. Some of the letters are very short, like Philemon, and others are much longer, like Romans.

These letters give us an insight into the beliefs and concerns of the first Christians and, just as people found them helpful then, so too do modern Christians.

The Visionary Book

The Book of Revelation is a weird and wonderful work written towards the end of the first century CE. It claims to be a series of visions, full of symbols and strange events. Its theme is that good will eventually win over evil, and that Christ is going to return to earth in victory. Most Christians accept it as poetry, and do not take it literally word for word.

Evil powers are symbolised as beasts that rise from the sea to torment the human race, and Christ returns on the clouds, in glory, to slay the beast and set the people free. It is a poetic way of talking about the final victory of good over evil.

Activities

Key Elements

1 What does the word 'Gospel' mean?
2 Why did the first Christians call them that?
3 Which book tells the story of the beginning of the Church?
4 a) Who wrote the letters in the New Testament?
   b) What does '1 Corinthians' mean?
   c) Why were the letters written?
   d) Why do you think they are included in the New Testament?
5 What is the book of Revelation about, and what type of writing is it?

The two parts of the Bible are called **Testaments** because both Jews and Christians believe that God has made a special agreement with humankind. (Testament here means agreement or promise. Another word for it is a covenant.) In the Old Testament God promised to guide the Jews and reveal his laws to them. In the New Testament, Christians believe that God has shown how much he loves all people through Jesus dying on the cross, and promises them life after death.

The Bible, therefore, is a collection of different books, written at different times by different authors. It did not fall out of the sky one day, and it was not written by just one person! It is like a library of religious books, some by Jews, some by Christians, between its covers. In fact, the word 'Bible' comes from the Greek word *biblia* meaning 'the books'. They would have been copied out on individual scrolls before the book format was invented.

Canon is a Greek word which meant 'a measuring rod'. It then came to mean a list of

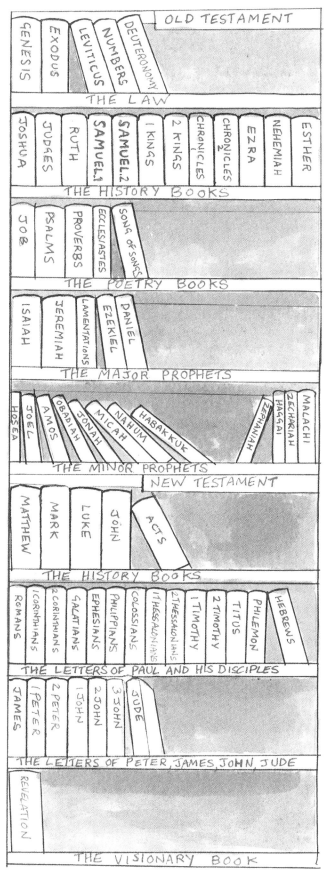

books accepted as genuine. The canon of the Bible means the correct list of books that are in it. The canon of the Old Testament has been fixed as the books of the Law, of the Prophets and the Writings, by the time of Jesus. The canon of the New Testament was settled by about 200 CE. In order to be included, books had to be widely read by Christians, had to be considered helpful, and either had to be written by one of the apostles or thought to be faithful to their teachings.

The Apocrypha

There is also a collection of writings which some Bibles include with the Old Testament, and which other Bibles print as a separate section in between the Old Testament and the New Testament. They are called **Apocrypha**, which means 'hidden (books)', because they are disputed. Some think they should not be in the canon.

There are 15 writings – some are lengthy books, some are short letters or extracts. They were included in the Greek translation of the Old Testament that was made in the Ancient World, but not in the Hebrew canon. The early Christians used the Greek Old Testament widely and carried on using the extra writings in their Bible. In the fourth century, the Christian scholar Jerome called these extra writings the Apocrypha and doubted whether they should be of the same standing as the rest of the Bible. He thought the events in them were more doubtful. Protestant Christians do not print the books as part of their Bible, but Roman Catholics still do, as in the modern *Jerusalem Bible*.

The Apocrypha were composed between 300 BCE and 100 CE. The writings contain stories of the Jewish ancestors, Tobit and Judith; the stories of the Maccabees – Jewish freedom-fighters in the century before Jesus; wise sayings; and additions to the Old Testament book of Daniel, such as the comical detective story called 'Bel and the Dragon'.

Activities

Key Elements

1 What special agreements to Christians think God made with humanity in the Old and New Testaments?
2 When was the canon of the Bible fixed?
3 How was the New Testament canon fixed?
4 What does the word 'Apocrypha' mean?
5 How many books does the Apocrypha contain?
6 Which ancient copies of the Bible included these books and which excluded them? Which Christians still include them in their Bible?
7 Who was the first Christian to doubt the accuracy of the stories in the Apocrypha?
8 When were the books of the Apocrypha written and what sort of things are they about?

Young Christians are encouraged to read the Bible.

The Bible in Christian Life and Worship

The Bible is used in a variety of ways in Christian life and worship. It is not just an ancient book, an old classic, read out of interest, as people might read the works of Julius Caesar or the ancient Greek writers. Christians read it to try to find out more about their faith, to find ideals for living, and even to try to hear the voice of God within them.

In church services, lessons from the Bible will be read, and the congregation will listen. Maybe much of it goes in one ear and out the other, but sometimes something might strike a chord or connect up in a person's mind. A saying, a verse, a phrase might jump out at them and suggest an answer to a problem, or help to guide them in making a decision. Or perhaps this will click into place during the sermon, when the preacher might comment on various aspects of the passages that are read out.

The Bible is also studied in small groups who meet in church or in someone's home. The minister, or some other member of the congregation, will read through some passages, think about them, look them up in a commentary written by experts, and will then lead the group in study and discussion. This will give people the opportunity of asking questions and raising doubts, an opportunity they do not have in a formal church service.

The Bible studies might be applied to problems of everyday life, such as finding a goal in life, coping with depression or family life. Or social problems might be focused on, like racism, war or unemployment. In this way, Christians may come to a deeper understanding of their faith and its application to life.

The Bible will also be used for personal study or meditation. Christians might set aside a few minutes each day for prayer and study. They might just open the Bible at random, or work through a particular book, or use Bible reading notes which will guide them through passages and comment on them. Anglican, Orthodox and Roman Catholic Christians might use the daily offices of morning and evening prayer – these are collections of various prayers, Psalms and readings, some from the Old Testament, some from the New Testament. A particular passage might be read through slowly, several times, so that its meaning sinks in. After doing this for some time people will think about what they have been reading and perhaps say a prayer. This is a way of using the Bible in meditation. Besides finding out information about their faith, and looking for ideals, they hope to sense the inner guidance of God through reading the words of scripture.

Making Sense of the Bible

The Bible, for all Christians, is in some way the Word of God. They hope to sense the voice of God within them as they read it. Yet there are different ways of understanding this:

- Some think the Bible is the direct Word of God, passed down through the writers as if they were secretaries taking notes from a heavenly voice. Everything in it is true, and most things should be taken word for word, as they are written. *The Bible is the Word of God, word for word.*

- Some think that the Word of God came to the writers, but that their own personalities and writing styles were included. They interpreted the Word that came to them; they were not just secretaries. *The Bible is the Word of God interpreted.*

- Some take this further, and argue that the writers were human beings capable of making mistakes, and were influenced by ideas around them at the time

(such as seeing the world as flat). The Bible witnesses to, or contains, the Word of God, but is not directly the Word itself. *The Bible is the Word of God interpreted – and sometimes wrongly.*

So, opinions vary amongst Christians, and not all Christians accept everything in the Bible as being true.

These three basic attitudes need to be explored further. The three opinions can be summed up as those of the fundamentalist, the conservative and the liberal (not in any political sense!).

The Fundamentalist
(from 'fundamentals', a belief in basic truths and principles that are written down)

These Christians think that the Bible is free from all error because it is not the words of men, but the Word of God. If passages seem to contradict themselves in the Bible, then these can and must be explained away. In the stories of the resurrection, for example, John's Gospel has Mary Magdalene going to the tomb first, then Peter, and then Mary is the first to see the risen Christ. Matthew, Mark and Luke have a group of women going to the tomb first, and in Matthew the first appearance of the risen Christ is to the women as they are running back to tell Peter and the others. Fundamentalists would argue that John had simply not mentioned the other women, but knew they were there, and the other appearances took place on different occasions.

Again, if the Bible seems to contradict science then scientists must be wrong. A case in point is with evolution. Fundamentalists believe in a six-day creation and that Adam and Eve were the first people. They spend much time and energy arguing against evolutionary theories. (Some see the six 'days' as six 'eras' however.) Humans, they say, did not evolve but were specially created by God.

Their understanding of the inspiration of the Bible writers is something like this:

The Conservative
(from 'conserve', to guard certain traditions and ideas)

The conservative Christian believes that something of the personality of the writers came through in the Bible; it is not directly the Word of God. Therefore, they do not feel that the Bible teaches science. Instead it is a book about faith and knowledge of God; it is not intended to be a scientific textbook. Hence there is no difficulty in accepting some form of evolution, and seeing the six-day creation story as a poem, which says *why* the world was created, but not *how*.

Conservative believers do feel that there are a number of truths that were inspired by God in the Bible, though, such as that God guides the world, spoke through the prophets, that he came in Jesus born of a virgin, worked miracles, died for people's sins and rose from the dead. They are not too concerned about trying to make various contradictory stories match one another, such as in the details of the resurrection story; they

accept that different writers may have heard different versions of the same story, but the writers are all saying that the resurrection happened, and that is the important thing.

The conservative view of inspiration works something like this:

The Liberal
(from 'liberty', freedom of thought and expression)

The liberal Christian feels that the Bible writers were inspired like any great writer is, like Shakespeare. They have insights into human life that others do not have, and they are able to put these into words. The Bible writers also had deep insights about God that can help others to know what God is like and find their way to him. The writers might have had an experience of God, and they tried to put this into words. But they could make mistakes. They thought as they had been taught, and held the same ideas about science that other people in the Ancient World had, for example.

Liberals feel that many passages of the Bible are symbolic poetry and should not be taken word for word. Some think more passages are symbolic than others. For example, some liberals think that all the miracle stories in the Gospel are symbolic of great truths in the teaching of Jesus, but that they did not actually happen (thus, the healing of a blind man means that Jesus teaches people how to see spiritual things in life; he opens people's eyes, as it were). Other liberals may feel that many of the healing stories did happen but that the nature miracles, such as walking on water, are symbolic stories. Many liberals do not believe that the virgin birth happened, instead they see it as a story with a meaning – God was in Jesus more than in any other man. Also, they do not accept the story of the empty tomb, but think that Jesus only rose again spiritually.

Liberal Christians try to find the kernel of truth in the Bible stories which they think often contain errors or symbols that need to be understood properly.

Their view of inspiration is as follows:

HMMM HOW CAN I PUT THIS?

Many Christians are conservative in some of their beliefs and liberal in others. They move backwards and forwards between the two camps. There are various stances within the 'conservative' and 'liberal' wings of Christianity. A significant group of Christians are fundamentalist, particularly in the United States. They fear that once you question one thing in the Bible, you will not know where to stop. Other Christians fear that if you do accept all that the Bible says, it will mean believing in things that are impossible to believe any more, like the six-day creation. They think it is better to take what seems good and sensible, and to leave a question mark over the rest.

All Christians will agree, however, that the writings in the Bible tell of the existence and love of God, of how Jesus showed people what God was like, and how there is a life after death.

It might be useful to look at a few examples from the Bible to compare and contrast the fundamentalist–conservative–liberal viewpoints. The passages to be studied will be:

- Joshua and the walls of Jericho (Old Testament: Joshua 6)
- The feeding of the 5,000 (New Testament: Mark 6:33–44; Matthew 14:13–21; Luke 9:10–17; John 6:1–14)
- The healing of a blind man (New Testament: John 9)
- Paul and the role of women (New Testament: Ephesians 5:21–5)

JOSHUA AND THE WALLS OF JERICHO

Joshua leads the Hebrews against the Canaanite city of Jericho. God tells him to get the Hebrews to march round it once a day for six days and on the seventh day they are to march round it again, with the priests blowing trumpets at the front, and the men giving a loud shout. They do this, the walls collapse, and they rush in and kill everyone, men, women, young and old, and all the cattle they find. They set fire to the city and do not take any loot from it. Only a prostitute, Rahab, is spared, because she had allowed two Hebrew spies into her house earlier.

THE FUNDAMENTALIST

If it is in the Bible, then it happened. I know it sounds ruthless and cruel, but we musn't question God's word. Perhaps the people were very sinful, and they had to be conquered so the Hebrews could possess the land, as God promised. Of course, Jesus taught a new law, in which we should love our enemies.

THE CONSERVATIVE

It was cruel, but people were more barbaric then, and God could not get through to them with his full message of love. He was preparing a people whom he could teach over the centuries. A miracle might have made the walls fall down, or it could have been an earthquake in which case the timing was God's doing.

THE LIBERAL

I really find this a barbaric old legend with little religious worth at all. It's possible that Joshua was aware of God's command to be holy, and he thought this meant that he had to wipe out the city becasue they didn't follow his God. Very primitive! The walls might have fallen down because of an earthquake, but I can't believe that was God's doing - it's far too cruel. No, it's all probably just a legend, and far from the moral ideas about God that were taught later on.

Three opinions that (1) want to keep the story as it is, (2) partly chip away at it, and (3) largely dismiss it as barbaric and irrelevant to Christian faith today.

A. List all the points of disagreement between
   (i) the fundamentalist and the conservative
   (ii) the conservative and the liberal.

B. What do you think about this story?
   Which viewpoint would you take?
   Would you take a different one? Give your reasons.

THE FEEDING OF THE 5,000

All four *Gospels* contain the same basic story: a crowd of people follow Jesus, it gets late, and they are hungry. Jesus blesses five loaves and two fish, and shares them round with the crowd of about 5,000 people. Everyone eats their fill, and there are twelve baskets full of leftovers. John's Gospel adds the detail that the disciples got the loaves and fish from a young boy, who was in the crowd.

THE FUNDAMENTALIST

It was a miracle, and it has been recorded in God's Word. It was a sign that Jesus was the Messiah - he multiplied the food and satisfied everyone's need. The story can be given a spiritual meaning too: if we come to Jesus with what little we have, then it can increase our faith and our joy beyond all expectations.

THE CONSERVATIVE

This was a miracle. All four Gospels record it, and so it is very likely to have happened. God might have suspended the laws of nature to perform it, or he might have used a force that scientists have not discovered yet, like some form of mind over matter. It was a sign that Jesus was the Messiah, which helped people to believe in him. We can also give it a spiritual meaning - Jesus increases our faith, if we come to him.

THE LIBERAL

This story might not involve a miracle at all in the usual sense. None of the Gospels claim that Jesus miraculously multiplied the food - that's what people read into it. They just say that Jesus blessed the loaves and the fish, and then they all ate their fill. Perhaps Jesus set a good example by sharing out the food he had, and this made everyone else share their food too, so that there was enough for everyone! The real miracle is that Jesus stopped people being selfish and made them share with one another.

A. How does the conservative approach this story in a different way from the fundamentalist?
B. Why do liberals think there was no miracle of multiplying the loaves and the fish involved? What do they think really happened?
C. What do you make of the story? Give your reasons.

THE HEALING OF THE BLIND MAN

Jesus cures a blind beggar by touching his eyes with spittle and mud, and sending him to wash in the pool of Siloam. The Pharisees interrogate the man and his family, demanding to know if he is telling the truth, and if he had ever really been blind at all. The man insists that he had been blind from birth, and that he can see now. Later, Jesus warns some Pharisees that it is they who are really blind, because they will not allow him to help them to see spiritually.

THE FUNDAMENTALIST

If it is in one of the Gospels, then it must have happened exactly as it says. Jesus had the power to heal, which was a sign that he was the Messiah. The story also reminds us that Jesus can cure our spiritual blindness, too.

THE CONSERVATIVE

There is only one account of this story in the Gospels, but there are similar stories of blind people being healed, so it is likely that this happened. Jesus had power to heal, probably by using forces of nature that we do not understand yet, or by suspending the laws of nature. It also has a spiritual meaning, but this is secondary to the fact that it happened and that Jesus showed his power.

THE LIBERAL

Jesus might have used paranormal powers, but that is not really important. The inner meaning of the story matters most. It is a parable, a story with a meaning, saying that we are all spiritually blind because of our selfishness, and we are influenced to be like this from birth. Jesus can change all that; he makes you see things in a new way. That's the real miracle, that our self-centred nature can be opened up to God and other people.

A. Does the fundamentalist think the story is only about physical healing?
B. Why does the conservative think the healing probably happened? How is the healing explained?
C. What does the liberal make of the story? What is the real point of it to him?
D. What do you make of the story? Give your reasons.

Paul and the Role of Women

A final example involves a brief study of a section of Ephesians (5:21–5). This was written by Paul, or one of his disciples, and the chosen passage concerns advice to husbands and wives:

Submit yourselves to one another because of your reverence for Christ. Wives, submit to your husbands as to the Lord. For a husband has authority over his wife just as Christ has authority over the Church. . . . And so wives must submit completely to their husbands just as the Church submits itself to Christ. Husbands, love your wives just as Christ loved the Church and gave his life for it.

- The fundamentalist Christian will take this word for word: men should be in charge. The husband is the head of each home, and his word has final authority. Some feel that wives should not go out to work, but should look after the home. The ideal is that the husband should not abuse his power, but should be loving and sensitive to the wife, respecting her feelings and wishes.
- Some conservative Christians will accept this as God's revealed order for family life and society, but others do not. They think that the author was influenced by the times, when women were treated as second-class citizens, or as having set roles in society. He was right about husbands and wives loving each other, but not right about one being in charge. Husbands and wives should share authority and roles in the home as a partnership, and in society.
- All liberal Christians would see this passage as being outdated and influenced by the culture of the author. They do not see all of it as being the Word of God. The Word of God in the passage is that husbands and wives should love one another, but the rest of the words are Paul's. Men and women should be more equal now.

Assignments

1 Make a Bible library poster, showing the Old Testament and the New Testament and the different books in each.
2 Write an imaginary letter, as an apostle, to a church in Athens. They are making foreigners sit at the back of the church and they will not let them take part in the service. What advice will you give them, and why?
3 Write an essay on the use of the Bible in Christian life and worship: (i) say how it is used in services, (ii) in groups, and (iii) by individuals.
4 Write an essay on the three main ways of understanding the Bible as the Word of God: (i) describe the differences between fundamentalists, conservatives and liberals in understanding the authority of the Bible (taking a couple of sample passages as examples) and (ii) conclude with whether you think it is necessary to believe every word of the Bible in order to be a Christian.
5 Imagine you were a newspaper reporter at the time of the feeding of the 5,000. Write a report mentioning the various stories, or theories that were being told of what had happened, and add your own comments.

6

Beliefs about Jesus

It is impossible for Christians to spell out what they believe to the last letter, because their faith is a mystery; it rests upon the mystery of God, whom no one can ever hope to fully understand. Christians say that they are always discovering new things about their faith as they grow older, and some things they will not understand until they are in heaven! Yet there are important things that Christians believe in, and want to tell people about.

The Creeds

The Christian Church has drawn up lists of its important beliefs from time to time, and these are called **creeds**, from the Latin word *credo*, meaning 'I believe'. The three great creeds of the Church are the Apostles' Creed, the Nicene Creed and the Athanasian Creed. The Apostles' Creed was not actually written by the twelve apostles, but it was based on their teaching. It was certainly in existence by the fourth century CE. The Nicene Creed resulted from the Council of Nicaea, a meeting of Church leaders in 325, but the form that can be seen in Church service books is a slightly later version of it. The Athanasian Creed was based on the teachings of Athanasius, who lived in the fourth century CE.

The great creeds were written down to preserve important Christian teaching, because at that time many people were arguing about what Christians should believe.

This is the Apostles' Creed, as found in the Church of England's Alternative Service Book:

> I believe in God, the Father almighty,
> creator of heaven and earth.
>
> I believe in Jesus Christ, his only Son, our Lord.
> He was conceived by the power of the Holy Spirit
> and born of the Virgin Mary.
> He suffered under Pontius Pilate,
> was crucified, died and was buried.
> He descended to the dead.
> On the third day he rose again.
> He ascended into heaven,
> and is seated at the right hand of the Father.
> He will come again to judge the living and
>   the dead.
>
> I believe in the Holy Spirit,
> the holy catholic Church,
> the communion of saints,
> the forgiveness of sins,
> the resurrection of the body,
> and the life everlasting. Amen.

Christians believe that God is love, and that Jesus came to show this to the world. Creeds are an attempt to respond to that love, and to give it some meaning. They are an attempt to understand what God has done, and is doing, in Christ. Many Christians think that the Holy Spirit guided the Church when the creeds were written, so that important beliefs would be preserved and passed on.

But a creed should not be taken as a full and final list of all that Christians believe. Remember that their faith is a mystery at heart – the mystery of God, the mystery of why he made the world, and the mystery of his love for people, shown in Christ. Creeds just show some of the things that Christians believe, the things they consider to be very important.

Activities

Key Elements

1 What is a creed?
2 What are the three main Christian creeds?
3 a) Why is the Apostles' Creed so called?
   b) List all the things the Apostles' Creed says about Jesus.

Think About It

4 Do creeds try to answer all the questions about belief in God and Christ?

Activity

- a) It is hard to list all that you like, or believe about a person. Take your favourite pop group, sports team, or best friend, and try to list the good things about them: all the qualities that you think they have. (You will probably find that there are still many more sides to them, and many things that you don't know how to write down.)
- b) Do you think it is more difficult to write a list of beliefs about God?

The Son of God

The Apostles' Creed begins by calling Jesus God's only Son. This is a common and often misunderstood title that Christians use for Jesus.

This is a common response to the question, but it is misleading. It sounds as though Christians believe that Jesus is the physical offspring of God, just as a person has an earthly father. It even makes Mary sound like God's wife! Christianity is not really the story of 'God and son', but of God at work supremely in a human life.

What do the angels and the way in which Jesus is shown here suggest about Christian beliefs?

What does the golden halo in this icon suggest about the importance of Christ?

In the East, the phrase 'son of' is used in a variety of ways. It can mean somebody's actual son, but it can also be used in a symbolic way – to say that someone is like someone else. So, 'son of a camel' is an insult that suggests that someone is very rude and ill-mannered. To call someone a 'Son of God' means that they are very holy and God-like.

The title 'Son of God' is poetic. It is a metaphor: it stands for something that should not be taken word for word. To call someone *the* Son of God means that he is the holiest person ever to have lived, the person who shows what God is like more than anyone else. Jesus was therefore to Christians a man full of God (though the title came to mean much more later on).

The Background

At the time of Jesus, outstanding people were called 'Son of God' by the Romans. To the educated, this was just a poetic title to mean the person was special, but the more uneducated probably thought the person's father had actually been a god. The Greek and Roman myths had many stories of gods mating with human women and producing demigods (half god; half human) like Hercules. It is likely that some Christian converts understood the story of the virgin birth in this way: that Jesus was a demi-god or that he had been the heavenly Son of God who had come down to save people, something like this:

To find the meaning of 'Son of God' as understood by Christians, it is useful to start with the Old Testament, which was the only Bible the first Christians had before the New Testament was written. Here, we find that faithful Jews are sometimes called 'Son of God', and the whole people of Israel were called God's son (as in Hosea 11:1, where

God says, 'When Israel was a child, I loved him and called him out of Egypt as my son' – which refers to the Exodus from Egypt).

The Kings of Israel were called 'Son of God', too, as in Psalm 2:7, 'I will announce,' says the king, 'what the LORD has declared. He said to me: ''You are my son; today I have become your father.'' ' The king was the special servant of God, who was supposed to rule the people with justice and set an example for the people to follow. 'Son of God' was a metaphor, therefore, for a faithful, holy servant of God; it suggested that the person was very close to God.

The first Christians used the title 'Son of God' against this background. It meant the Jewish Messiah, the King of the Jews, the special Servant of God. It was only later that the title suggested that Jesus was divine, and more than an ordinary human. It was the belief in the resurrection that started the Church thinking that Jesus was *uniquely* one with God. When they thought of Jesus, they thought of God and man, together.

Question
• What did you think 'Son of God' meant before studying this chapter? Have your views on this changed?

Activities

Key Elements

1 What two different meanings can 'son of' have in the East?
2 What did 'Son of God' suggest to Romans and Greeks at the time of Jesus?
3 What did 'Son of God' mean in the Old Testament, for the Jews?
4 Write a paragraph on each of the following:
   a) Psalm 2:7 and the king as 'Son of God'.
   b) Why did some early Christians think Jesus was a demi-god and why did the Church say they were wrong?
5 When Jesus is called the Son of God by Christians, what does it mean, and what does it not mean?

The Incarnation

The word **incarnation** means 'in the body'. Christians have come to believe that Jesus was not just a good man, nor just the holiest prophet that has ever lived. They believe that God and man were joined together in his life and that Jesus was, in some way, God become man.

This does **not** mean that Christians think that Jesus was like a puppet controlled by God, or that God disguised himself in a human body, as though he were putting on a

suit of clothes. Jesus was not a mask, a secret identity for God, like Clark Kent is for Superman; Jesus was a real, complete human being with his own feelings and his own mind.

God Came Down to Earth in Jesus

Christians today take this as symbolic language, meaning that the presence of God was focused in the life of Jesus more than anywhere else on earth; God is supposed to be everywhere and in all things, but some things are vehicles for his presence more than others. The Church teaches that there was a deliberate and unique joining of God with the human being, Jesus, from the moment of conception in Mary's womb, so that the life of Jesus is a unique act of salvation by God in human history.

The manner and nature of the joining of God and man in Jesus is seen as a mystery that ultimately defies words. For the creeds, it was important to say that it was God, and not an angel or his deputy, that was in Jesus, and also that Jesus was a full human being, and not some strange Superman figure. The Gospels, for example, are clear that Jesus could feel pain like the rest of us.

The Developing Message

The first Christians did not think of Jesus as God incarnate, however. This belief developed gradually. Peter's message, soon after the Resurrection, was that Jesus was a man blessed by God as shown by the signs and wonders he had worked through him.

Mark's Gospel, the earliest of the four, presents Jesus as the Messiah whose words have a striking authority and whose miracles were seen as the first signs of the Kingdom breaking through. Jesus is a man full of the Spirit who has an unnerving effect on those around him. This is how people react when he preaches:

The people were all so amazed that they started saying to one another, 'What is this? Is it some kind of new teaching?'   *(1:27)*

As a man, Jesus shows people what a true human being is.

As God, Jesus shows what God is like in a way that people can understand.

The Gospels of Matthew and Luke, some 15 to 20 years later, present essentially the same picture. God had acted in a striking and unique way in his envoy, Jesus of Nazareth.

At the end of the first century CE, the presentation of the Christian message had changed. In John's Gospel, Jesus is the Word of God incarnate. He is God manifest in flesh. The prologue of John reads:

The Word became a human being and, full of grace and truth, lived among us.   *(1:14)*

The 'Word of God' is a metaphor for God acting in the world. It is God acting towards people. The Gospel closes with the confession of Thomas when he encounters the risen Christ: 'My Lord and my God!' (20:28).

As the years went by, people thought more and more about Jesus and why he could do the things he did. The Church came to see that there was more to it than they had realised, and so their message changed. Jesus had made people so aware of what God was like that God must have been living and working in him in a unique way. Jesus presented God in a human life. The Nicene Creed speaks of the Son as being 'God from God, Light from Light'. This does not mean the human being, Jesus of Nazareth, but the God who was present, or incarnate in him. The Creed was written to point out that it was wrong to teach that a lesser god was in Jesus than the true God. God the Son, then, equals the part of God that was in Jesus, united to him. Christians often confuse 'Son of God' with 'God the Son', but they were originally different. Son of God means the man full of God; God the Son means the God who filled the man. (Though Christians see these as two sides of the same coin: there is one person who is human and God.)

Activities

Key Elements

1 a) What is meant by the word 'incarnation'?
 b) What does this word mean for Christians?

Think About It

2 When the New Testament says that Jesus did not know when the Kingdom would arrive, or says that he felt pain on the cross, what does this suggest about Jesus?
3 What do Christians think Jesus shows people about God and humanity?
4 Write a paragraph about how Christians try to explain the incarnation in modern language.
5 Compare what Peter said about Jesus in Acts 2:22 with what John's Gospel says about him in 1:14. How are they different?

The Cross

The cross is the most important Christian symbol. The story of the crucifixion of Jesus stands, with that of his resurrection, at the centre of the Christian faith. Christians understand the story of the cross in various ways. There is no one way of seeing it, but all say that God was doing something in Jesus on the cross. Here are some ways that modern Christians have of understanding the cross:

- God came in Jesus and showed people how to live. God would not force anyone to listen, and he gave them the freedom to reject him. They did, and nailed him to a cross. The cross shows people, today, that *God is love*, and that he will forgive people if they will turn to him, no matter what they have done. Looking at the cross should make people sorry for their sins.
- The cross shows that *God can suffer*; he is not a million miles away in Heaven. God is involved in the struggles of everyday life. God stands alongside people who suffer and gives them courage. There is a story told about the Day of Judgement, when all the innocent victims of torture and disease rise up to challenge God, but when they see the wounds in his hands and feet, they realise he is one of them.
- The cross shows that God has entered all the darkness in the world. He has gone through death, and come out the other side. He has shown that the darkness can be transformed, and that *good is stronger than evil* in the end.

These are modern ways of understanding the story of the cross. The following are some much older ones that sound strange to modern ears at first.

A Sacrifice for Sin

An early way of understanding the death of Jesus was as a sacrifice. The Jews had various sacrifices, such as the communion sacrifice, where an animal was slaughtered, offered to God, and most of it was eaten by the family and by the priest who offered it. This was a way of showing gratitude for the meat.

This symbol is sometimes used for Jesus as the 'Lamb of God'. Lambs were used as sacrifices at Passover time by the Jews. The banner suggests victory. Why do you think this symbol was used for Jesus?

But it is the **atonement** sacrifice that is relevant to the story of Jesus. Atonement means to make up for something. The blood of various animals was sprinkled on the altar and was thought to purify people from sin. This sounds strange to us, but people in ancient times thought that blood contained the life force, and that an animal's blood offered to God could pay the price for human sins. Jesus had died and shed his blood. The blood of the Son of God was more powerful, and could purify the whole human race. It was the best sacrifice that could ever be offered, and so the Christians stopped offering ordinary sacrifices. (Other people used to think they were mad to stop since sacrifices were so common then.)

This seems to be a curious piece of old mythology to some modern Christians, and they explain the rise of this idea in this way: the first Christians were Jews who were used to offering atonement sacrifices. The question of what sacrifice God would find acceptable was very important to them. Through Jesus, they felt the forgiving love of God taking away their guilt. They tried to make sense of this by seeing Jesus' death as a *super* atonement sacrifice, which was logical to them, but seems strange to us today. It was a powerful idea, though, that God had done something to forgive people when they did not deserve it. He had shed his blood to purify them even when they had turned against him.

We still use the word 'sacrifice' today when people give up something they value for someone they love. In this sense, the death of Jesus can still be described as a sacrifice, because he gave up his own life out of love for people.

A Victory over Evil

The cross probably sounds more like a victory of evil over good. However, the early Church teachers argued that Jesus had defeated the devil by dying on the cross. Some said that this was because Jesus had shed his magical blood to purify the human race. The devil thought he had destroyed the Son of God, only to have his plan backfire.

Others argued in a different vein. The early Christians thought that people died because they sinned, and sinners were slaves of the devil in the Underworld, Hell. Jesus was killed by the devil's agents, and the devil took Jesus' spirit to the Underworld. However, Jesus had no sin in him, and so he burst free taking many lost souls with him. Anyone who followed Jesus would then be *his* slave, and not the property of the devil.

This idea sounds strange today for a number of reasons. Not all Christians believe in a personal devil any more. No one thinks that there is an Underworld directly beneath us. And science tells us that we die to make room for others.

Perhaps the power of this old story lies in the idea that in the story of the death and resurrection of Jesus, good and evil are seen to be struggling, and good eventually wins in the resurrection. This gives people a hope for the future, and lessens their fear of death.

Why do you think this idea would have been a popular and powerful one in the past?

The Justice of God is Satisfied

Another way of understanding the cross was to use the language of the law courts. People have sinned, therefore they stand guilty before God. God is their judge. God is holy and demands justice, but he is also love, and so he became man and took the punishment for sin himself.

Many Christians found this to be a deeply moving idea, and they felt a burden of guilt roll away when they first heard it preached. They believed they could be forgiven because of what Jesus had done.

Why do you think this idea is powerful?

Other Christians, however, found this idea too mechanical. It makes God too much a slave of his justice. Why should he have to suffer before he can forgive?

There are numerous ways of understanding the cross. Yet, all Christians agree that:

- On the cross, Jesus did something to save people.
- God came close to human life and

entered its darkness to transform it into glorious light, in the resurrection.

- The burden of guilt rolls away when confronted with the forgiving God on the cross.

Activities

Key Elements

1 What are three modern ways of understanding why Jesus died on the cross?
2 List briefly the three older ideas of why Jesus died on the cross.
3 Write a paragraph on each of the following:
   a) Why did the first Christians understand the death of Jesus as a sacrifice for the sins of the world?
   b) Why do many people find the justice idea of the cross helpful, and why do some find it a problem?

Think About It

4 What does a picture of Jesus on the cross suggest to you about God? Why do you think that some people think it says more about God being cruel than loving?
5 Why do *you* think that Jesus died on the cross?

Activity

- Imagine that you are a Christian preacher and you have to explain why Jesus died on the cross:
  a) to a Jewish person at the time of Jesus;
  b) to a modern-day criminal;
  c) to someone who has been through a great deal of suffering.
  What would you say to each one?

The Resurrection

The resurrection belief is mentioned in every New Testament book. It is the central belief of Christianity. Indeed, the whole of Christian theology – all its reflection on God and Christ – come from that belief.

The disciples were frightened and ran for their lives when Jesus was crucified, and yet something made them regroup in Jerusalem and boldly go out preaching their message.

The New Testament letters do not describe the resurrection in any detail. In the main, they refer to it as the victory of Jesus over death, and as the new life that Christians felt inside:

If the Spirit of God, who raised Jesus from death, lives in you, then he who raised Christ from death will also give life to your mortal bodies . . . (Romans 8:11)

More information is given in 1 Corinthians 15, where Paul describes the appearances of the risen Christ to the Twelve and other disciples. Paul describes the resurrection life as being in a spiritual body, the nature of which is beyond human understanding: 'When the body is buried, it is mortal; when raised, it will be immortal.'

The four Gospels give the fullest accounts, adding the story of the empty tomb and giving more details of the appearances:

- The resurrection is seen as God's blessing on all that Jesus said and did, when, in the eyes of many, he was a failure for having been crucified.
- The resurrection is not simply about a dead man coming back to life, but a transformation. Jesus lives *in God*.
- The resurrection is seen as a pledge that all the darkness in life will one day be turned into glorious light. All that has happened in the universe will not just fade away and be lost; it has a fulfilment to come in God.

St Paul says in his letter to the Romans:

I consider that what we suffer at this present time cannot be compared at all with the glory that is going to be revealed to us.   (8:18)

The resurrection is seen as a triumph, a transformation and as a future hope.

The Background

The belief in the resurrection of the dead developed quite late in the Old Testament. The early writings in it suggest that the ancestors of the Jews believed in a shadowy Underworld called Sheol. All people went there.

But as the Jews thought more about the love of God, they could not believe that death could separate them from him. There must be more 'on the other side'. Also, so many people seemed to suffer unfairly in this life. Surely it must be made up to them in the afterlife. Some of the Psalms show a trust and confidence that God will be there 'on the other side': 'I have served you faithfully, and you will not abandon me to the world of the dead.' (16:10)

The belief in resurrection first appears in the Book of Daniel, composed in the second century BCE:

'Many of those who have already died will live again: some will enjoy eternal life, and some will suffer eternal disgrace. The wise leaders will shine with all the brightness of the sky.'   (12:2–3)

Not all the Jews at the time of Jesus believed this, though. The Sadducees accepted only the early writings in the Old Testament as scripture to be believed, and not the later writings.

The Pharisees did champion the idea of resurrection, but they taught that this would happen to everyone at *the end* of history. The Christians were saying that it had already happened to one outstanding man *within* history.

Did Jesus Rise from the Dead?

Someone Stole the Body

It's a suggestion, but there's no evidence that that is what happened. It is hard to see how the empty tomb alone could have made the disciples believe in the resurrection. It was the appearances as well, and the feeling of new life inside. And, don't forget that some Christians don't believe in the empty tomb story. They think Jesus only rose spiritually.

Jesus Didn't Really Die

He did die sooner than expected (in six hours; crucifixion victims could linger on for a day or two). But this could be explained by the fact that he was whipped before being crucified. Some people died from the whipping alone, and people did not usually have both punishments together.

If Jesus had recovered in the tomb, he would have been a physical mess, and would not have been able to move the huge tombstone, or convince anyone that he had risen in glory!

The Disciples Felt Guilty

A clever idea, this! This might just explain seeing appearances of Jesus – i.e. they were produced by their guilt at deserting Jesus or their sorrow at losing him (as some people claim to 'see' dead relatives because they are so sorry to lose them). However, it cannot really explain the sense of new life and courage they felt, and that the early Christians felt who joined the Church later on. Guilty people do not make other people feel free, but guilty too.

Dead People Don't Rise

This is the hardest point to tackle. There is no scientific proof of a life after death, and the bodies of people just lie in the graves and rot. But this does not mean that people cannot live on spiritually in some new form in another world, or level of reality. This would be beyond investigation by science. Science cannot prove it or disprove it. It is a question of faith. The disappearance of Jesus' body is seen as a 'one off' by Christians, because he was so special as the Son of God.

Jesus Lives on in his Teaching

A noble idea, and there are some people who go to church and call themselves Christians and who believe just that. They are committed to the ideals of peace and love that Jesus taught, and that is a good thing. Yet that is not the official teaching of the Church, or of the New Testament. It teaches that Jesus of Nazareth somehow *survived death* and promised his followers that the same could happen to them.

Activities

Key Elements

1 What is the central belief of Christianity?
2 What do the New Testament letters say about the resurrection of Jesus? Write a short summary.
3 What details do the four Gospels add to the story?
4 Write a paragraph on each of the following:
 a) What does 1 Corinthians 15 say about the resurrection of believers?
 b) Why is the resurrection of Jesus seen as a sign of hope for the whole universe? (Refer to Paul's comments in Romans 8.)

Think About It

5 Why do people say that the resurrection is the most important belief in the New Testament?
6 Do Christians believe that the resurrection of Jesus was just a dead body coming back to life again? If not, what do they see it as?

Assignment

• Interview some church members as to their beliefs about who Jesus was, why he died on the cross and what the resurrection was. Write up a report afterwards.

The Ascension

The writer of the Acts of the Apostles includes a short story describing how the risen Christ left his disciples by rising up into the air, known as the **Ascension**:

After saying this, he was taken up to heaven as they watched him, and a cloud hid him from their sight. (1:9)

The New Testament letters speak of Jesus being raised up and exalted. St Paul, for example, quotes from an early Christian hymn in Philippians 2:8–9.

*He [Jesus] was humble and walked the path of obedience all the way to death –
his death on the cross.
For this reason God raised him to the highest place above
and gave him the name that is greater than any other name.*

Many ordinary, uneducated believers would have mixed up all this symbolic language with factual language, rather like little children today when they hear someone say something like, 'I'm over the moon about this!' They think that people have really flown over the moon!

The popular idea of the shape of the world in the past was that the earth was at the centre, with Heaven up above, Hell below, and the stars and planets moving around the dome of the sky in their various orbits. Many of the early Christians would have pictured Jesus going back to God in the way Acts describes it: he would go up to Heaven above. To us, this is ridiculous, for there is nothing but miles and miles of empty space above the earth.

The idea of Jesus ascending on high and sitting at the right-hand side of God does mean a great deal as picture-language, however. The writer of Acts probably understood the ascension story as a symbol, for he was an educated man and would have known more about the nature of the world than many.

The idea of going up on high suggests power and success. The athlete who wins a

Why do you think people thought like this?

gold medal stands above the others on the podium. The best-selling record is called the 'top of the pops'. To say that Jesus ascended is to say that Jesus had become the most important person in human history; that he now lives in God and has a cosmic significance. It means that Jesus reigns over all the forces in the world, that good has won over evil.

Question

• Why did ancient people think that heaven was up in the sky? Where do modern believers think it is?

Activity

• Tell in your own words the story of the Ascension in Acts 1.

The Parousia

Christians believe that Jesus is reigning over the earth, but that the Kingdom has not yet come. Many people suffer, and evil is still at work. Christians think that Christ will return in some way; he has not finished with the world yet. The special word for the return of Christ is the **parousia**. This is a Greek word meaning 'the presence'; and was used of kings and rulers returning to their court. This area of Christian belief is called **eschatology**, which means the study of the last things, or the end of time.

Various New Testament passages describe the parousia in very vivid and striking poetry:

'In the days after that time of trouble the sun will grow dark, the moon will no longer shine, the stars will fall from heaven, and the powers in space will be driven from their courses. Then the Son of Man [Christ] will appear, coming in the clouds with great power and glory. He will send the angels out to the four corners of the earth to gather God's chosen people from one end of the world to the other.' (Mark 13:24–7)

Then I saw heaven open, and there was a white horse. Its rider is called Faithful and True; it is with justice that he judges and fights his battles. His eyes were like a flame of fire, and he wore many crowns on his head.... Out of his mouth came a sharp sword, with which he will defeat the nations.... On his robe and on his thigh was written the name: 'King of kings and Lord of lords'. (Revelation 19:11–12, 15, 16)

Very few Christians take all this word for word. It is obviously poetry, full of symbols and hidden meanings. Many Christians do think that Jesus will actually return in some way, however, and that everyone will see him. He will come again in glory; he will not be reborn as an ordinary person.

Other Christians find this hard to believe. Instead they think Christ will return as a spiritual force that will cover the earth.

Others just take the whole parousia idea as a symbol for the final victory of good over evil, but they do not pretend to know where, when or how this will take place. Some think that it will take place in Heaven, in the next life, and the earth will eventually die as the sun fades away, having run its course.

The vivid poetry that the parousia hope is expressed in is a style called **apocalyptic** (which means 'revealing hidden things'). It was popular amongst the Jews at the time of

Jesus. It developed from the Book of Daniel onwards, and one passage in that book lies behind most of the imagery in the parousia idea:

During this vision in the night, I saw what looked like a human being. He was approach-ing me, surrounded by clouds, and he went to the one who had been living for ever and was presented to him. He was given author-ity, honour, and royal power, so that the peo-ple of all nations, races, and languages would serve him. (7:13–14)

Activities

Key Elements

1 What does 'parousia' mean?
2 How do Christians understand it?
3 a) How is the parousia of Jesus described in Mark 13?
   b) How do many Christians under-stand the language used in this passage?

4 How do Christians understand the symbols of:
   a) the Ascension, and
   b) Jesus sitting on the right-hand side of God?
5 How does Paul try to express the same ideas in Philippians 2:6–11?

Think About It

6 Ancient people often mixed up facts and symbols, like little children do today. Discuss any modern-day examples.
7 Write a paragraph explaining three of

the ways that modern Christians have of understanding the parousia.
8 What hopes and fears do you have for the future? Have a class discus-sion.

Assignments

1 Write a paragraph about how and why the early Christian view of Jesus developed in the way that it did. Explain the difference, if any, between 'God the Son' and the 'Son of God'.
2 Write an essay on the idea of the cross as a victory over the devil: (i) Explain why many Christians find this hard to believe today and (ii) dis-cuss whether there is anything that can still make sense, and come alive, in this old way of understanding the cross.

3 Write an essay on the development of Jewish belief in resurrection: (i) explain how belief in it developed in the Old Testament; (ii) why the Sad-ducees rejected this belief; and (iii) why the Pharisees found the Christ-ian claims surprising even though they believed in the resurrection.
4 Design a collage or poster entitled Parousia, showing good winning over evil.

7

Lifestyles

The young people found that some people were cold and unfriendly when they attended their local church. They also found that some people were very friendly indeed, and chatted to them about their school project. Most churches will have a mixture of these types of people. Some people go to church because they think it is a respectable thing to do. Others have problems and go for comfort and help – and they might not always feel like being talkative and friendly. Others are committed members who contribute to the running of the church in many ways. They take their faith seriously and apply it to their lives.

The young people chatted to a husband and wife who made coffee each week. They had to be there early to set things up, and they bought the coffee, milk and sugar as a gift for the church. Then there were the Sunday School teachers, and a woman who ran the local Guides in the church hall each week. There was a doctor who tried to live out his faith by helping people to get well, and by having the patience to listen to them. There were some who ran a group for one-parent families, and a playgroup for the children, and the vicar organised a social action team which visited the homes of the elderly and did odd jobs for them.

All these people were trying to help others in some way, either in their jobs or in some of their spare time. They felt that going to church and praying helped them to do this. Of course, anyone with a kind streak can do things for others – you don't have to be a Christian to care for other people – but these church people felt their faith helped. Their faith is about love of neighbour and the good news that God is forgiving and loving.

Questions

- What different reasons might people have for going to church? Try to think of other reasons as well as those mentioned in the passage above.
- How were the young people trying to work out their faith?
- What is the basic moral at the heart of Christianity?

The following pages survey the lives and achievements of some famous Christians who have been in the news, or had bestselling books that have influenced people. They each show how the teaching of Jesus helped them to face certain challenges.

People staying behind for coffee after a service. Why do some churches do this? Is it a good idea?

Mother Teresa

Mother Teresa was born Agnes Gonxha Bojaxhiu in Yugoslavia in 1910 of Albanian parents. She was a Roman Catholic. She felt that she wanted to give her life to God's service from the age of 12. When she was 17, she went to join the Loreto Nuns at their headquarters in Dublin, Ireland. She had heard about this group at school, and the work that they did in India. After initial training in Ireland, she was sent to Darjeeling in India where she became a novice (a person training to be a nun). When she took her final vows to be a nun she took the name Teresa, after a favourite saint of hers.

She was then sent to Calcutta to teach geography in a school. The pupils were from rich families, and the work was easy. However, the school and the convent were in a poor part of the city. Many people lived out on the streets, in shelters made out of old boxes, or in rows of simple huts. These people had travelled into the city after famine had struck their village and they were desperate for food and work. They begged what they could, and a few were lucky to earn a little money now and then. There were sick and elderly people just dying in the streets, with dogs and rats amongst them looking for food scraps.

Gradually, Teresa felt that she should leave the convent to work amongst the poor. It was two years before she was allowed to go. She had to train as a nurse with a different order of nuns, and then she returned to the city. A family gave her a room, and she started to tend sick people there. She taught the local slum children how to read, write and how to keep themselves clean, by holding her classes in the street, drawing in the dust because there was no blackboard. Gradually, others joined her, and she called them her Sisters.

After five years of begging for medicines, and having no room to treat patients properly, she went to the Calcutta Council. They offered her an old rest-room next to a Hindu temple where pilgrims used to rest. She moved in and began to take very sick people off the streets. She called the place Nirmal Hriday, 'Place of the Pure Heart'.

In 1950, she and her Sisters were allowed to form a new order, the Missionaries of Charity. More money was donated and more helpers came until her work has spread over India and the world. There are Homes for the Dying and Children's Homes, as well as Leprosy Homes. Mother Teresa's example seems to have sparked off compassion in many other people. She was awarded the Nobel Prize for Peace in 1979. She died in August 1997.

The Sisters do not try to convert people to Christianity. There are daily services for the Sisters, and they will instruct people in the Christian faith if they desire it, but their job is to be helpers to anyone, no matter what their race or creed. The aim in the Homes for the Dying is to let people die in a loving environment, even if they have not known love at any other time in their lives. The motive for all their work can best be summed up in Mother Teresa's own words:

Let no one ever come to you without going away better and happier. Let there be kindness in your face, kindness in your eyes.... In each suffering person you can see Jesus.

Mother Teresa.

Her work can best be understood as an imitation of that of Jesus:

Christ's life was not written during his lifetime, yet he did the greatest work on earth. He redeemed the world and taught mankind to love his Father. The work is his work and to remain so, all of us are but his instruments who do our own little bit and pass by.

Compassion for Outcasts

Mother Teresa's story highlights the compassion that Jesus showed for the poor and the social outcasts of his day, like the lepers whom most other people would not dare go near. This love for other human beings is a central part of the Gospel message.

Mother Teresa's story also highlights another issue: that of innocent suffering. The people she helped have done nothing to deserve the troubles that they face. They were just unlucky being born where and when they were. Christianity teaches about a God of love, so why does this suffering go on in the world? Christians have been trying to answer this question for ages. The usual answer is that human beings are a 'fallen' species. Basically, this means that they are out of tune with God because they often go their own selfish way. They are not functioning as they should be, and many things go wrong with the world. Wars and famines can be caused by humanity's own greed; they are not God's doing. God does not step in to force people to change because he gives people free will, freedom to choose good or evil. God has sent teachers, and has come specially in Jesus, to teach people the way to live, but he will not force anyone to listen.

This means that we live in a world where things can and do often go wrong, where tragedies happen that are not part of God's plan for people. That is how the world is, but Christians like Mother Teresa feel it is their job to help people to feel the love of God in the midst of the problems of life, and to take courage and to work to make the world a better place.

Martin Luther King

Martin Luther King was born into a respectable family in Atlanta, Georgia, USA, in 1929. His father was a Baptist minister, and King was ordained a Baptist minister himself in 1947. He went on to study at Boston and Harvard universities and became a Doctor of Philosophy at the age of 26.

In his youth, he had been made aware of the colour problem in the USA when he was not allowed to play with some white children along his street, and he remembered seeing the secret all-white organisation, the Ku Klux Klan, beating up blacks on the streets. When he became pastor of a church in Montgomery, Alabama, he became active in the National Association of Coloured People. In 1955, King became the president of another organisation, the Montgomery Improvement Association. This group led a boycott of the buses by all blacks for 382 days. This was over the arrest of an old black woman. She had refused to give up her seat on the bus to a white person because she was tired.

The Civil Rights Movement was made up of people who wanted change in American society and equal rights for blacks. They pressed King to preach the use of violence, if necessary, to help change things more quickly. He refused, and followed a policy of non-violent protest. He would organise petitions, demonstrations and sit-ins, but there must be no violence. He took this both from the teachings of Jesus and from the Indian

Martin Luther King at the Civil Rights March in 1963, on the steps of the Lincoln Memorial in Washington.

leader, Gandhi, who had used non-violence to try to end the British occupation of India some years earlier.

King often suffered unfairly. Once, he was arrested for driving at 30 mph in a 25 mph area; his house was bombed; he was stabbed by an unstable black woman, and he received many offensive phone calls or letters each day. Some white people felt angered and threatened by him; this was because he was making them face up to their prejudices, and trying to get them to change their way of life.

In 1962 he met President Kennedy, and a year later, in August, he led a march on Washington of 250,000 people (60,000 of whom were whites). This was a demonstration in favour of the Civil Rights Bill that was being debated by Congress (the American Parliament). It was passed in 1964, but King did not think that it went far enough. He carried on negotiations with the new President, Lyndon Johnson.

King was awarded the Nobel Peace Prize in 1964, and he donated the 54,000 dollars to the Civil Rights Movement. His life was ended suddenly on 4 April 1968. He was shot in the head while standing on the balcony of his hotel in Memphis, Tennessee, by a sniper in the crowd.

Question

- Should the Christian Church speak out and involve itself in politics, or should it just get on with church life? Have a debate about this, thinking about examples of Christian action in places such as Nicaragua, South Africa and Britain (see also p. 190).

He had succeeded in winning better conditions for the country's blacks, such as desegregated buses in areas of the South (blacks and whites used to have to sit separately). He summed up his work in a speech he made when he received the Nobel Peace Prize:

I have the audacity to believe that peoples everywhere can have three meals a day for their bodies, education and culture for their minds, and dignity, equality and freedom for their spirits. I believe that what self-centred men have torn down, other-centred men can build up. I still believe that one day mankind will bow before the altars of God and be crowned triumphant over war and bloodshed.... I still believe that we shall overcome.

Non-violent Social Change

King's story highlights the need some Christians feel to be involved in politics. They do not see Christianity as just being about saving people's souls to get them to heaven. An important part of the Gospel message is love and justice for human beings. If things in society rob some people of love and justice, then these things are to be challenged. Politics is then brought in, because politicians have the power to change things.

Some Christians are wary of this; they think that priests and pastors should stick to their prayers and leave social change to politicians and social workers. But other Christians feel that they cannot help but be involved in politics if they really love their neighbours.

Some Christians feel that it is sometimes right to use violence to stop a corrupt government, but King disagreed. He preferred non-violent action. The benefit of this is that you do not repay evil for evil, hurt for hurt, and that gains public support because it shows the authorities up for what they are. However, many people may suffer in the process and it might take a long time to win. King was trying to follow the words of Jesus:

'You have heard that it was said, "Love your friends, hate your enemies." But now I tell you: love your enemies and pray for those who persecute you.' (Matthew 5:43–4)

King's story also highlights that racism is anti-Christian because all races of people have been created by the same God and are equal in his sight. Christianity is not just a white person's religion; Jesus, the founder, was coloured himself.

Activities

Key Elements

1 a) What did Martin Luther King do to help blacks in the USA?
   b) What inspired him to do this?
2 What is meant by non-violent social change?

Think About It

3 Which part of the teaching of Jesus influenced King?
4 What issues does King's story raise for Christians today?
5 Do you think it is a sign of strength or weakness to refuse to retaliate when attacked?

David Wilkerson

David Wilkerson was a Pentecostal minister in a small village, Philipsburg, in the USA, when he read an account of the trial of seven teenage boys from New York. They were charged with the murder of a 15-year-old polio victim, Michael Farmer. They were members of a street gang called the Dragons. Michael had been stabbed in the back and beaten over the head.

The year was 1958, and it was a turning-point in Wilkerson's life. He felt an inner voice urging him to do something to help. He travelled to New York and tried to attend the trial, but he was thrown out of the court room and his picture was printed in the newspapers – they made him look like a Bible-waving fanatic. He did not give up, and tried to get permission to see the boys in jail. He had to get this from the parents, first, and, even then, when he reached the jail, the chaplain did not think it was wise for a stranger to see the boys that were under his care. Wilkerson seemed to have failed.

But he still felt an inner urge to help the teenagers in New York, and, one day, when walking around one of the slum areas, he met a group of youths on a street corner. They recognised him from his picture in the paper and started chatting. They thought he was to be trusted because he had tried to help the boys on trial, and they introduced him to various gang members in their hideouts. He talked to them, and listen to their problems, and he was made to feel welcome by most as they appreciated someone taking an interest in them – no one else seemed to care. Once, after he had preached about the forgiveness of God, four gang leaders knelt down on the street and turned their lives over to Christ.

Wilkerson was threatened and hated at times, though. One gang member flicked all his buttons with a knife, and then rested the knife on his stomach, warning him what would happen if he ever turned against them. Another character, Nicky Cruz, slapped him in the face, spat at him, and told him to go to Hell, when he first met him. (Nicky Cruz is now a minister himself, working with young people!)

Despite successes, Wilkerson realised that more needed to be done. He and a few members of a local church had helped some young people to come off drugs, but, once back on the streets, they had picked up the habit again because all their friends were addicts. Also, one youth called Israel had become a Christian after being a gang leader. Several months later, however, Wilkerson heard that Israel was on trial for murder. Apparently, Israel had been forced to join a gang when they were low on numbers, after months of going straight. (If you refused to join a gang, you would be beaten, then a limb would be broken, and then your life would be threatened.) Israel was in a gang fight, someone was killed, and he was on trial, although he had not done the actual killing.

This made Wilkerson realise the need for special homes or centres for young people when trying to escape from gang life or to come off drugs. This meant him leaving his church in Philipsburg and, in 1959, he went to work full time in New York. He took over a house and called it a 'Teen Challenge Centre'. There were problems and failures, such as the case of Carlos, an ex-member of the Suicides gang. The leader of the gang threatened him with a knife. Carlos snapped off a car aerial and was about to hit out with it when he changed his mind and snapped it over his knee. He was stabbed in the ribs, and nearly died.

Other teenagers have gone 'cold turkey' – the painful sudden withdrawal from drugs – and have been cared for at the Centres, only to become addicts on the streets again later. It has been estimated, however, that 2,500 young people were successfully helped at the first Teen Challenge Centre in its first six months. It is a success story overall. Teen Challenge Centres have since spread over the USA and into Europe.

Run Baby Run: a book written by Nicky Cruz, telling the story of his life.

Forgiveness

David Wilkerson's story touches upon the theme of compassion for fellow human beings, even when they might be guilty of serious crimes and murder, or might be hopelessly addicted to drugs. He did not condone any of these things, but he wanted the young people to know that they could start again with a clean slate. He preached that God was a forgiving God who offered a second chance. He thought it was better for a killer to be changed into a caring citizen, than to be punished. His example of love won the respect and the trust of many of the young people. It must also be remembered that the social conditions that these youths lived in – poverty, hunger, unemployment and loneliness – all helped to make them aggressive and turn to crime, or seek an escape through drugs.

Wilkerson was imitating Jesus who was prepared to welcome tax collectors into his band of disciples, as well as ex-prostitutes. Jesus on one occasion also helped a Roman centurion, who worked for the enemies of the Jews (see Luke 7:1–10). Wilkerson's story points out the power of love and forgiveness to transform people who are self-centred, full of hate, or hopeless. He also highlights an area of Christian belief – that God will sometimes guide people in special ways through an inner voice or prompting, and they will achieve much if they have the faith to respond.

Activities

Key Elements

1 Describe David Wilkerson's work amongst New York gangs.
2 What made him begin his work?
3 In what ways did Jesus show compassion for drop-outs as Wilkerson did?

Think About It

4 Do you think that it is easy for adults to work with teenagers? What problems might they find? What particular difficulties did Wilkerson have?

Dietrich Bonhoeffer

Dietrich Bonhoeffer was born in 1906 in Germany. He became a teacher of theology in Berlin, and a minister in the Lutheran Church (the national Church in Germany). Bonhoeffer was deeply shaken when Hitler came to power in 1933. He was horrified by the Nazi party's anti-Semitism (hatred of the Jews) and he tried to get his fellow ministers in Berlin to go on strike, refusing to carry out funerals until the Nazis toned down their policies. He failed, but he took courage at the Barmen Declaration in 1934. Representatives from the German Free Churches met there to agree to

Dietrich Bonhoeffer in London in 1939.

struggle. He also revolutionised the teaching style of the students by insisting that they spend half an hour per day in silent prayer and meditation on the scriptures. He realised that these future ministers would need to have a thorough grounding in the spiritual life, and to learn the value of the support of a loving community for the years to come.

In 1939 he went on a lecture tour in the USA. He was welcomed with open arms, for his writings had become famous. Yet, when the Second World War broke out that year, he felt that he had to return to Germany, even though he could have stayed in America. He wrote:

> *It was a mistake for me to come to America. I have to live through this difficult period in our nation's history with Christians in Germany. I will have no right to participate in the reconstruction of Christian life in Germany after the war if I do not share the tribulations of this time with my people.*

When he returned he became more and more disillusioned with the Confessing Church. It seemed to lack the courage of its convictions. Many of his students had not refused military service when it had been their right to do so as Christians, because they were eager to prove their patriotism. Many Lutheran pastors had been forced to swear an oath to be loyal to Hitler, and little opposition to this had been voiced. Bonhoeffer felt more must be done. One verse he quoted from the Bible sums this feeling up well, 'Speak up for people who cannot speak for themselves.' (Proverbs 31:8).

He became involved with a group of conspirators against Hitler. These included high-ranking members of the German military as well as Bonhoeffer's brother-in-law, Hans von Dohnanyi. This caused much heart-searching because of his pacifist (anti-war) views. But he felt that this was a crisis and if Hitler was killed, thousands of innocent lives would be saved.

The first bomb attempt on Hitler in 1943 failed. Bonhoeffer and his brother-in-law were arrested on 5 April 1943. He went to Tegel prison in a Berlin suburb where he

renounce any attempts by Hitler to get the Churches to serve him rather than God. Their first loyalty was to Christ. From this the Confessing Church was formed, and its ministers acted unofficially and illegally.

Bonhoeffer ran a training seminary for future Confessing ministers at Finkenwalde from 1935 to 1937, when the Gestapo closed it down. He carried on teaching his students in an old vicarage and in a country house, which was closed in 1940.

Bonhoeffer's faith and beliefs matured during this period. He attacked the official Church for teaching 'cheap grace'. **Grace** means receiving a favour that you do not deserve, from God in this case. Bonhoeffer taught that the grace of God was costly; a person had to be prepared to stand up and be counted to be a real disciple. By 'cheap' grace he meant the idea that God would forgive you no matter what if you kept up church attendance and said 'sorry' every week.

He wrote his most famous book at Finkenwalde – *The Cost of Discipleship*, and it was becoming obvious to him that the Church was going to be involved in a life and death awaited trial. A second attempt by Bonhoeffer's friends on Hitler failed in July 1944, and then he was transferred to Flossenburg concentration camp. On 9 April 1945 Bonhoeffer and other prisoners were hanged in the woods nearby. The prison doctor wrote:

> On the morning of the day, some time between five and six o'clock, the prisoners were led out of their cells and the verdicts read to them. Through the half-open door of a room in one of the huts I saw Pastor Bonhoeffer still in his prison clothes, kneeling in fervent prayer to the Lord his God. The devotion and evident conviction of being heard, that I saw in the prayer of this intensely captivating man, moved me to the depths.

Violent Social Change

Bonhoeffer's story spotlights the challenge of the Christian life if a person is to be a true disciple of Christ. It is costly, not cheap or glib. Jesus warned that the path of discipleship would not always be easy:

> 'If anyone wants to come with me,' he told them, 'he must forget self, carry his cross, and follow me. For whoever wants to save his own life will lose it; but whoever loses his life for me and for the gospel will save it.'
> (Mark 8:34–5)

Bonhoeffer died a martyr's death, dying for the principles he believed in. His story raises the question of whether Christians should ever use violence, in the light of Jesus' words about loving one's enemies. Bonhoeffer did not decide to do so lightly; he thought he was in an extreme situation, like someone who sees a man driving a car towards a mother and child. Should you shoot the cruel driver and save innocent lives? He decided it was better for the corrupt Hitler to die and for thousands to live.

Bonhoeffer's writings also raised the question of the involvement of the Church in society and in politics. He thought the Church should side with the oppressed minorities. If Christians did not speak out and just got on with their church life, then it was the same as siding with the oppressors. In 1945 he wrote:

> The Church was silent … when it should have cried out because the blood of the innocent was crying aloud to heaven.

His experiences made him rethink the basics of the Christian faith, and his thoughts about God have inspired many Christians since. He did not see God as a powerful judge demanding people's obedience, but as giving himself to the human race in humility in the life of Christ; God stands alongside people, urging them on. God influences the world from a position of weakness, not power. 'God lets himself be pushed out of the world on to the cross.' God gives people freedom to choose, but he has demonstrated his love in the example of Jesus' suffering on the cross. He also spoke of Jesus as 'the Man for others', stressing the need for the Church's involvement with social change for the better.

In spite of his pacifist views, Bonhoeffer thought that it would be right to kill Hitler if thousands of innocent lives could be saved by doing so.

Activities

Key Elements

1 What made Bonhoeffer support the Confessing Church?
2 Describe Bonhoeffer's work at Finkenwalde. What was he trying to achieve?
3 Why did Bonhoeffer agree to take part in the attempt on Hitler's life? Do you think it was right for him to do so?
4 In what way did Bonhoeffer live out his teaching about the cost of discipleship?
5 What new ideas about God and Jesus did his experiences give him?

Think About It

6 Do you think his life was wasted? Discuss this.

Questions

- Arrange a debate about the use of violence. One side to argue that sometimes violent means are justified to achieve social change, and the other side to agree with Martin Luther King that violence is never justified and that only non-violent means can be used.

- Do some more research on one of these Christians, then write an imaginary interview to find out what motivates/motivated them.

Christian Guidelines

The lives of these famous Christians have raised a number of issues to do with how Christians try to live and what they think is really important. A survey of some of the teaching of Jesus follows, as well as an important passage from Paul, and one from the Old Testament. These will give more information about the morals and values of Christians.

The Sermon on the Mount

(Matthew 5–7) This is a collection of various sayings of Jesus that he probably spoke on separate occasions, but the Gospel writer has put them together to form a summary of Jesus' moral teaching. It is called the Sermon on the Mount because the writer introduces it with Jesus going up a hill to teach his disciples.

The Sermon falls into two sections: the **Beatitudes**, and teaching about various topics.

The Beatitudes (Matthew 5:3–15)

These are short sayings, and there are nine of them. 'Beatitude' means 'happy saying'. Jesus explains that the kind of lifestyle which is truly happy is one that is honest and does not give in when the going gets tough. Being happy, for Jesus, did not mean being lazy, well off and selfish.

1 Happy are those who know they are spiritually poor . . .
2 Happy are those who mourn . . .
3 Happy are those who are humble . . .
4 Happy are those whose greatest desire is to do what God requires . . .
5 Happy are those who are merciful to others . . .
6 Happy are those who are pure in heart . . .
7 Happy are those who work for peace . . .
8 Happy are those who are persecuted because they do what God requires . . .
9 Happy are those who when people insult them and persecute them and tell all kinds of evil lies against them because they are my followers.

The first three Beatitudes are reversals of traditional expectations. They sound strange at first. Jesus means that people who know their needs, who are not locked up in themselves and cold to others, will be truer human beings. They can feel, hope and love. They will be more open to God, too, than someone who feels self-sufficient, or who manipulates others. These people have their place in the Kingdom. Martin Luther King's struggles for the blacks in America, or David Wilkerson's support for drop-outs and drug addicts, were inspired by this teaching.

Beatitudes 5 and 6 are about a true search for God and its rewards, and 4 and 7 are about a true search for justice. 'Pure in heart' means to have singleness of vision, not being distracted by selfish concerns. Mother Teresa's life is an excellent example of this.

Beatitudes 8 and 9 are about suffering at the hands of others for doing what you believe to be right. If a person suffers in this way they are counted 'happy' because they are keeping their integrity and God will reward them. The only difference between 8 and 9 is that 9 speaks specifically about being persecuted for being a follower of Jesus. Bonhoeffer's example can be recalled here. He found that discipleship was not an easy path, but to be honest to his own convictions he had to follow it. King opened himself up to insults and harassments, and eventually lost his life because of the work he did. Yet their example lives on and inspires others.

Activities

Key Elements

1 What does the word 'beatitude' mean?
2 List the nine Beatitudes in your own words.
3 a) Does anything surprise you about the Beatitudes?
   b) What points was Jesus making?

Think About It

4 Do you think the Beatitudes can make sense for people today?

Activity

- Design a poster about the Beatitudes, using photographs from newspapers and magazines.

Teaching about Various Topics

The rest of the Sermon concerns teaching on the Jewish Law; anger; adultery; divorce; vows; revenge and love of enemies; charity, prayer and fasting; riches and possessions; and judging others.

The Law (Matthew 5:17–20)

Jesus said he had come to make the teachings of the Law come true. He seems to be saying that all its commandments are to be kept, but he ignored the food laws (like not eating pork) when he taught, for example, that it did not matter what food you ate. It is the state of a person's heart that makes them 'clean' or 'unclean' (see Mark 7:14).

It is difficult to know what he meant by the Law not being done away with, but perhaps he meant that all its commandments of love were eternal and could not be cancelled. On another occasion he summed up the Old Testament Law as being love of God and love of neighbour. That was what really mattered.

Anger (Matthew 5:21–6)

Jesus teaches that it is what is in a person's mind and feelings that is the real issue. He points out that anger in itself can be dangerous as it can lead to murder. The Old Testament law only dealt with the act of murder, not the inward feeling of hating someone. Other people should not be treated as 'good-for-nothings' because all are the children of God. On another occasion, though, Jesus himself showed anger, when he cleared the traders out of the Temple (see Mark 11:15–19); perhaps righteous anger, speaking out against injustices, is all right, but not anger that hates someone else and might secretly want to see them dead.

WHAT IS THE SERMON ON THE MOUNT ALL ABOUT?

Jesus taught that wrong actions are the result of wrong thoughts and feelings.

Murder starts with anger, a rage that wants to see someone hurt.

Adultery begins with lustful thoughts that get the better of the person. ...When you want to use someone else just for your own pleasure.

Jesus taught that people should repay evil with good, and should try to love their enemies rather than wanting to hurt them back.

Jesus taught that it is a person's inner motive that counts; a person who gives a little money in secret is purer than one who gives much and tells the world about it.

Money should be used wisely, not worshipped as a god. That makes people selfish.

Jesus taught that people should be careful when passing judgement on others. No one is perfect. When you point a finger at someone else, three more are pointing back at you.

Adultery (Matthew 5:27–30)

Again, Jesus goes behind the outward action and points to what a person is thinking or feeling inside. Adultery, strictly speaking, means a married person having sex with someone other than their spouse. But adultery starts with a lustful look. Jesus did not just understand sin as wrong actions, but also as the wrong thoughts that start these off. He might have been speaking tongue in cheek, here, for many married people have cast a lustful look at someone in their life! Perhaps he was warning people not to be too judgemental of those who committed adultery. It is a weakness many people can fall into if they are not careful, and people should not pretend to be righteous and condemn others when they often feel the same way inside. The story in John 8:1–11 shows Jesus being very understanding and forgiving to a woman caught in the act of adultery. In no way was he condoning it, though. There is nothing wrong with sexual desire; it is natural, but lust means wanting to use someone rather than wanting to love them. It means caring more about selfish pleasure than the whole quality of a relationship. Adultery breaks the trust in a marriage.

Divorce (Matthew 5:31–2)

The Law of Moses allowed divorce if a man found something shameful in his wife. There were two schools of thought about the meaning of this. One school claimed that it meant anything that displeased the husband, such as the wife being a bad cook, or always nagging; the other said that it referred to adultery.

Jesus sided with this second school and allowed divorce only if adultery was involved. Some Christians today feel that if Jesus said that one thing could break a marriage, then there might be other serious things that could, like cruel treatment or desertion. They follow Jesus' teaching that divorce should not be a cheap and easy option, however.

Vows (Matthew 5:33–7)

Jewish people at the time made many promises by swearing oaths. People were more superstitious about such things then, and it was a way of trying to persuade someone you were telling the truth, or even a way of trying to cover up a lie. The name of God was often used in these oaths, which Jesus found to be offensive. He taught that God's name should not be dragged into petty disputes; people should speak the truth plainly and say what they mean.

Revenge and Love of Enemies (Matthew 5:38–48)

Jesus went beyond the strict letter of an Old Testament law. Many Rabbis felt uneasy about applying 'an eye for an eye' literally, preferring a payment of compensation. Jesus based the command to love one another on Lev. 19:18. Hating the enemy was not a part of Jewish tradition, but was a common human failing. Jesus goes further than this: he wants love to be shown to offenders. This should have more power to change them. David Wilkerson lived by this principle, trying to reform the gangs he worked with.

Many Christians argue that the purpose of prison sentences should be to try to reform the criminal, and not to hurt him or her. But they also feel that letting an enemy insult you personally is one thing; then you can take it, but if other people are threatened then it is a different matter. Hence, if a criminal will not respond to reform, he/she must be locked away for the protection of society.

Some Christians would be prepared to fight in a war if they thought it was in a just cause (e.g. like stopping the Nazis in the Second World War), but other Christians would not go this far and would refuse to fight in a war, because many innocent people would suffer. They might, like Bonhoeffer, use violence against corrupt individuals if they can save others by doing so, however.

Charity, Prayer and Fasting (Matthew 6:1–18)

Jesus criticises people who make a show of religion, telling people how good they are: some giving to the poor only in public so all can see; some praying on street corners so all can hear; some going around in sackcloth when they fast so everyone will know. Jesus advises people to give money in secret, to pray in secret and to dress normally and be cheerful when fasting so no one else knows. He teaches that it is sincerity that matters, not the actions of giving to charity, praying or fasting in themselves.

Jesus also teaches that prayer should be to the point, and not said like a form of magic that uses a great number of phrases, thinking that you are more likely to be heard that way. It is here that Matthew inserts the Lord's Prayer, with its themes of God as a loving Father, of hope for the Kingdom and forgiveness of one's enemies.

Riches and Possessions (Matthew 6:19–24)

Jesus teaches that true riches are spiritual realities because these last for ever. Values such as love and freedom are more important than having plenty of money. People are easily tempted to give up their values if they will benefit financially, such as walking over others to get to the top, taking bribes, or fighting to keep their possessions. Jesus sees a life spent on earning wealth as a waste of time if spiritual values are ignored. He points out that money can easily become an idol, to be worshipped rather than God. If money becomes a person's master, then it will make the person selfish. It is all right to have money, however, so long as it is used wisely; money should be a servant, not a master.

Judging Others (Matthew 7:1–6)

Jesus warns that if a person is quick to accuse someone else of a failing, then they are forgetting that they are only human too. When they point a finger at someone, three are pointing back at them! No one is perfect. This should make people more sensitive to each other, and more ready to forgive. This is not to say that you should never speak out, but it is a general principle for Christians to remember, because it keeps things in perspective: 'There but for the grace of God go I.'

The teaching in the Sermon on the Mount is a summary of a Christian lifestyle. Some of the details and circumstances in the teaching of Jesus here are perhaps irrelevant and out of date because he was dealing with certain situations in first-century Galilee and Judaea – like people standing on street corners to say their prayers, or the teaching about oaths. But there are eternal principles contained within these teachings which Christians believe still apply today:

- Sin is not just a wrong action, but the inner feelings and thoughts of the person are involved too. That's where people have to change. This teaching may also make it hard to say what is sinful in every situation. For example, supposing a woman, trying to bring up a baby on her own and suffering from lack of money, stress and isolation on a large housing estate, batters her baby – is she really to blame when she is so affected by her circumstances?
- Sincerity is what matters in religion, not how well prayers are said, nor how often people fast, nor how much they give to charity. A person who hardly knows any prayers but says them with meaning is worth more to God than experts who can recite long prayers full of long words, but do not say them from the heart.
- People should strive for peace, and develop a forgiving attitude, remembering that they often do wrong, too.

• People should not be self-centred but open to others and to God. That way they will find true happiness.

Activities

Key Elements

1 What point was Jesus making in his teaching about adultery and murder?
2 What does Jesus say about sincerity in his teaching on prayer and fasting?
3 What did Jesus have to say about judging others? Did he mean that people should never speak out when they think someone else is doing wrong?
4 What did Jesus teach about the use of wealth in the Sermon?

Think About It

5 What good deeds might people show off about today? What do you think Jesus' message to them would be?
6 Discuss whether you think that in this modern world ordinary people can put Jesus' teaching into practice, or whether his teaching is too unrealistic for most people to attempt.

The Great Commandment

(Mark 12:28–34) A teacher of the Law of Moses asked Jesus which commandment was the most important of all. (The Law ordered a number of rituals to be followed and also commanded spiritual things, such as only worshipping one God.) Jesus replied that the greatest commandment was to love God with all a person's heart, soul, mind and strength, and that the second most important commandment was to love their neighbour as themselves. The first is from Deuteronomy 6:4–5, and the second is from Leviticus 19:18 (both are books of the Torah, or Law).

Here, Jesus showed his skill in dealing with the Old Testament scripture, drawing out what he saw as its central teaching – love. Love of God and love of humanity cannot be separated. They are two sides of the same coin.

The teacher was pleased with this answer, and agreed that love was more important than the other commandments which ordered various types of sacrifices. Jesus told him he was not far from the Kingdom of God.

Jesus ignored many of the commandments in the Law, such as the food laws, but he regarded himself as a faithful Jew. It is likely that there were a number of Jews who thought that the spiritual commandments of the Law were more important than the ritualistic laws about sacrifice and diet, and that Jesus sided with them. He might have been more radical in his dismissal of some aspects of the Law, though, and probably believed he had the authority to do this as the Messiah.

Activity

• Read Mark 12:28–34 and describe in your own words the incident when Jesus said what the greatest commandment was.

Question

• How does this passage show that Jesus was more concerned with inner motives than with external rituals? Was he the only Jew to think this?

Love

(1 Corinthians 13) Paul wrote his first letter to Christians in Corinth, in Greece, because he heard that they were having problems. Some of them liked to think they were wiser than the rest and more spiritual. Some of them seemed to have paranormal gifts, such as faith healing and the ability to speak in strange languages when they praised God.

Activity

- Write out 1 Corinthians 13:4–8 in your own words.

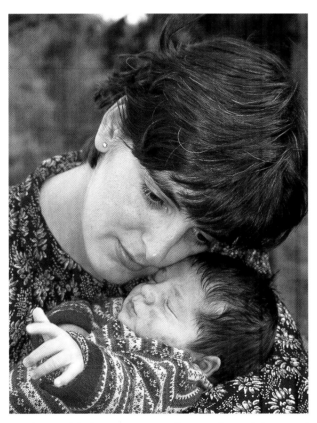

Mother and baby: an image of unconditional love and trust.

Paul pointed out that all their wisdom and all their gifts were utterly worthless if they did not have love. Any gifts that people had were God-given to build up their community, to help each other, and not there to show off with.

His teaching about love forms the thirteenth chapter of his letter, and it is often called the hymn to love. The word for love that he uses in Greek is *agape*, a suffering love. It is the word used of the love Jesus showed when going to the cross. It is a love that is prepared to be hurt in the service of others, not asking for anything in return.

Paul argues that only love is eternal; all other gifts will pass away when the Kingdom comes. He is saying the same thing as Jesus in Mark 12:28–34, in his own way:

I may have all knowledge and understand all secrets; I may have all the faith needed to move mountains – but if I have no love, I am nothing.

Activities

Key Elements

1. What Greek word does Paul use for 'love' in 1 Corinthians 13? What kind of love does he mean?
2. What was happening in the Corinthian Church when Paul wrote to them?
3. What was the greatest gift of God, according to Paul? How would it show itself to be the greatest?
4. List the ways he has of defining love. Can you add some of your own?

The Ten Commandments

RELIGIOUS COMMANDMENTS

(1) Serve God alone.
(2) Do not make any images of God or worship any idols.
(3) Do not use God's name for evil purposes.
(4) Keep the Sabbath day holy.

SOCIAL COMMANDMENTS

(5) Respect your father and mother.
(6) Do not murder.
(7) Do not commit adultery.
(8) Do not steal.
(9) Do not accuse anyone falsely.
(10) Do not desire to take another man's possessions.

(Exodus 20:1–17) The Ten Commandments are probably one of the oldest sections of the Old Testament, and one of the first sections of the Law to be written down by the Jews. It is a short set of principles for living. Four of the Commandments concern religion, and six concern other people and society.

1   The Commandments were written at a time when people worshipped many gods, and thought that each tribe had its own god. Here, the Jews were told to worship only one God.

2   The danger in making images of God is that people will think that they can understand God. God is a mystery and beyond human knowledge, and so, Jews believed, he cannot be pictured. Also, some ancient people used to think that if they made an image of a god, then it gave them some power over it, and this was foolish superstition.

3   The Commandment about God's name refers to a time when people thought that just saying his name was powerful, like magic, and would make things happen. People used to utter curses in this way, hoping to bring harm to someone. Hence, the Commandment forbids this. Jesus was referring back to this when he told people not to use God's name in oaths (see p. 113).

4   The Sabbath day for Jews is Saturday. They are supposed to rest from all kinds of work. This idea was introduced as a humanitarian idea so that people would be sure of getting a day off each week, and also spend some time worshipping God. Over the years various extra rules and regulations were added to the observance of the Sabbath so that people dared not do the least thing for fear of God's punishment. Jesus criticised this idea of the Sabbath, saying, 'The Sabbath was made for man, and not man for the Sabbath.' Christians changed the Sabbath day to Sunday because that was the day of the resurrection.

5   The idea of respecting father and mother was connected with the old custom of children looking after their parents in their old age because there was no Welfare State or Old Age Pension system. This is irrelevant to Christians in the West, now, but family life is still seen as being important, for it is a loving base where children can be reared.

7   The Commandment against adultery was also conditioned by the lack of a Welfare State and of adequate contraception. There were strict ideas about marriage and the duties of the children who legally carried your name. If you were not married and had children, they might not feel they had to be responsible for you in your old age. Christians now condemn adultery because it is breaking a basic bond of trust.

The other Commandments speak for themselves. Respect for other people's feelings and possessions is essential if society is to work peacefully. People cannot just do as they please if they are going to live with others.

These Jewish Commandments are still used by Christians, even though some details in them might belong to a bygone age. Jesus drew much inspiration for his teaching from them.

Activities

Key Elements

1 a) List the religious Commandments.

   b) List the social Commandments.

2 What is the meaning of the second Commandment about not worshipping idols?

Think About It

3 What did the third Commandment mean? Does this still apply today at all?

Assignments

1 Imagine you are *either* one of Mother Teresa's helpers in Calcutta, *or* one of David Wilkerson's helpers in New York. Make up entries in your diary for a week.

2 Have a debate on the following: 'The Ten Commandments are the best set of rules the world has ever had.' (Think about whether some of them no longer apply to today's world; whether some of them are clearly true for all ages and societies, etc.)

3 What do you think is the basic theme behind the Ten Commandments?

4 Make up your own list of Ten Commandments that you think people should live by.

5 Write an essay on the Sabbath: (i) explain the original reason for having a Sabbath day, as given in the Old Testament; (ii) the way the use of the Sabbath had changed by the time of Jesus; (iii) Jesus' teaching about the Sabbath; and (iv) whether you think a Sabbath day is needed and what kind of things should not be allowed to happen on it, for example, should Sunday trading, horse racing and betting be allowed?

8

A Cycle for Life

There are points in people's lives when they feel that they have passed from one stage of life to another. This might seem gradual or sudden. Some societies and religions have special ceremonies to mark these changes. They are called **rites of passage**. Family and friends can then join in the celebrations when someone passes from one stage to another. It helps it to sink in for all concerned, and helps people to think about the meaning of the various stages of life. Christianity has a series of rites of passage that form a cycle for life. They begin with birth, go on to growing up, marriage and death.

Questions

- What is meant by 'rites of passage'?
- What special times are kept each year in your family? Why do you do this?
- What types of things make you feel more adult?

Baptism

For most Christians, the first stage begins with baptism. Roman Catholic, Orthodox and Anglican Churches baptise babies (this is called 'infant baptism'), as do some Free Churches like the Methodists and United Reformed. Other Churches will only baptise people when they are old enough to know what they are doing. Couples with new-born children in those Churches will usually take their babies to the front of the church where the minister will pray for it, hoping that God will bless it. This is called **dedication**.

A dedication service. Why do some denominations hold this kind of service?

The Service

In an infant baptism, holy water is poured from the font on to the child's head by the priest. This is water that has been blessed by the priest first. It is poured over the child's head three times while the priest says the baby's name and then: 'I baptise you in the name of the Father, and of the Son, and of the Holy Spirit.'

An Anglican baptism.

The people answer these questions not only for themselves, but also in the name of the child who cannot speak for itself yet. The parents are expected to bring the child up in the Christian faith, and it will be given a chance to make up its own mind to accept the Christian faith later on in the ceremony known as **confirmation** (see pp. 122–3).

Roman Catholics and some Anglicans rub blessed oil (called chrism) on to the child's forehead. This indicates that the Holy Spirit has come to the child in baptism and has started to work in his or her life in a quiet way.

The priest then may take a candle that is lit from the large Paschal Candle and hands it to the parents, saying: 'Receive this light. This is to show that you have passed from darkness to light.' The congregation then replies: 'Shine as a light in the world to the glory of God the Father.' Then the priest says: 'God has received you by baptism into his Church.'

In the Anglican service, the people then say:

> 'We welcome you into the Lord's Family. We are members together of the body of Christ; we are children of the same heavenly Father; we are inheritors together of the Kingdom of God. We welcome you.'

All Churches will have some formula of welcome.

Before the actual act of baptism with water, the priest asks the parents and friends who are presenting the baby for baptism certain questions:

> 'Do you turn to Christ?'
> 'Do you repent of your sins?'
> 'Do you renounce evil?'

Orthodox Christians immerse the child three times in the font. They point out that the first Christians probably immersed people in the water rather than sprinkling them.

The Meaning

Water is used in baptism because it is a symbol of three things: washing, death, and new life.

Baptism is done to children on trust, like buying them an expensive present that they can choose to open later on if they wish to. Baptism is the sign of having joined the Church.

Christians baptise people because Jesus instructed them to:

'Go, then, to all peoples everywhere and make them my disciples: baptise them in the name of the Father, the Son, and the Holy Spirit.'
(Matthew 28:19)

John the Baptist baptised before Jesus, as did other Jewish movements at the time. The baptism was for Jews who turned from their sins to await the coming Messiah (see p. 12). Christian baptism means that a person is joining the followers of the Messiah, and it is seen as taking a first step into the Kingdom of God.

Christians are divided on their understanding of baptism. Roman Catholics, Orthodox and Anglicans see baptism as a sacrament – a special action that channels God's Spirit and blessing to a person. So, they think that something happens inside a person when the outward action is done to them. God's Spirit starts to come to life in their lives. This is called regeneration, which means a new start or a new birth. The idea is that people are changed within, and made more sensitive to God's call and presence. They turn from their old way of life, and open up to God.

Of course, it is harder to understand what this means for a baby. Babies are thought to be cleansed from original sin, which to many people today means that the baby is surrounded by many sinful influences that were in the world before its birth which affect it. The baby will be met by God's spirit and opened up to his love.

Other Christians understand baptism as a sign or symbol that people have changed inside. They commit their lives to Christ, and show this publicly by being baptised. Baptism does not make the change inside, but Jesus commanded that it should be done, as an act of witness.

Activities

- Write a paragraph explaining how some Christians justify infant baptism when the child cannot speak for itself.
- Visit an infant baptism and arrange to talk to some of the people involved. Prepare a questionnaire to find out what you think is important to know about infant baptism.

Activities

Key Elements

1. a) Explain how water is used in baptism.
   b) What three things does the water in baptism suggest?
2. What does the priest say when someone is baptised?
3. What is the difference between infant baptism and dedication?
4. How do Orthodox Churches baptise babies?
5. How and why is the symbol of light used in baptism?
6. What words of welcome are said by an Anglican congregation to the newly baptised? What do you think these mean?
7. Why do Christians baptise?
8. How is Christian baptism different from that of John the Baptist and other Jewish sects at the time of Jesus?

Confirmation

In Churches where infant baptism is practised, there needs to be a ceremony where people can make their own decision to belong to the Christian faith. This is called confirmation, as in confirming that the person wants to be in the faith. It also helps to make any young people doing this feel a little more grown-up and responsible since they are making up their minds.

Methodists and United Reformed Christians do not have confirmation. People become Church members in a service where they publicly confess their faith.

The age for confirmation varies from church to church, but it is usually around the age of 11 or 12. However, adults can also be confirmed if they did not get a chance when they were younger.

Roman Catholic children are usually allowed to take Holy Communion before they are confirmed, often at about the age of seven.

The Preparation

Candidates are usually expected to join a confirmation class which meets one evening a week or a fortnight. This might last for a few months to a year. They will be taught the basics of the faith, discuss some issues and probably learn the Apostles' Creed. The group leader (usually the priest) will explain the service of confirmation to the candidates so that they will understand what is happening.

The Service

The candidates will be asked to answer certain questions as a group. These will include the questions their parents had to answer for them when they were baptised as babies.

These are the Anglican words:

> 'Do you turn to Christ?'
> 'Do you repent of your sins?'
> 'Do you renounce evil?'

The Bishop will be present and he will ask questions like:

> 'Do you believe and trust in God the Father,
>   who made the world?'
> 'Do you believe and trust in his Son Jesus
>   Christ, who redeemed mankind?'
> 'Do you believe and trust in his Holy Spirit,
>   who gives life to the people of God?'
> (Anglican Service)

They then come to the front of the church and, one by one, kneel at the altar rail. The Bishop will place his hands upon the head of each of them and pray: 'Confirm, O Lord, your servant N [the candidate's name] with your Holy Spirit.' (Anglican) or, 'N, be sealed with the gift of the Holy Spirit.' (Roman Catholic)

In the Roman Catholic Church, and in some Anglican churches, the Bishop also smears a small amount of chrism oil on their foreheads. This is a symbol of the blessing and richness of the Holy Spirit. It is called the anointing with holy oil.

In the Orthodox Church, this prayer for the blessing of the Holy Spirit takes place immediately after baptism at a ceremony called chrismation. The priest anoints the child and says: 'Be sealed with the Holy Spirit.' The oil, or chrism, has been blessed by a bishop and he prays that people marked with it may 'bear Christ in their heart, in order to become a dwelling of the Trinity'.

The Meaning

Confirmation is a way of saying 'Yes' to a person's baptism. It is a conscious act and decision to join the life of the Church.

It is also a ceremony that calls God's Spirit into a person's life – to bless them and help them to live the Christian life. Some Christians say that the Spirit brings certain gifts at

Saul, to do the work to which I have called them.' They fasted and prayed, placed their hands on them, and sent them off.

A prayer from the Roman Catholic confirmation service draws out the significance of the ceremony well:

God our Father, you sent the Holy Spirit upon the apostles, and through them and their successors you give the Spirit to your people. May his work begun at Pentecost continue to grow in the hearts of all who believe.

There is a slight problem in understanding confirmation, for the gift of the Holy Spirit is supposed to be given to a person at baptism. The usual argument is that the Spirit lies dormant like a seed until a person's confirmation, and then it springs into life. Confirmation puts the cap on everything, completing the act of baptism done years before.

It is a further blessing of the Spirit, starting people off consciously on their Christian life. The Spirit is then expected to help and guide them through life, helping them to be more sensitive people. This process of making someone holy is called **sanctification** – making into a **saint**.

Some Churches feel that this runs the risk of being too formal. They stress that people can come to believe in Christ and feel the Spirit at work within them at any point in their lives, without a priest or a bishop around. These Churches do not have infant baptism, or confirmation, but believers' baptism.

this time, such as *wisdom, understanding, right judgement, knowledge, reverence, wonder* and *courage*. These are the sevenfold gifts of the Spirit, either helping people to make sense of their faith and the direction of their lives, or giving the strength to live it.

The Bishop places his hands on the heads of the candidates for three reasons:

1   To touch the candidates and make them feel wanted, so that they belong. They are joining the Church family.
2   To show that the ceremony is being carried out with the blessing of Christ himself. (Churches with bishops believe that the authority of the bishops can be traced back to the apostles, and it was Jesus himself who sent them out.)
3   The apostles and early Christians used to lay hands on people when they prayed for them to receive special gifts, as in Acts 13:1–3.

In the church at Antioch there were some prophets and teachers.... While they were serving the Lord and fasting, the Holy Spirit said to them, 'Set apart for me Barnabas and

---

Activity

• Write a paragraph on each of the following:
  a) How do Christians explain the coming of the Spirit at confirmation if the Spirit was already there at baptism?
  b) How do some of the Free Churches react to the idea of confirmation?

Believers' Baptism

People will approach the minister of a Baptist Church, House Church, Pentecostal Church or Evangelical Church if they feel that they want to be baptised. The minister will want to be sure that they understand what they are doing, and that they have a sincere and personal faith in Christ. Some teenagers or adults in this position might have just come to believe in Christ for the first time. They might have to attend baptism or membership classes for several weeks before the baptism, in order to be instructed in the faith.

The Service

The person will descend into a pool half-filled with water, and will be asked to make a pro-fession of faith. This might be a formal response to something like, 'Do you believe that Jesus is Lord and that he died for your sins?', or people might be asked to say a few words of their own, saying how they came to believe in Christ. This is called a testimony. They will have a sponsor who will have back-ed their application for baptism, and who will stand by, holding a towel ready.

The minister will lower them completely under the water for a few seconds and say, 'I baptise you in the name of the Father, the Son and the Holy Spirit.' Some might say instead, 'I baptise you in the name of Jesus.'

If the church does not have a pool they will either use someone else's church nearby, or the local swimming pool, or even have an open-air service in a river or in the sea.

Men will usually wear old clothes, and women will usually wear a long, white robe.

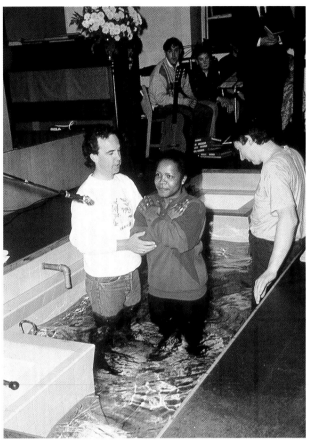

A believers' baptism. What type of Church is this probably being held in?

The sacrament of baptism is just a symbol to these Christians, a sign that the person has made a decision for Christ. It is not a special channel for God to work through.

Activities

- Visit a Baptist church and watch a believers' baptism. Talk to the people afterwards and write up a report.
- Design a poster or write a poem called 'New Life'.

Activities

Key Elements

1 What opportunity does confirmation give to people who were baptised as infants?
2 What is the usual age for confirmation? What do you think it should be?
3 What preparation is needed from confirmation candidates?
4 What are the two sets of questions that the bishop asks the candidates?
5 What does the bishop do to confirm someone, and what does he say?
6 How is it different in the Roman Catholic and Orthodox Churches from the Anglican Church?

7 What is the meaning of confirmation?
8 What gifts do many Christians think the Spirit brings at this time?
9 What are the three reasons for the bishop laying his hands on people's heads?
10 What does believers' baptism mean?
11 What preparation is needed?
12 Describe what happens at a believers' baptism.
13 What do these Christians think is happening when a person is baptised?
14 Which view do you agree with, infant or believers' baptism?

Marriage

People can be married in a register office (or registry) but Christians are expected to marry in church. Most ministers of religion are authorised to perform marriages, but some Free Church ministers are not, and they have to ask a registrar to attend the service and sign certain documents.

The Preparation

A couple wishing to be married will visit the minister and talk things over with him. He might arrange a few meetings, to try to get to know them a little. He will try to make sure that they understand what a serious step marriage is, and will answer any of their questions.

The Service

There are certain traditions about weddings, such as the bride wearing white, and that her father 'gives her away' during the service. These do not have to be followed, though, if the people are not happy with them. There are parts of the service that cannot be changed, such as where the couple make their vows, and the minister pronounces them man and wife. A marriage service has to have certain contents.

a) The minister asks if there is any reason, in law, why the people should not marry.
b) The couple have to give their consent to each other.
c) The couple exchange the marriage vows.
d) The couple are proclaimed as husband and wife.
e) The Register has to be signed, as a legal record of the marriage.
    (The giving of a ring, or rings, is usual, but not essential.)

A wedding ceremony in an Anglican church. Which part of the service is shown here, and what is its significance?

The most sacred part of the ceremony is the exchange of vows. This is what actually marries you.

The minister says to the bridegroom:

'N, will you take N to be your wife? Will you love her, comfort her, honour and protect her, and, forsaking all others, be faithful to her as long as you both shall live?'

Then he says to the bride:

'N, will you take N to be your husband? Will you love him, comfort him, honour and protect him, and, forsaking all others, be faithful to him as long as you both shall live?'

After they have both replied, 'I will', they face each other. The bridegroom says:

'I, N, take you, N, to be my wife, to have and to hold from this day forward; for better, for worse, for richer, for poorer, in sickness and in health, to love and to cherish, till death us do part, according to God's holy law; and this is my solemn vow.'

The bride either says the same back to the bridegroom, or a slightly different version that changes one line 'to love, cherish and obey'. This is regarded as old-fashioned by many modern couples. In the past the man was thought to be the head of the household, and the wife was subordinate to him.

The ring is then presented, and the bridegroom says to the bride:

'I give you this ring as a sign of our marriage. With my body I honour you, all that I am I give to you, and all that I have I share with you, within the love of God, Father, Son, and Holy Spirit.'

The ring is a token of the love between the couple and is worn as a reminder by the bride (and maybe the bridegroom as well). It is also a symbol of eternity, being a circle – a symbol of unending love.

After the giving of the ring, the minister says, 'I therefore proclaim that they are husband and wife.' And then adds, 'That which God has joined together, let not man divide.'

Orthodox wedding services are slightly different. The couple exchange rings at an engagement before the wedding. The priest blesses the couple, and there is a party afterwards. During the wedding service itself, a silver crown (a *stefana*), or a garland, is held over each of their heads. These are then placed on their heads, the priest joins their hands and he blesses their future life together. Almond sweets are shared out, and then there is a full feast.

A Ukranian Orthodox wedding, showing the crowning ceremony. What is the significance of this?

Orthodox, Roman Catholic and some Anglican weddings will have a Eucharist after the marriage service.

The wedding reception after the service gives friends and family a chance to celebrate with the couple and to give them a send off into their new life together. Feasting is a common way of celebrating because everyone has to eat and drink, and it brings people together.

Activities

Key Elements

1 How do a couple have to prepare for a marriage in church?

2 a) What things are only traditional, and what things *have* to happen in a marriage service?

   b) Do you know of any other traditional things that take place at Christian weddings? Do they have a religious meaning?

3 What do the vows mean that the couple make to each other?

4 What does the wedding ring symbolise? Do you think men should wear one as well?

5 What does the priest or minister say when he joins the couple in marriage?

6 Describe how Orthodox marriages differ from Anglican marriages.

Think About It

7 Why do some brides choose to omit the words 'to obey' from their vows? What do you think about it?

8 Why do you think it is traditional to have a reception after a wedding?

The Meaning

Roman Catholics, Orthodox and many Anglicans see marriage as a sacrament. The couple are spiritually joined together through the service. This idea comes from the story in Genesis where Adam and Eve are created. Adam looked at Eve and said, 'At last, here is one of my own kind – Bone taken from my bone, and flesh from my flesh.' The author goes on: '...a man leaves his father and mother and is united with his wife, and they become one.' (2:23, 24)

Jesus also talked about the special union that God fashions between a man and his wife: 'Man must not separate, then, what God has joined together.' (Mark 10:9)

Other Christians interpret these passages to mean that God created marriage as a deep way of sharing between a couple, and that God blesses their relationship.

Christians believe that the difference between the vows taken in a church and those taken in a register office, is that they are made before God. His name is called upon as a witness to the marriage, and his blessing is sought.

Christians in the past used to think that the main reason for marriage was so that the couple could have children. For some time, many of the Churches were wary of ways of birth control except for natural methods. The Roman Catholic Church still takes this position officially, though some Catholics disagree with this and use contraceptives. But marriage is now seen, by all Christians, as being about companionship first and foremost. Sexual activity is part of that deep relationship. Most couples do have children, and feel fulfilled in having them. It seems to some to be the crown of fruition of their marriage, but they want to be able to plan responsibly when to have them, and how many to have.

It is interesting to compare two Service Books in the Church of England to see the changing attitudes. The seventeenth-century Book of Common Prayer has these three reasons for marriage: (1) to have children, (2) for sex, (3) for companionship. The 1980 Alternative Service Book has the reasons in this order: (1) for companionship, (2) for sex, (3) to have children, if the couple want to.

The marriage service helps the couple psychologically to feel more committed to each other because they make a public commitment. They feel they have the support of their family and friends and the Church.

Divorce

All Christians agree that marriage should be intended for life. That is the ideal. If a minister felt that a couple were not sure that they wanted to spend the rest of their lives together, he would talk them out of it. Yet not all marriages are successful. Some do break down. It is here that Christians are divided on what to do next.

Roman Catholics do not allow divorce. They argue that since marriage is a sacrament, it is binding for life, and a couple cannot be un-married. They can live separately, but they cannot divorce and remarry. They refer to Jesus' words in Mark 10:9 and to the view of Paul expressed in 1 Corinthians 7:10–11 where he allows separation but not divorce.

Catholics do allow annulment. This is a declaration that a marriage never in fact took place, and there are strict conditions, which show that at least one of the couple did not intend to make the vows properly at the time of the wedding.

Most other Christians do allow divorce. They point to Jesus' words in Matthew 5:31–2 where he says that divorce can happen because of adultery. If one thing can break a marriage, then other things can, too, such as cruel treatment, desertion or a complete breakdown in relationship.

Orthodox Christians are sometimes **excommunicated** for a time after divorce (meaning that they cannot take the sacraments in

church) if they were the guilty party and then re-admitted after a service in which they express their sorrow over contributing to the ending of the marriage. They believe that marriage is a solemn union that should be for life, but it can break down from within.

Some Christians feel that divorced people should not remarry because their first marriage failed. Others feel it is only humanitarian to allow people to remarry, especially if they were the innocent party. Orthodox Christians can remarry, but without the full marriage ceremony. In the Church of England, a blessing of a second marriage is allowed, once this has taken place in a Register Office, though a full second marriage in Church is allowed in some places.

Activities

Key Elements

1   Write a paragraph on the teaching of Jesus about marriage in Mark 10.
2   What does it mean when some Christians say that marriage is a sacrament?
3   What different opinions about divorce do Christians have? List them.

Think About It

4   Do you think divorce is always wrong? Write a paragraph about what you think.

Funerals

The Church has a special service for the end of life as well as for its beginning. Friends and relatives will gather together for the funeral service. It will usually open with the minister saying some words of Jesus, such as:

'I am the resurrection, and I am the life; he who believes in me, though he die, yet shall he live, and whoever lives and believes in me shall never die.' (John 11:25–6)

After some singing and praying, the minister will say a few words about the deceased person, summing up the value of their life and how they will be missed; and then if the person is to be buried, as the coffin is lowered into the grave, the minister says the committal (these are the Anglican words):

'We have entrusted our brother/sister N to God's merciful keeping, and we now commit his/her body to the ground: earth to earth, ashes to ashes, dust to dust: in sure and certain hope of the resurrection to eternal life through our Lord Jesus Christ, who died, was buried, and rose again for us. To him be glory for ever and ever.'

These are the Roman Catholic words:

'Father, into your hands we commend our brother (sister). We are confident that with all who have died in Christ he(she) will be raised to life on the last day and live with Christ forever . . .'

The Orthodox service has similar words, but adds, later on:

'May Christ give thee rest in the land of the living, and open unto thee the gates of Paradise, and make thee a citizen of his Kingdom.'

If the person is cremated, only slightly different words will be said.

There will be a meal afterwards for all the guests, and this will allow them time to share their sorrows and share memories, as well as meeting people they may not have seen for some time.

In some Churches there will be a Eucharist said in memory of the dead person as a part of the service.

A funeral helps people to face up to the loss of a friend or relative. It is a public act of saying farewell, and all the people there share in the sorrow to some degree.

Christians believe in a life after death. They believe that a deceased person's body might rot away in the grave or be cremated into ashes, but their personality lives on, somehow, raised to new life by God in another place that is really impossible to imagine. The story of Jesus rising again helps to give them confidence in this hope.

Activities

Key Elements

1   Explain what the priest or minister does at a funeral.

Think About It

2   What comfort do you think some of his words will give to the people?

3   Do you think it is better to be buried or cremated?

Assignments

1   Write an essay on baptismal regeneration: (i) explain how Christians think this is caused in (a) infants and (b) adults; (ii) describe how other Christians, who reject this view of baptism, understand baptism; then (iii) conclude with what you think.

2   Write an essay on Christian marriage: (i) give the reasons why Christians think marriage is good; (ii) the reasons why the Roman Catholic Church officially bans contraception; (iii) explain how the view of marriage has changed in the Anglican service of 1980 compared to that of 1666, and (iv) conclude with whether you think there is still a place for marriage in today's world.

3   Hold a class debate on the advantages and disadvantages of marriage: 'Marriage is unnecessary and old-fashioned.'

9

Experiences and Pilgrimages

Experiencing God

Most Christians do not claim to have had any special, remarkable experiences of God, such as you might find reported in a Sunday newspaper, but most feel that God is with them in a quiet way. This may be felt when they pray: it feels as though someone is listening. Words from the Bible may seem to come alive as they are read, and there may be a sense of peace during a service, a sense of feeling refreshed inside.

There are more striking feelings and experiences which some Christians claim to have, though:

- A sense of God's presence, or a deep inner joy.
- A sense of being saved.
- Being cured by faith.
- Experiencing a vision of God, Christ, Mary, or one of the saints.
- Experiencing paranormal gifts and abilities as a result of prayer.
- Feeling inner promptings from God, or hearing 'loud thoughts'.

A Sense of a Presence, or Deep Joy

This can happen quite suddenly, during a time of personal prayer at home, or in a church service. It can even happen when the person is not doing anything religious.

One person wrote:

I began praying, not really sure that there was a God. . . . a great relaxation came upon my mind and everything fitted together. It only lasted for a moment, perhaps four to five seconds . . . I really felt that God was communicating with me.

Another person recalled:

In adolescence, after receiving instruction for confirmation one day in church I prayed for Christ to come into my life. A sense of relief, the peace of God, something fantastic.

One person was just walking in the garden when he experienced this:

I was walking by an apple tree that was in blossom – light pink and bright. I suddenly looked twice at it and the combination of the fresh green of the leaves, and the colourful blossom made me stare at it. I was suddenly aware of a presence that was within the living tree and within me, too, and somehow in the space between us. We were all part of one force.

John Hick, a professor of theology, has written about an incident that happened when he was a student:

It happened . . . – of all places – on the top deck of a bus in the middle of the city of Hull, when I was a Law student at University College, Hull. . . . It was as though the skies opened up and light poured down and filled me with a sense of overflowing joy in response to an immense transcendent goodness and love. I remember that I couldn't help smiling broadly – smiling back, as it were, at God – though if any of the other passengers were looking they must have thought that I was a lunatic, grinning at nothing. And there have been a number of less intense, usually much less intense, moments from time to time, varying from a background sense to a momentarily more specific sense of existing in the unseen presence of God.

Questions

- Although most Christians do not claim to have any special religious feelings, what benefits do many of them feel from prayer and church services?

- List the different types of special experience that some Christians have.

Activity

- Read through the above examples again:
  a) What did each experience feel like?
  b) What common features are there in all the stories?
  c) Do any of them seem different?
  d) What situations were these people in? Were they all doing something religious?
  e) Have you ever felt anything like this? What did you make of this experience?

Being Saved

Many Christians are baptised as infants and are brought up in the Church. Their faith means something to them, and they carry on with it quietly. Some, however, who are not brought up in the Church, might have a conversion experience where they feel that God has come to them. This might be a sudden, unexpected encounter. Some Christians say that this happened to them when they went to hear a preacher and they began to understand who Jesus was for the first time. They felt challenged to make a decision for Christ, and went to the front of the meeting to be prayed for and advised on what to do next. They felt a sense of new life inside, and a sense of being loved and forgiven.

John Wesley, the founder of the Methodist Church, had a similar experience when he was listening to a reading from Paul's letter to the Romans. He felt his heart 'strangely warmed' and he felt that he did trust in Christ, 'and Christ alone', for his **salvation**. This was not such a sudden experience for him, however, for he had been searching for God for some time. He had been very religious, and worked hard at trying to be good to others, but he felt a constant sense of guilt – he was so aware of his failings that he could not feel God's love. This wall of guilt was washed away in an instant.

Some people make a sudden decision for Christ and feel renewed within; this feeling of being loved and forgiven comes to others only after a long period of searching. Such Christians talk about 'being saved' or about being 'born again'. They are enthusiastic and lively believers, but some other Christians become impatient with them if they assume that everyone else should share the same experience as them, and doubt that others are really Christians if they have not.

Activities

Key Elements

1 a) Describe what usually happens when a person feels 'saved'.
   b) What do they feel like inside?
2 This experience sometimes happens to very religious people. What happened to John Wesley?

Think About It

3 How can people like this benefit the Church? What problems might some of them cause as well?
4 You may have read about famous people who say they are 'born again' Christians, such as some American politicians or pop stars. How do you react to these people? For example, do you feel they should be quieter about their faith?

Cured by Faith

A healing service. Do you think this type of service helps people?

The Gospels are full of stories of healing miracles (see p. 18). People have claimed to be healed in this way in recent times as well. The Reverend Colin Urquhart is an Anglican priest who holds services of healing. People come to him to be prayed for, and some of them claim to be healed. Here are two cases.

The first is that of a Scottish woman who was losing her hearing because of a childhood illness. She was deeply distressed. Colin Urquhart placed his hands on her and prayed:

We asked the Lord to forgive her, to heal the misery in her life and fill her with the Holy Spirit. She was immediately liberated and began praising and thanking him. It was almost as an afterthought that I placed my hands over her ears: 'Lord, please restore the hearing of your child.' Until then, I had needed to shout to make her hear me when speaking to her. . . .

'Can you hear, now?' I asked quietly.

She turned and looked at me, her face radiant. 'Did you shout then?' she asked.

I went on talking quietly, until my voice was drowned by her saying: 'I can hear, I can hear. Oh, thank you Lord, thank you.'

The second case, also from his book, *When the Spirit Comes*, concerns a man with cancer. He came to a prayer group in the vicarage lounge, and the people prayed for him. Nothing seemed to have happened. He had not felt any change. But when he went into hospital a few days later, it was discovered that all the cancer tumours had disappeared.

There are other stories of healings that are gradual or not complete, rather than split-second 'cure-all' miracles. For example, James Moon went to Lourdes with his wife. He was suffering from a stroke and diabetes. He could hardly walk, and was put in the baths there. He suddenly felt a strange feeling come over him, and he knew that he could walk. He did so, much to everyone's amazement, but he still dragged a foot and was told to be careful. He had not been completely healed.

In the Acts of the Apostles, there are stories of the early Christians praying for the sick and healing them, as in the case of the lame man in Chapter 3. Paul mentions in his first letter to the Corinthians that some have the gift of healing, and there have been stories of faith healing all through the history of the Church. This is seen as the Spirit of Christ carrying on his earthly work.

Christians have different ways of understanding such healings. Some think that God intervenes in the normal course of nature to do something amazing and new. It is a force that cannot be investigated by science.

Other Christians think that the power of faith, of belief, itself unlocks certain powers in a person's mind and body that science is only just coming to realise exist. The presence of God helps to create the faith necessary to unlock these abilities. James Moon, for example, suddenly felt that he believed he could walk. Jesus often told people, 'Your faith has cured you.'

Marvellous though these stories are, some people pray for healing and nothing seems to happen. They stay sick, suffer, and sometimes die. True, prayer might help them feel stronger emotionally, so that they can cope with their illness better. It does not affect their physical condition at all, though. Christians suggest reasons why this might be:

- Maybe the person had a sin in their life that they had not confessed.
- Maybe it was not God's will for the person to be healed – perhaps they can learn something through their suffering: 'It is good for their soul.'
- Maybe certain people are not as receptive to the power of faith and the abilities of the mind over the body.

Whichever, Christians regard healing by faith as an exception that might happen occasionally, and so normally they will go to the doctor like anyone else. They cannot really explain why some are healed and some are not.

Activities

Key Elements

1 a) Describe what happened in each of the cases reported by Colin Urquhart.
   b) What happened to James Moon at Lourdes?
   c) What explanations do Christians suggest for these stories?
2 What reasons do Christians give to explain why some people are not healed in this way?

Question

- Have you heard of anyone being cured by prayer? What do you make of such stories?

Seeing Visions

This is much more rare than feeling a sense of a presence, or 'being saved', or of being healed through prayer. Yet there have been cases of it throughout the history of the Church. The first case recorded in the New Testament is of the visions the disciples saw of the risen Christ. The most dramatic of these was that seen by Paul. Before this experience he had been an enemy of the new Christian movement and was having some Christians arrested or even put to death. Read the account in Acts 9:3–9. Note what Paul saw and heard. Did he actually see Jesus?

A famous story of a vision in more recent times is that of St Bernadette of Lourdes. On Thursday 11 February 1858, when she was 14, Bernadette was out walking by a grotto. She heard what sounded like a gust of wind, but the trees did not move. Then she heard it again, and noticed that the branches of a rose bush in front of the entrance to the grotto were moving. By this was a gentle light that contained the figure of a beautiful woman, dressed in white, and she was smiling. Bernadette tried to move but could not at first. She made the sign of the cross, and stared at the woman. Then she felt at peace. She knelt down and said her rosary. The woman said hers, too, then vanished. The apparition appeared several more times, and when word got around many other people came to watch. They saw nothing, only Bernadette smiling, looking up as if in a trance. Eventually, the figure told Bernadette that she was the Virgin Mary and that a spring that appeared near her was to be visited by people who sought healing. Thousands of pilgrims now go to the spot, which has been built over with a huge church and chapel. (There is more about Lourdes on p. 142.)

Visions obviously happen to people, but what are they seeing? Some Christians think that these people see an actual spiritual form that appears briefly in this world.

Others think that they see a picture projected by their own minds. This is not quite the same as hallucinating. It is as though very deep feelings and ideas in their minds are turned into pictures that their eyes somehow see. The feelings inside are very real; and Christians believe they are given by God. There are also cases of emotionally troubled people having very unpleasant visions projected by their minds.

The statue of Our Lady of Lourdes. What is hanging from her arm? Find out what the inscription means.

Question

- What do *you* think happens? Discuss this in class.

Activities

Key Elements

1 a) Describe what happened to Paul on the road to Damascus (Acts 9:3–9).
   b) Describe Bernadette's vision.
   c) What effect did these experiences have on the people concerned, and on those with them?
2 What are the two ways in which Christians explain these visions?

Strange and Wonderful Gifts

Pentecostal Christians, and members of the charismatic movement, believe that God has given them certain extraordinary gifts to use to help other people, and to help them to worship. Paul lists these gifts in 1 Corinthians 12:4–11. These are examples of some of the gifts he mentions:

- *Healing* – through the power of prayer.
- *Prophecy* – to speak out words which come from an inner sense of what God feels about a situation. They might be words of encouragement, or of warning.
- *Knowledge* – a person might suddenly have an insight into a person's problem.
- *Speaking in tongues* – an ability to speak in a language for the purposes of prayer and praise that the speaker has never learned. Some think that these are actual foreign languages. Others think that it is the same thing as happened to the disciples at Pentecost (see pp. 64–5). Paul might have something different in mind, though, such as a special prayer language. It seems likely that it is a special subconscious language that enables people to express deep feelings that they cannot easily put into words.

These gifts will be used in services in Pentecostal or House Churches, where the service has no formal structure, and anyone can take part. They will also be used in prayer groups held in people's homes by members of the charismatic movement, because the Churches they belong to have a formal service with no room for spontaneous gifts. If someone speaks in tongues out loud, then the people will wait to see if someone can interpret the message. Sometimes, people will sing in joyful harmonies in their special prayer language.

Activities

Key Elements

1 List some of the gifts mentioned in 1 Corinthians 12:4–11 and explain what they are.
2 Which groups of Christians believe in these gifts and practise them?
3 How would you explain 'speaking in tongues'?

Think About It

4 Have you heard or seen any of these gifts in action? If so, how did you react to them? If not, how do you think you would feel?

Loud Thoughts from God

Some Christians feel that God guides them in making a major decision by popping sudden ideas or thoughts into their minds. This might feel like an inner voice, or an inner prompting. It might just be a sudden idea that appears as if from nowhere and makes everything click together. David Wilkerson experienced such inner promptings when he went to help the gangs in New York (see pp. 104–5).

Another example involved Dr Frances Young, a teacher at Birmingham University, who was ordained a Methodist minister on 3

July 1984. This is how she describes her decision to be ordained:

> *I was driving home and stopped at the traffic lights in Dudley, and suddenly I had another loud thought which was simply, 'You should get ordained.' An extraordinary thing happened after that. I just don't know how I drove back – I'm not aware of the journey at all – I must have been on automatic pilot or something. . . . But during the course of that drive home . . . I had the whole of my life laid out in front of me; and all its peculiar twists and turns which hadn't seemed to make very much sense suddenly fell into a pattern, as though this was all leading up to that moment and that conclusion.*

Inner promptings or flashes of insight seem to help some Christians work out the direction of their lives.

None of the experiences mentioned in this chapter are claimed as out-and-out proofs of the existence of God. A sceptic could argue that the loud thoughts, visions, and joyful presences are all created by the person's own mind. The gifts of the Spirit could be akin to things like ESP – products of powers in the mind that people tap into; and people might get well because they want to enough.

Christians would respond that it feels different from things happening in their own minds, that it is not like forgotten thoughts popping into their memories again. The sense of a presence, they say, feels like something or someone else being with them.

Also, the result of all these experiences is often a deep change in the person concerned. They are not just weird experiences – they claim that they alter a person's outlook, and usually change them for the better. So, a person feeling an inner prompting might do something very brave that they would never have dreamed of doing on their own, or a person healed through prayer will feel spiritually refreshed within as well as physically better. It is all a matter of faith; of what a person believes. There is no direct proof of God in these experiences, but Christians argue that there is no proof that God is not involved either.

Activities

Key Elements

1 What is actually meant by 'loud thoughts'? Do people hear a voice inside their heads?
2 Read through Dr Young's experience again. What loud thought struck her? How did it affect her? Is there another explanation for it that you would put forward?

Question

- How would sceptics explain these experiences? How would Christians answer them?

Pilgrimage

Christians sometimes go to places to try to feel closer to God. There are special places of **pilgrimage** such as Lourdes in the south of France, and the Holy Land (Israel). Making the effort to travel to a place in order to pray, study and meditate, helps people to take their faith seriously. It is also a way of stepping aside from the daily toil that becomes so commonplace in order to spend some time resting and thinking.

All life is like a pilgrimage as people move through time from birth to death. We move along, and learn new things on the way. Going on a religious pilgrimage helps some people in their spiritual life. The great religions of the world all have places of pilgrimage. Hindus, for example, go to the sacred River Ganges. Muslims visit Mecca, their holy city. Christians visit places in the Holy Land where Jesus lived and preached, or famous shrines where saints are buried, or where people say the Virgin Mary has appeared. Going on a pilgrimage benefits a religious person in three ways:

Christian places of pilgrimage have special connections with great figures or events in the Christian faith, and Christians believe that these places have a special feel about them, an awe, a special holiness that comes from being used and prayed in for centuries. For generations, pilgrims have treated these places with respect as holy places. Many pilgrims feel that something of this rubs off on them during their stay there.

One elderly lady was on a pilgrimage to the Holy Land. She felt deeply moved as she visited places connected with the life of Jesus; they brought home to her how real a person he had been in history. In the Church of the Holy Sepulchre, where Jesus' tomb is thought to lie, she knelt down in prayer, tears streaming down her cheeks. She felt the suffering and rejection that Jesus must have gone through and the mystery of the resurrection seemed all around her – somehow, he *was* alive. Her priest was with her, and a group of others. He had not felt anything in particular on the visit, but he knelt alongside her in the church and prayed too. He was moved when he saw her tears and her faith, and he marvelled at the fact that he had had to come all those miles to see that and be moved.

Activities

Key Elements

1 Why do Christians go on pilgrimage?
2 Why do certain places become pilgrimage centres?
3 How does going on pilgrimage affect some Christians?

Bethlehem – the Church of the Nativity

Bethlehem boasts the Church of the Nativity. This is the traditional site of the birth of Jesus. Although rebuilt in the sixth century, much

Life is like a journey – why? What important things have happened to you on your journey so far? Do a drawing of a road and plot them along the way. What other things would you like to happen? Plot them in a different colour.

1 It helps in their search for God; they often feel closer to God and more involved with him on the pilgrimage.
2 It helps people to be more aware of the passing away of their life, of their limited time on earth. It sets them thinking and helps them to work out a sense of priorities.
3 It is making an effort, and this helps them to have a disciplined spiritual life. People feel they are getting up and doing something to draw closer to God.

Inside the Church of the Nativity, in a grotto at the eastern end. The star marks the spot where Jesus is thought to have been born. Why are there so many incense burners hanging above it!

of the original church survives. It was built by the Emperor Constantine at the urging of his mother, Helena. He became the first Roman Emperor to convert to Christianity, in the fourth century. But the site was regarded as holy for some time before that. Early in the second century, Emperor Hadrian built a shrine to a Roman god on it to discourage the Christians, and a Christian writer, Justin Martyr, in the second century, mentions the site as that of Jesus' birth. In 614 the Persians invaded Palestine and destroyed many churches, but the Church of the Nativity was spared, some say because the mosaic over the entrance shows the three wise men wearing Persian dress.

Various Churches have altars in it, including the Orthodox, Roman Catholic and some smaller Eastern Churches – the Armenians and the Copts.

Nazareth

Nazareth was where Jesus grew up, and where he worked until becoming a preacher. There are two Christian sites of interest: the Basilica of the Annunciation and the Greek Orthodox Church of St Gabriel. Both claim to be the site of the Annunciation. The Basilica is modern but it stands on the site of earlier churches which were built around the cave-dwelling believed by some to have been Mary's house. Inside the Orthodox church is a well at which another tradition claims Gabriel appeared to Mary.

Jerusalem – the Church of the Holy Sepulchre

A shrine has existed on the spot of the Church of the Holy Sepulchre from early in the Christian period. Emperor Hadrian built a temple to a Roman goddess there in 135 CE in an attempt to remove traces of Christianity. St Helena persuaded Constantine to build two churches on the site. They were begun in 326 and finished in 335. One of these was a domed building that housed a tomb cut out of the rock; the other covered the traditional site of Calvary, where Jesus was crucified. (Calvary is the Latin translation of Golgotha; see Matthew 27:33.) The site of Calvary was thought to be very close to the tomb because Jesus was crucified outside the city walls, and tombs were also outside. Jesus was buried in a rich man's tomb, and this would have been near the city gates, near the place of execution. Helena's churches were destroyed by invaders and then rebuilt by the Crusaders, but all under one roof.

It is now under the control of six churches. The Greek Orthodox have the most influence, and the others are the Roman Catholics, the Armenians, the Syrians, the Copts and the Ethiopians.

The Church of the Holy Sepulchre in Jerusalem, thought to be built on the sites of Jesus' crucifixion and burial.

The Church of the Holy Sepulchre – this photo shows the stone upon which the body of Jesus might have rested. The original stone has been covered with marble. A Coptic shrine stands to the rear of the tomb. There is evidence of other tombs in the area, confirming that this was an ancient burial ground. The site of Calvary is to the right of the tomb area. Why do you think the original cave that contained the tomb was cut away? What feeling do you think a worshipper would have in here?

Rome

St Peter's and the Vatican Palace. Thousands of people have gathered to receive the Pope's blessing. Why is this place so special to many Christians?

The city of Rome contains a small area called Vatican City, the headquarters of the Roman Catholic Church. Its huge, domed St Peter's rests upon the foundations of a much older church built by Emperor Constantine in the fourth century. Constantine believed that St Peter was buried beneath his church. Vatican hill had been a cemetery in earlier Roman times, and tradition held that Peter had been crucified in the reign of Emperor Nero and buried there by the early Christians.

There is a legend that Peter was fleeing from Rome during the first great persecution of Christians, when he met Jesus walking towards the city. Peter asked, 'Domine quo vadis?' ('Lord, where are you going?') And Jesus answered, 'I go to be crucified again.' Peter felt ashamed after seeing this vision, and returned to Rome where, on his insistence, he was crucified upside down because ordinary crucifixion was too good for him as that had been done to his master. (There is a little church called Domine Quo Vadis? on the supposed spot.)

St Paul is also said to have been killed at Rome during Nero's persecution in about 64 CE. As a Roman citizen he would have been beheaded outside the city wall. The traditional site was at the third milestone along the Laurentian Way, by the Salvian Marsh. A monastery was founded there in the seventh century. His body is thought to have been buried nearer to Rome, under the church of St Paul-without-the-walls.

Rome is also an important pilgrimage site because that is where the Pope lives. Roman Catholics believe that he is Peter's successor as head of the Church (see Matthew 16:18–19).

Question
- What is the evidence that St Peter might be buried at Rome?

Lourdes

The grotto at Lourdes, where St Bernadette saw her visions. The people have gathered to hear Mass beneath the statue of the Virgin, where Bernadette stood. What hopes and fears do you think these people will have?

Lourdes, in the south of France, is a very popular place of pilgrimage. This is where St Bernadette is said to have seen the Virgin Mary. (The story is on p. 135.)

Since Lourdes became a centre of pilgrimage in the last century there have been about sixty-four cases that have been declared as miraculous cures. If a person reports a cure, they are examined by a medical team at Lourdes, and the team will refer to the patient's home medical reports and doctor. The person will only be pronounced as cured if the complaint has totally disappeared and if there was no chance of the problem gradually getting better on its own or with normal medical treatment.

There are many people, however, who say that they felt very much better after going there, though they are not completely cured. Many also say that the experience helped them spiritually or emotionally, even though their physical illness remained unchanged. One woman was afraid of losing her eyesight. She went to Lourdes and returned full of life and self-confidence, although her eyes had not improved. She felt that she had been given the strength to cope with her problem.

The pilgrims gather at night with lighted candles to sing praises to God. The Lourdes hymn is sung, 'Immaculate Mary! Our hearts are on fire, that title so wondrous fills all our desire. Ave, ave, ave, Maria!' (Note that Catholics call Mary immaculate because they believe that she was kept free from the effects of sin when she was born. This was to prepare her for giving birth to Jesus.) This photo shows part of the route taken by the candlelit procession. Why do you think the pilgrims hold candles?

Santiago de Compostela

The shrine of Santiago (St James) of Compostela was one of the most popular places of pilgrimage in the Middle Ages, ranking with Rome and the Holy Land. It is still a popular site for Roman Catholics.

Compostela lies in north-western Spain. A local bishop ordered a site to be explored and excavated early in the ninth century when reports came to him of visions granted to an old hermit and to local peasants. The hermit had a dream in which he was told that the tomb of St James, the brother of St John, and son of Zebedee, and one of the 12 apostles, was in a wood near his home. The peasants reported seeing a star above the wood, and hearing heavenly music. An old Roman grave was found, and the bones were declared to be those of St James.

James was executed in about 44 CE in Jerusalem (see Acts 12:1–2). An eighth-century legend said he had preached in Spain after the resurrection, and that after his death his body had been taken there for safety. The presence of his tomb was even said to have converted a princess who built a shrine over it. This was forgotten about and it became surrounded by the wood.

A stone church was built over the shrine in the reign of Alfonso II (864–910) and it soon became a popular place of pilgrimage, whatever the truth behind the various legends. Spain needed a shrine and a patron saint at this time, as they were fighting the Muslim Moors for control of the land, and the idea of St James of Compostela rallied them and gave them hope.

Compostela became a place of international pilgrimage when Benedictine monks set up a community there after the defeat of the Muslims. Many came by sea, or by land through France ('The Way of St James'). There were many stories of miracles, such as one about an innocent boy who was framed for stealing a gold cup and was hanged. He was found alive on the gallows because St James was holding him up!

The cathedral of Compostela, the centre of the pilgrimage.

Walsingham

Walsingham in Norfolk is known as 'England's Nazareth' because it is said that in the Middle Ages a replica of the Virgin Mary's home in Nazareth was built there. In 1061, the Lady of the Manor, Richeldis de Faverches, had a vision of the Virgin's home in Nazareth, and was instructed to build a copy nearby. Various legends surround the story of the building of the original shrine. One says that the builders had numerous problems in constructing the shrine. Then one day they found that it had moved 200 yards away and miraculously built itself. Augustinian brothers became the guardians of the shrine in about 1169. It became popular because the way to the Holy Land was blocked by Muslim conquests, and so 'England's Nazareth' was visited instead. There were two attractions: a statue of Our Lady of Walsingham, and a phial said to contain milk from Mary's breasts. (There were many such relics around at the time and a learned man of the day, Erasmus, said that the phial probably contained a chalk mixture instead!)

The pilgrims would remove their shoes to walk the last mile to the shrine at the Slipper Chapel at Houghton St Giles (which is now a Roman Catholic church). The Red Mount Chapel was built to house pilgrims at King's Lynn in 1485, and the shrine seems to have been at the height of its popularity in the fifteenth century. It was destroyed by a Protestant mob in Henry VIII's reign, when many shrines and monasteries were demolished in order to seize their money and stop any influence by the Pope in England. The statue of Our Lady was taken to Smithfield in London and burnt.

The story of the renewal of the shrine begins when the Reverend A. Hope Patten became vicar of Little Walsingham parish church in 1921. He had a copy of the statue made from an image on the seal that had survived and he placed it in the parish church. A copy of the shrine was built ten years later, and the image was placed there. Crowds of pilgrims have flocked there ever since. The Orthodox have a small chapel with the Anglican Shrine Church. The Roman Catholics have converted the old Slipper Chapel into a shrine. Many Christians who go there say they find the experience restful and that it is spiritually refreshing to have a few days away from the normal pace of life. There were many stories of healings in the Middle Ages and there are still some claims made today. Thanksgiving plaques are placed in the wall for answered prayers.

The restored image of Our Lady of Walsingham holding the infant Jesus. Many pilgrims pray before this hoping for unity between the Anglican and Roman Catholic Churches. What do you think she is holding in her right hand, and why?

Canterbury

St Thomas Becket, Archbishop of Canterbury, was murdered by four knights in Canterbury Cathedral on 29 December 1170. He was declared to be a saint only three years later because of his deeds of charity and the stories of miracles performed by asking for his prayers, or drinking water from St Mary's well into which his blood was said to have flowed. There were stories of the blind receiving their sight, of the lame walking, and of a drowned boy being restored to life.

This saint became so popular that King Henry II, who had been responsible for his murder, performed a penance by walking barechested and barefooted through the streets of Canterbury to the Cathedral. Monks whipped him along the way as he went to pray for forgiveness.

Pilgrims' ways were established, people travelling via Portsmouth, Southampton, Sandwich or Winchester. Chaucer's pilgrims in *The Canterbury Tales* (written in the fourteenth century) went along the old Roman road, Watling Street, via London.

A Pilgrim's Hall was set up at Aylesford near Canterbury. A religious order has recently been established there again, and the hostel has been restored. Besides Henry II, Kings Richard I, Henry VIII, and Louis VII of France visited Becket's tomb in the Cathedral, and about 100,000 pilgrims visited the tomb in 1420, a sizeable proportion of the population then.

Becket's tomb was so popular because he was a symbol of resistance against tyranny – against rulers who did not have the interests of the common people at heart. Henry VIII was particularly eager to destroy this shrine after his break with the Pope. Twenty-six wagons of gold and jewels were taken from it to fill Henry's treasury.

The photo on the right shows the modern shrine at the site of the murder. Notice the cross and the swords.

The pilgrims' steps leading up to Trinity Chapel where Becket's shrine used to stand, covered in jewels, to the left. Why do you think that the steps up to the shrine are so worn? Pilgrims still visit the site of the shrine to pray today. The Pope prayed here with the Archbishop of Canterbury on his visit in 1982.

Taizé

Another international place of pilgrimage is Taizé in south-east France. This community of monks is made up of members from several different Churches and was formed after the Second World War by Roger Schutz (Brother Roger). During the war he had helped Jewish refugees in his house in the village. He had a vision of a Christian community where young people could visit to worship and discuss problems. Taizé community can be visited by members of all the Churches, all religions and by people who have no religion. Many young people camp out in the fields nearby and join in prayer, worship and discussion groups. Some might help in the kitchens, or do other odd jobs on the land. The food is simple, and the hospitality is warm and friendly. The worship contains simple songs in Latin and in other languages (mainly French, English and German). Candles blaze at the front of the church, and icons are all around it. The Easter vigil is held each Saturday evening, while the congregation hold flickering candles. Taizé is an opportunity for young people to make friends from different countries in Europe.

Brothers from Taizé hold meetings for young people throughout the world. Here they are surrounded by some of the 70,000 who gathered in Stuttgart, Germany in December 1996.

Lindisfarne (Holy Island)

This island is a few hundred yards off the Northumbrian coast, sixty miles north of Newcastle. At high tide, the island is cut off from the mainland for about five hours. It is about a mile and a half long, and a mile wide. It has a population of about 200, most of whom earn their living from fishing and tourism.

St Aidan came there with a group of monks in 634 at the request of King Oswald of Northumbria. He wanted Christianity to spread in his kingdom, so he gave the monks a base to work from. The monks lived in simple huts, and a large monastery was built there in the Middle Ages, which was closed by Henry VIII. It is now in ruins, but pilgrims meet there to hold services or to visit the small island church.

Activities

- Is there a particular place that means a lot to you – perhaps somewhere you go on holiday, or a corner of a garden? Write a paragraph explaining what is so special about it, and what you feel when you are there.

- a) List three important places of Christian pilgrimage in the Holy Land, and describe one of them.
  b) List two places of pilgrimage connected with visions of the Virgin Mary, and describe one of them.

- Write a paragraph saying what the special attraction of Rome is as a place of pilgrimage.

- What evidence is there that the site of Jesus' birth was known and respected from early on by Christians?

Iona

This is an island about a mile off the coast of West Scotland. It is three miles long and about a mile and a half wide. St Columba came there in 563 with a group of monks. They lived in simple huts, and set out on to the mainland to teach the people about Jesus. They converted some of the Saxon kings, some of whom were buried on Iona. The island was regarded as a holy place. A larger monastery was built on the island in the Middle Ages, but this was closed by Henry VIII. The island was owned by the Dukes of Argyll until the eighth Duke gave it to the Church of Scotland in 1899.

The island became a centre of pilgrimage again in the 1930s. A minister in a church near Glasgow, George Macleod, came there in 1938 with a group of young ministers and craftsmen. They stayed for a time, and then returned to the mainland to live ordinary lives. Other people came, sharing their lives together, and then returned home later. The process of coming and going has carried on since. The idea was to mix ordinary working people and church ministers together so that they could learn how to understand each other better. Many young people go to summer camps on the island every year to pray, discuss issues, and work.

The ruined monastery has been largely restored and members of any Church are free to hold services there.

Spring Harvest

Evangelical Christians enjoy travelling to special Praise or Bible weeks. These use showgrounds and holiday camps which church groups take over. One of the most popular is 'Spring Harvest' which uses several Butlins Holiday Camps around Britain at Eastertime. There are speakers, huge praise meetings with modern instruments, and fun activities. People try to learn something new about God, or find what their next step should be in their faith journey.

Graham Kendrick performing on stage. Music is an important feature of Spring Harvest and other modern Christian gatherings.

The Greenbelt Festival

The Greenbelt Festival runs on August bank holiday weekend, and encourages the Arts. It is like a smaller scale, Christian Glastonbury festival. This is a more youthful event than weeks such as 'Spring Harvest', with a main stage in the evenings presenting Christian and secular bands who use contemporary styles – Rock, Dance, Techno and so forth, such as 'The World Wide Message Tribe'.

There are fashion shows, circus tents, an art gallery and a full film programme as well as worship times, Bible studies, and speakers who explore what it means to believe in God today.

Though this festival was started by Evangelical Christians, it is popular with many different denominations and styles. There are Anglican monks and nuns present, and a Roman Catholic mass is held on site.

Assignments

1. Do some research into the site of Calvary/Golgotha and of Jesus' tomb. Do you think the Church of the Holy Sepulchre does stand on both sites?
2. Write a diary of an imaginary visit to Lourdes. You are disabled and cannot walk very well. Try to describe what you see and how you feel during the pilgrimage.
3. Design a collage called 'Healing at Lourdes', using the themes of water, lights, motherhood, sick and healthy people.
4. Do some research on Walsingham as a place of pilgrimage today. Find out from your local Anglican or Roman Catholic church if there are organised pilgrimages. Is there a particular time in the year when most people go?
5. Write a paragraph explaining why the shrine of St Thomas Becket was so popular in the Middle Ages, and why king Henry VIII was so eager to destroy it.
6. Do a project on Taizé and say what you think about it.
7. Find out how Iona is trying to bring Christians of different traditions together today.
8. Write an essay called 'The Pilgrim's Way': (i) cover the reasons Christians have for going on pilgrimages; (ii) describe two places of pilgrimage, and (iii) the hopes and feelings of Christians visiting them.

10

Beliefs of the Worldwide Church

THIS CHAPTER WILL EXPLORE CHRISTIAN BELIEFS ABOUT: GOD; THE HOLY TRINITY; SIN; SALVATION; THE CHURCH; SAINTS; THE LIFE OF THE WORLD TO COME; AND JUDGEMENT.

Christians think that God is the creator of the universe. They think God is the mystery behind life, the universe and everything. God is vast, and cannot be seen with human eyes or understood by the human mind. God fills everything, and is everywhere at once.

They believe that this vast, mysterious God is at work in the world, and can reveal himself to people. God is called Father, Son, and Holy Spirit; Christians believe that God has three ways of being God.

The Church teaches that humans have free will to choose good or evil. Turning away from God is called sin; turning back to God, with his help, is called salvation.

The Church is made up of people who believe in Jesus Christ. They form a worshipping family together.

Christians believe that this worshipping family exists in heaven, also, on the other side of the grave, in the Communion of saints.

The Church teaches that this world is not all there is; there is more to come. There is a life and a hope after death.

There must be something better than this!

Christians believe that there will be a final judgement, when everyone will have to give an account of their lives. Good will win over evil, and tears will be wiped away from every eye.

God

Christians do not believe that God is an old man in the sky, like a very wise, cosmic Superman who lives on the right-hand side of the Milky Way. God is not a human being, but a force that is *everywhere* at once, invisible and eternal. In John 4:24, Jesus says, 'God is Spirit.' Spirit is more like love, peace and freedom than like a man or woman. But God is more than these: Christians also believe that he can be prayed to and communicated with in a personal way, as two friends or two lovers would relate.

God, for Christians, is beyond human understanding, and is a mystery. When people think about life and the universe, there seems to be a grey mystery – why should anything exist? What is the point of it all? If there is a force behind all this, then what is it, how does it work, etc? God is the name given to this mystery, this puzzle in life.

Christians believe that God is the Creator. Only fundamentalist believers think that God made the world in six days, and that the human race sprang from an actual couple, Adam and Eve. Most Christians take all this as symbolic poetry, an ancient attempt to say that the world came about because of the mystery of God, and not just by chance. It might have taken millions of years for the universe to form, and God has been at work creating it all that time, and is still at work, for the universe is still changing and growing.

The Ground of Our Being

Christians do not think that God is one object among all the others in the universe – even a superior one. God is different, and contains all the universe within himself. He is not just one lump or shape of some kind in one corner of the galaxy, but present in all things. God is therefore of a different order of being. The theologian, Paul Tillich, coined the term, 'the ground of our being', to suggest that God is not floating about 'up there' somewhere, but is to be found deep within people, as the source of our life and very being. God is deep at the centre of all things.

God is thought to be infinite (without limit) and eternal (without beginning or end). Humans are both finite and temporal. This means that we have limits and have a start and a finish (we are born, and we die). Christians therefore argue that God has to be a mystery, for finite and temporal beings can never fully understand the infinite and the eternal. They think of God as like a vast, mighty ocean, and humans are just able to see the shore, and splash about in it, but beyond, there is darkness and mystery.

The Ancient of Days by William Blake.

What feelings does this photo suggest? Why is an ocean a fitting symbol for God?

The Holy Trinity

Speaking of God as 'the ground of our being' sounds impersonal and makes God seem remote. Yet Christians believe that God is involved in the world, and in a personal way with individuals. They speak of God as 'Father, Son and Holy Spirit'. This is the **Trinity** (from tri-unity, 'three-in-one'). To think how three things can be one, they suggest a triangle, with three sides or angles but it is one shape.

The three sections of the Trinity do different things, though they all work together:

- The Father is the Creator.
- The Son is the Saviour or **Redeemer**.
- The Spirit is the one who gives new life and makes holy.

This can be seen from the questions asked Anglican candidates at confirmation:

'*Do you believe and trust in God* the Father, who made the world*?*'
'Do you believe and trust in *his Son* Jesus Christ, *who redeemed mankind?*'
'Do you believe and trust in *his Holy Spirit,*
who gives life to the people of God?'

The Father is the Creator, the Son is the Redeemer, and the Spirit is the Life-giver, or **Sanctifier** (one who makes holy). These are not taken to be three gods, but one God working in three ways.

Activities

Key Elements

1 What did Jesus mean, in John 4:24, when he said 'God is Spirit'?
2 Christians see God as an almighty force but also as personal, why?
3 What is the mystery that everyone feels in life? What has God got to do with this for Christians?
4 What does it mean to call God infinite and eternal?
5 What does God as 'the ground of our being' mean?

Think About It

6 Can God 'up there' still have any meaning in a symbolic sense?

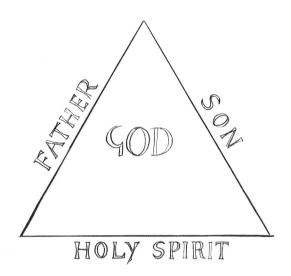

This threefold pattern to God's activity can be seen in various New Testament writings, such as a prayer of St Paul, known as 'the Grace':

The grace of our Lord Jesus Christ, the love of *God*, and the fellowship of the *Holy Spirit*, be with us all, ever more.

In the story of the baptism of Jesus, a three-fold pattern can be seen, too:

As soon as Jesus came up out of the water, he saw heaven opening and the Spirit coming down on him like a dove. And a *voice* came from heaven, 'You are my own dear *Son*. I am pleased with you.'

(Mark 1:10–11)

When the creeds were being written, people began to talk about the three *persons* in God – of Father, Son and Holy Spirit. Some people think of three *minds*, or spirits, which are all part of God and which all love each other perfectly: Father loving the Son, and the Spirit as the bond of love uniting them. This can be very moving, and helps some Christians to imagine God as personal, warm and friendly, but it runs the risk of seeing three gods cemented together by a spiritual 'super-glue' of love. It makes people think of God as being like a team of three people.

Christians believe in one God, not three, and so some think that it is simpler to think

not of three individual persons in God, but of three *roles* in God; i.e. that God has three ways of being God:

• The Father is the Creator, the power behind the world.
• The Son is God coming in Jesus, working to bring the world back to himself.
• The Spirit is the presence of God living inside people, bringing them new life.

There is a danger here that people will think that Father, Son and Holy Spirit are only three temporary ways of God being God. Each role, or person, is then seen like an actor's mask which he wears and discards: he wears the Father's mask to create the world, the Son's mask to save it, and the Spirit's mask to work in people.

The Church teaches that the three ways of being God, call them roles or persons, are eternal. God is threefold in himself, and not only in the world as people experience him. God's threefoldness suggests that God is dynamic, able to relate with himself and to act outwards into the world. The writers of the creeds did not understand 'person' to be an individual mind, but a distinct existence in God that could relate to other parts of God. These three relations, or existences, lived in each other and shared the same being, that of God. God is seen as being like a round dance, dynamic and alive.

In John 14–16, Jesus speaks of the Spirit as the **Paraclete** (in the Greek) that he would send in his place on earth. It is usually translated as helper, comforter, or even counsel for the defence. Literally it means 'one who comes alongside someone else'. The work of the Spirit is seen as being to bring new life to Christians and to inspire them to follow Jesus and to understand his teaching. The Holy Spirit is God's presence in the world, and in the believer.

This dome at Mount Athos in Greece depicts the Trinity at Creation. How is the Holy Spirit represented?

Activities

Key Elements

1 What does the word 'Trinity' mean?

2 Do your own diagram or drawing to express the Christian idea of the Trinity.

3 How does a triangle help some Christians to understand the doctrine of the Trinity?

4 a) What roles do each of the persons in the Trinity have in Christianity?

   b) How is this seen in the questions confirmation candidates are asked?

5 How is the threefold activity of God seen in the story of the baptism of Jesus?

6 a) What are two of the ways that Christians have of understanding the Trinity?

   b) Each of these has certain strengths but can cause problems and misunderstandings. Explain these.

7 What did Jesus mean by the Paraclete?

Sin

For Christians, sin means to turn from God and put self first, in the sense of being self-centred and therefore careless about the needs and feelings of others. The Greek word for sin in the New Testament is *hamartia*, which means 'to miss the mark'. This suggests that people are not fulfilling God's goals or their own.

Sin is not seen as a list of dos and don'ts in the New Testament. A sin is not just an individual action, but the inner attitude of the person that does it, and the effect on other people. It means to go against what a person feels to be right, wilfully, and to hurt someone else in some way.

What have Adam and Eve got to do with it?

It's just a story, I think. But it means that if you put yourself first, then others get hurt.

So people cause wars, and crime and things...!

Most Christians see the story of Adam and Eve as symbolic of the meaning of sin. The couple are placed in the garden of Eden, a paradise where they have all kinds of trees to eat from, including the Tree of Life. They are told that they must not eat off one tree – the Tree of Knowledge of Good and Evil. The serpent, representing evil, tempts them to eat from the forbidden tree, and they are changed inside. They are no longer conscious of God's care and love, and they start to scheme to cover up their disobedience. God finds them out, and banishes them from Eden to the world outside, where life will be hard. This is known as **the Fall**, i.e. the fall into sin.

The Tree of Life stands for the path of life and goodness. The Tree of Knowledge stands for the path of death and destruction. Adam and Eve disobey God and become selfish, caring for their own desires only. Things start to go wrong; they feel guilty, and then life gets hard.

Catholic Christians talk about two different types of sin, venial and mortal:

- Venial sins are not as serious; for example, telling a lie. A person can confess these privately to God; though they can also be confessed to a priest if people find that more helpful.
- Mortal sins seriously affect the person's relationship with God; for example, murder; and the Roman Catholic Church teaches that these must be confessed to a priest. He will be able to help the person to receive God's forgiveness, through his or her wall of guilty feelings, and speak with the authority of the Church behind him.

Christians also talk about original sin. There are many different interpretations of this. Here are three:

- In the past, it was thought that it was a moral stain passed down through the generations from Adam and Eve's first sin. Therefore, people were born with a wicked streak in their genes, somehow. Some Christians still believe this.
- Orthodox Christians believe Adam's fall led to mortality – death and suffering. There is no moral taint handed down, but our mortality makes us morally weak and it is a struggle to be good.

SIN AND SALVATION

Desmond Palethorpe was a hardworking family man. One day, he received a letter from his company.

Great! My boss has retired and I've been promoted!

Everything went fine; Desmond worked with his old friend Bob in charge of a busy department.

He made lots of money and his family enjoyed themselves.

But then things started to go wrong. Desmond stayed at the office longer and longer hours, hoping to get further promotion.

Sorry Dear, I won't be home for dinner tonight. ...Look, I said I'm sorry!

Desmond even managed to get his friend Bob fired for a few mistakes that he could have helped him to sort out.

But one day, he had pushed things too far...

He found that his wife and family had left him.

She says I'm not the person she married anymore...I've become selfish and cold!

Oh God, what have I done?

Desmond vowed to change and to put his home before his work. Having lots of money wasn't everything.

His wife was overjoyed to find that he was his old self again.

He had come to his senses.

In this story, Desmond turned his back on his family and friends. He became selfish and self-centred. Christians call this sin, and see it as turning away from the God who created everyone and who is within everyone.

Christians believe that people are affected by all the sin in the world from the moment they are born, the accumulated sin of past generations. This drags people down and makes it hard to be good. This is called original sin.

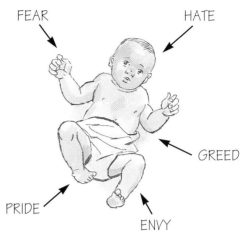

FEAR

HATE

GREED

PRIDE

ENVY

Sin can exist in systems of government, not just in people. Policies that keep poor nations poor and hungry, while millions are spent on weapons, are sinful. Policies that divide people according to race, giving one race a better deal than another, are sinful.

When people come to their senses and do an about turn, Christians call it salvation. The Gospel is about turning to God who will forgive, letting people start again.

Christians believe that Jesus died to bring people back to God, to turn people from their sins. Baptism is a sign that sins are washed away. It also brings God's Spirit to people, to help them live new lives, and to help to put things right in the world.

A. What do Christians mean by sin and salvation?
B. What have Jesus on the cross and baptism got to do with it?
C. How did Desmond's actions hurt himself and other people? What made him come to his senses?
D. Make up a story like that of Desmond and his family, to make the same points.

- Others do not believe that there ever was an Adam or Eve, they are just symbols of Everyperson, of humans being confronted by the choice between good and evil. For them, original sin means the negative influence in the world that is built up over the ages from all the individual sins of people, that starts to work on people from birth, turning them away from good and dragging them down. It does not matter if this started with an original human couple or not, for it was started by someone, somewhere, and carries on. This is why it is often hard to do what you think is right, and, even worse, it might blind people to what is right.

Perhaps death is meant to be in God's plan, and is not a curse. We die to make room for others, and to move on, closer to God. Our sinfulness makes it something to fear, though, when it should be a letting go, a door opening to eternal life.

Questions

- What do Christians mean by sin and salvation?

- What have Jesus on the cross and baptism got to do with it?

- How did Desmond's actions hurt himself, and how did they hurt other people? What do you think made him come to his senses?

- Can you make up a story like that of Desmond and his family, to make the same points?

Salvation

Sin is falling short of God's standards, and going against what a person feels to be right; a broken relationship results. There is a break in the relationship with God; with anyone the person has hurt; and with the person's own self. If a person is not being true to himself and doing what he feels is right, then he will be leading a disordered, double life, divided against himself, against his neighbour, and against God.

Salvation means turning to God and being open to God. Christians feel that a healing process begins as the relationship is restored. There is a feeling of being forgiven, of peace of mind, and a resulting openness and friendliness to others – a person wants what is best for them, and is not just thinking of himself. Salvation is about being made a whole person, a complete human being, at peace with himself, others, and with God. Christians believe that God has to come to people's aid, as they are not strong-willed enough to save themselves. Salvation – being made whole – is a life-long process, and not a split-second affair. It involves a struggle.

Baptism

Most Christians feel that this process begins with baptism (see pp. 119–121, 124). This is seen as a way of bringing God to the human soul, to help cut off the evil influences in the world. Some think this helps by washing away original sin that is inherited from 'Adam', and others just see this as a loving channel for God's Spirit to work in the soul. This is only the beginning of the process, though, as people need to go on responding to God throughout their lives, and opening themselves to his Spirit. Baptism starts a good work, but it must be completed by personal acts of faith later.

Personal Conversion

Other Christians feel that baptism alone is not important in itself. A person needs to have a conversion experience. This happens when people come to believe that Jesus died for them personally. They feel challenged to submit their lives to him and to ask God for forgiveness. They say they feel a sense of new life within and they believe that they will eventually go to heaven because Jesus died for their sins. Salvation, in this view, is still a process, though, and not an 'instant mashed potato' idea for people are not made good and perfect overnight. People need to respond to God for the rest of their lives. Salvation is a process of sanctification (being made holy, or complete) that is life-long.

Social Liberation

Christians do not think that salvation only comes to people, but to society as well. Sin can exist in systems and structures of society. This is called 'structural sin'. For example, the old political system of apartheid in South Africa encouraged racism against blacks and coloureds. Or, think of the unfair trading system that makes the Third World countries

Activity

- Find out about a structural sin in today's world, such as the exploitation of the Third World. Produce a small project on this.

poorer and leaves them with vast debts. Christians believe that salvation needs to affect these structures.

These structures were all started off by individuals, but they have a life of their own, in a way, as the sin carries on from generation to generation in the systems people created. People are caught up in them and affected by them. Most Christians feel that these structures should be challenged by prayer and non-violent protest, but some are prepared to use violence in extreme situations if people are suffering greatly. People can co-operate with God in bringing salvation to the world – but their hearts must be changed first.

Activities

Key Elements

1 What does *hamartia* mean?
2 How is sin defined in the New Testament?
3 Which Christians teach about mortal and venial sin? What is the difference?
4 What do Christians mean by original sin?

5 Try to define salvation in a sentence.
6 Explain how some Christians think salvation begins with baptism.
7 In what way do others think salvation is more personal?
8 What does sanctification mean?
9 How can sin and salvation affect society? Give examples.

The Church

The Greek word *ekklesia* was used for the Church in the New Testament. It means an assembly of people, a believing community. The people who make up the Church are each trying to carry on the work of Jesus in some way in response to his teaching, and so the New Testament calls the Church the Body of Christ, i.e. a group of people trying to follow Christ on earth, with the Spirit within them.

> *All of you are Christ's body, and each one is a part of it.*   *(1 Corinthians 12:27)*

The Church is described in the Nicene Creed as being *one*, *holy*, *catholic* and *apostolic*. This means that although there are many different denominations, or national Churches, it is all the same faith, following one God through Jesus.

'Catholic' does not mean 'Roman Catholic', but 'worldwide'. **Apostolic** means that it is based on the teachings of the apostles, which were handed down in the New Testament. Roman Catholics, Anglicans and Orthodox feel that they are truer to the teachings of the apostles, because they have bishops who can trace their lineage and authority back to them. These Churches also have similar beliefs about baptism and the Eucharist. They believe these are also based on the teaching of the apostles.

Free Churches feel that they can call themselves apostolic because they follow the teaching of the Bible and they do not think it matters if you don't have a line of bishops going back to the apostles. They do not think, either, that the understanding of baptism and the Eucharist that the above Churches have, came from the apostles, but is a later interpretation. Hence the divisions within the world-wide Church.

Activities

Key Elements

1 What does the word *ekklesia* mean? What does this suggest the Church really is?
2 a) What does the New Testament mean when it describes the Church as the Body of Christ?
  b) What implications does this idea have for society and questions of race relations?
3 What does it mean when the Church is described as 'catholic'?
4 What does it mean when the Church is described as 'apostolic'?
5 Why do some Churches claim to be more apostolic than others? How do the others react to this charge?

Saints

The word 'saint' means someone who is holy, or set apart for God. In this sense, all Christians who believe that God's Spirit is at work within them as they strive to be good are saints, even though they are far from perfect.

'Communion of saints' means the fellowship of all Christians, alive and dead. Christians are part of a family, or a community, of believers. They are not meant to be loners. They believe they share the life of Christ through the Spirit. Christians do not think that death stops their sharing in Christ's life, or with one another. It all carries on, for eternity.

When Christians usually talk about saints, however, they mean especially holy people

Activity

• What saints have you heard of? Make a list and say what you know about them.

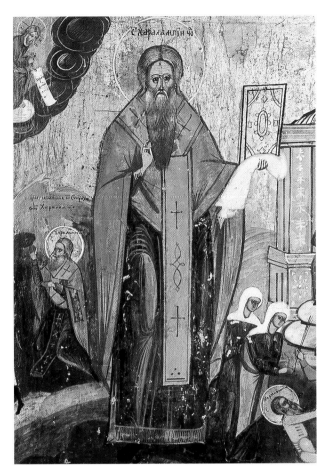

Part of a Russian Orthodox icon. Images of the saints are a source of inspiration, and are treated with great respect.

who lived lives very close to God and who set examples for others to follow.

Roman Catholic, Orthodox and some Anglican Christians believe that they can ask the saints in heaven to pray for them, just as a Christian might ask someone on earth to pray for them if they are going through a difficult time. The saints are thought to be closer to God, and therefore their prayers are stronger. Mary, the mother of Jesus, is honoured above all the other saints because she gave birth to the Redeemer, and is thought to be especially close to him. In the Orthodox Church there is a saying, 'The Lord is wonderful in his saints!' This means that the saints present God to people by setting an example and letting God shine through their lives. Icons are special, painted images on wood of the saints

that not only have a halo of light around their heads, but also have light shining out from the face in order to put the idea across of them being witnesses to the reality of God.

A recent case of the canonisation of a saint by the Roman Church was that of Maximilian Kolbe, a Polish priest and member of the Franciscan order. He was in a concentration camp in 1941 when he volunteered to die in a punishment squad to let a married man with a family go free.

Some Christians started to be honoured as saints when they were martyred in the Roman Empire. A local cult of a martyr grew up around his or her homeland or place of death. The same honours were then extended to all outstanding Christians. The people mentioned by name in the New Testament were automatic candidates as they were close to Jesus.

The Roman Catholic Church has a complicated procedure for pronouncing people saints. It is called **canonisation** (which means formal admission to the *list* of saints). A case is heard for and against a person in a council held in the Vatican, and the Pope has the final word.

In the Orthodox Church, saints are pronounced by local councils of bishops. The Anglican Church honours the saints that were established before their split with Rome. It does not proclaim any new saints, though many people are honoured as saints unofficially, and added to the Church's calendar.

Protestant Christians are wary of the cult of the saints. They feel that a person should pray to God through Jesus alone. Otherwise it might cause confusion and people might start to treat the saints as gods themselves. Other Churches would argue, however, that although it is true that some more superstitious believers might treat the saints as divine beings, or be afraid of approaching Jesus directly and prefer to go through a saint, this is certainly not the official doctrine of the cult of the saints. People can ask for their help, but they are not a substitute for Jesus. Jesus can still be approached directly, and should be.

Activities

Key Elements

1 What does the phrase 'the communion of saints' suggest about the Church?

2 How do Christians think this communion is affected by death?

3 Why do some Christians ask the saints to pray for them? Which Churches do this?

4 How do the Orthodox show the significance of the saints in their icons?

5 Write a paragraph on each of the following:
   a) How did the practice of honouring the saints begin?
   b) How are new saints made?
   c) Why do some Christians have reservations about this?

The Life of the World to Come

The Bible presents a number of striking images of the life of the world to come, or the afterlife as it is more commonly known. It is described as a state of bliss or glory. Some passages have ranks of singing angels, shining light, dazzling objects and magnificent colours:

There in heaven was a throne with someone sitting on it. His face gleamed like such precious stones as jasper and carnelian, and all round the throne there was a rainbow the colour of an emerald.... From the throne came flashes of lightning, rumblings, and peals of thunder. In front of the throne seven lighted torches were burning, which are the seven spirits of God. Also in front of the

throne there was what looked like a sea of glass, clear as crystal.

(Revelation 4:2–3, 5–6)

This passage gives a disturbing feeling of the terrible and utter strangeness of the presence of God in heaven. It should not be taken literally for it is a piece of poetry. It is full of symbols:

- the lights – rainbow, the gleaming face, torches – suggest God's purity and goodness;
- the noises – thunder, rumblings, lightning – suggest tremendous power;
- the throne also suggests power and authority;
- the sea of glass suggests truth, beauty and purity.

The passage goes on to describe four living creatures that surround the throne – they suggest the terrifying otherness of God – the force of life beyond description.

All the descriptions of the afterlife in the Bible are poetic or symbolic because such a state of existence is beyond human knowledge and imagination. St Paul believed that the afterlife would come as a surprise and be beyond people's wildest dreams:

as the scripture says,
'What no one ever saw or heard,
what no one ever thought could happen,
is the very thing God prepared for those who
*   love him.'   (1 Corinthians 2:9)*

In the past, many people believed that heaven was up above the sky somewhere, and that a person's spirit floated up to be with God. But some Jews believed that, instead of this, the dead were raised up in new bodies and lived on a renewed earth where there was no more death or suffering. Both of these ideas can be found in different parts of the Bible, although the writers are careful to stress that 'the life of the world to come' was really beyond description, and they were just using symbols to express it.

St Paul seemed to combine these two ideas into one idea of being raised up in a new body to a spiritual place. He talked about a 'spiritual body' (read 1 Corinthians 15:35–54):

This is how it will be when the dead are raised to life. When the body is buried, it is mortal; when raised, it will be immortal. When buried, it is ugly and weak; when raised, it will be beautiful and strong. When buried, it is a physical body; when raised, it will be a spiritual body. (15:42–4)

Many Christians believe that a person has an immortal soul, and that this lives on after the death of the body, as a mind, or in a new spiritual body of some kind. Modern science cannot prove or disprove the idea of an immortal soul, but the mind and the brain do seem to be very closely interwoven.

Some Christians think, however, that the immortal soul idea is wrong, and that our minds and feelings are a part of the working of the brain. Resurrection therefore to them means that God creates a new life for people. God has had their individual personality stored in his memory, like a musical composer who remembers the notes of a piece and can get musicians to produce the sounds again. This way, there is nothing in people that automatically survives death; the afterlife is an act of God.

Modern Christians are influenced both by the Biblical images and by modern scientific knowledge. They tend to believe that a person lives on spiritually with God in another level or dimension of reality, beyond this physical universe. What shape or form this has, if any, is unknowable. This is the modern version of the floating up to the spirit-in-the-sky idea. The soul, or personality, lives on in a new, spiritual body.

The modern Christian version of living on a renewed earth echoes what some scientists are suggesting: that the universe will stop expanding and may collapse in on itself, which will push matter out again in a new creation, with a new and possibly very different universe forming. This might be the new earth promised in poetic passages like Revelation 21:1–4, 'Then I saw a new heaven and a new earth. The first heaven and the first earth disappeared, and the sea vanished', and the dead will be raised up to live in this new world.

Activities

Key Elements

1 How is the afterlife described in the Book of Revelation?
2 How do Christians interpret some of the symbols in this description?
3 Why is the afterlife a mystery if it exists?
4 Write a paragraph describing what St Paul says about the kind of body people will have in the afterlife, in 1 Corinthians 15:35–54.
5 Why do some Christians think resurrection will happen even if people do not have an immortal soul?
6 What are the two basic ideas that modern Christians have about the afterlife?

Judgement

Christians feel that God cannot let evil go unpunished, or suffering not be made up for. Otherwise, God would not be just and fair. This is the origin of ideas of Hell and of punishment in the next life. In the Book of Daniel in the Old Testament, some are raised to eternal life, but others are raised to eternal disgrace.

In the Synoptic Gospels (Matthew, Mark and Luke), Jesus talked about the fire of Hell (see Matthew 5:22 for example). Revelation has graphic descriptions of the state of the damned, such as:

Whoever did not have his name written in the book of the living was thrown into the lake of fire. (20:15)

This gave rise to the idea of Hell as a terrible place of fire and eternal torture.

Many modern Christians feel very uncomfortable with this idea, though. If God is a God of love, how could he reject people in such a cruel and final way? God would then be responsible for running an eternal Chamber of Horrors. The Bible verses might not have meant such an idea, however:

- They were symbolic. The fire suggests God's power and anger purifying sin, as rubbish burnt up by flames, or germs killed off by heat. The word for 'hell' in the Gospels as used by Jesus is 'Gehenna' (in the Hebrew) and this was a symbolic reference to the Valley of Hinnom outside Jerusalem where the city's rubbish was burned. Jesus used this as an image of God's coming judgement; he did not mean it to be taken literally. *Hell is therefore a state of being cut off from God*, and not a place of physical flames.
- The Bible language is open to interpretation – is the purpose of the 'fire' for punishment or for correction? If for correction, then it has the idea of God purifying the evil out of sinners to make them worthy of living in his Kingdom. This means that *Hell is a temporary affair,*

until the person is ready for Heaven. The eternal element of the judgement is then upon evil, destroying that for ever.
- Many modern Christians believe that *it is people themselves who put themselves into Hell*, and not God. At the Judgement, all they have done and all that they are is revealed to them, and some will not be able to stand it. The presence of God's holy light will be a burning fire to them and a joy to others.

The Roman Catholic Church developed a belief in **Purgatory**. This is thought of as an in between state for the majority of people who are not very good or very bad. People in Purgatory are saved, but have to be prepared for Heaven. In medieval times, it was a place of less suffering than Hell. Now, Catholics see this as being purified and healed by the love of God.

Modern Christians stress the love of God and the fact that he will not easily give up on anyone that he has created. While there is anything in a person that can be redeemed they are redeemable and not lost for ever.

The parable of the Last Judgement in Matthew 25:31–46 draws together many of these themes. The righteous stand on the right-hand side of the Son of Man (Jesus) when he returns to judge the earth and they are sent into the blessed Kingdom. The unrighteous are sent into the 'eternal fire which has been prepared for the Devil and his angels'. This is after the inner motives and deeds of all concerned have been revealed: some visited Christ (in other humans) when he was sick, hungry or naked; others closed their hearts to their fellow humans.

It is possible to interpret this parable in the old way – God sending some into eternal damnation; or to see it in a more modern light

---

Activity
- Design a collage called 'Heaven and Hell'.

– of people's own consciences casting them into the purifying fire.

The parable also points out that salvation was not only for those who called themselves Christians, but for those who 'did the will of God' by being open to their neighbour.

Hence, many Christians believe that there is a place in the Kingdom for many members of other faiths, and for many who have not even believed in God on earth, but have unknowingly done his will in various ways.

A 15th century painting of the Last Judgement with Christ returning in glory. Who is seated around him, and how are the people being raised reacting?

Activities

Key Elements

1 Why do some Christians need to have a belief in some kind of judgement after death?
2 Summarise what is said about the Judgement in the Book of Daniel, in the teaching of Jesus and in the Book of Revelation.
3 Why are many modern Christians uncomfortable with this teaching if taken at face value?
4 What is Purgatory, and which Christians believe in it?
5 Write a paragraph on each of the following:
  a) How do many Christians interpret the Bible teaching about Judgement and Hell today? (Cover the three aspects of symbols, correction and putting yourself into Hell.)
  b) How can Matthew 25:31–46 be interpreted in the old way, and in the modern way?

Think About It

6 Discuss whether you think that Matthew 25:31–46 suggests that members of other faiths and good atheists will have a place in the Kingdom.

Assignments

1 Write an essay: 'The Christian idea of God is not about a "good fairy" in the sky.' Include: (i) God as Spirit; (ii) God as everywhere at once; (iii) God as infinite, eternal and a mystery; (iv) God as within – the ground of being; and (v) conclude with your reactions to these Christian ideas.

2 Write an essay: 'The Trinity is not three gods but one God.' Include: (i) the triangle image and parts of a whole; (ii) threefoldness in the New Testament; (iii) three persons or three roles?; (iv) dangers with three roles and the teaching of the Church; and (v) conclude with whether you think the idea of the Trinity is helpful or confusing when thinking about the Christian God.

3 Tell the Adam and Eve story. What does this teach about sin, and how do modern Christians take this story?

4 Ask a group of church members what they believe about the afterlife. Write this up in a report.

5 Write an essay on the Christian view of the afterlife, mentioning: (i) the old ideas of floating up and of living on a new earth; (ii) modern views on the soul and the body; (iii) the modern version of 'floating up to the sky' and (iv) the modern version of the new earth. Conclude with what makes the most sense to you, and why.

11

A World Faith

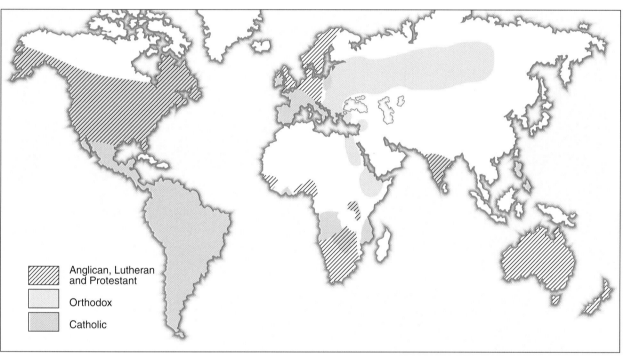

Anglican, Lutheran
and Protestant

Orthodox

Catholic

Christianity has spread to various parts of the world from
its beginnings in ancient Galilee and Judaea. This map
shows the distribution of the three main branches of
Christianity according to which denomination the
majority of Christians belong to.

How did the teachings of
one man make a religion
that has spread all over
the world?

Bit by bit, as people carried the message
around, I suppose...but what I want to know is
how come there are so many different churches
if they all follow the same person?

Soon after the death of Jesus, the Christians travelled about the Holy Land, and out into the Roman Empire, teaching that Jesus had risen. They believed that they had Good News to spread.

One of the most outstanding early missionaries was Saint Paul. He thought that the Christians were wrong until he said he had a vision on a journey to Damascus, a vision of the risen Christ.

Gradually, the Christians increased in numbers and the faith spread among the Gentiles (non-Jews). Disagreements arose between the Jews and the Christians, and they split into two religions.

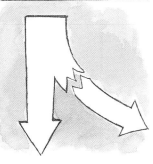

Christians suffered at times at the hands of the Romans, until the Emperor Constantine made Christianity legal in CE 313.

THE CHURCH BREAKS APART!

The Western and Eastern churches separated in 1054. The Eastern Christians felt that the Pope was trying to lord it over them when he should have been an advisor and a servant.

Some wrong things happened in the West. Relics were the remains of holy people, but many forgeries were sold to simple people who thought it would bring them luck or help them in the afterlife.

GENUINE SAINT'S BLOOD

A group of people argued against these practices and against the Pope. A German, Martin Luther, started the ball rolling. Some Christians in the sixteenth century started new churches. They were called Protestants.

Catholics and Protestants each thought they were right, and would not listen to each other. They tortured each other, and burned people as heretics (people who went against the teaching of the church).

GETTING TOGETHER

The 20th century saw attempts to bring different Christians together, like the World Council of Churches, and their motto, 'All One in Christ'.

Christians have learnt to pray together, no matter what church they belong to.

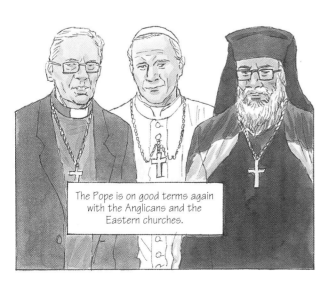

The Pope is on good terms again with the Anglicans and the Eastern churches.

Christians feel it is important to stand together wherever possible, so that they can help the poor and try to change the world for the better.

Christians in Kerala, South India, parade to celebrate St Thomas' Day. Why is St Thomas important to them?

The Church Spreads Out

The Acts of the Apostles in the New Testament gives information on how Christianity spread after the death of Jesus. It presents a pattern of growth that starts in Jerusalem and spreads northwards into Samaria and beyond as far as Antioch in Syria (now in Turkey), which became a major Christian centre. From here, missionaries went west, establishing churches all through Asia Minor and into Greece. The story in Acts ends with the faith having spread to Rome.

This does not present the whole story, however, for Christianity also went east, with churches being established in the Persian Empire and in India. Church tradition says that the Apostle Thomas took Christianity to India, and the Mar Thoma Church there regards him as their founder. The Church spread more successfully in the west, though, because of the Roman Empire. This provided:

- Good roads from one corner of the Empire to another, making travel quicker and easier.
- Safe travel between frontiers because of the Roman guards keeping the peace.
- A common language, Greek, to preach the faith in.
- The Empire was corrupt and weakening at the time, and many people were tired of the old way of life and looking for new hope.

Gentile Believers

The first Christians, in Jerusalem, thought of themselves as being Jews who followed the Messiah. They did not think that they belonged to a different religion at all. They were hoping that all the other Jews would come to believe in Jesus, and that this would give new life to the old faith. The first crisis they faced was whether to allow non-Jews – Gentiles – to become members of the Church. Acts 10 tells the story of Peter's visit to Cornelius and his family – Gentiles who were friendly to the Jews and worshipped only one God. As soon as they heard about Jesus, the family believed in him, and felt the Holy Spirit bringing them new life. Peter was taken aback, but allowed them to be baptised.

The apostles eventually agreed that Gentile converts did not have to be circumcised like Jews. But this agreement did not happen without a struggle, and it seems that there were still some Jewish Christians who believed that a Gentile convert had to become a Jew as well as a follower of Christ.

Paul

According to Acts, it was Paul who was the most active in spreading Christianity in the Empire, and he became the great missionary to the Gentiles.

Paul and his helpers followed the trade routes throughout the Empire to spread the faith. It was the obvious and easiest path to take. He went to the Jewish synagogue in each place first. (There were settlements of Jews living in the major cities of the Empire.) He preached the coming of the Messiah to them, and if the Jews didn't listen he then went to the Gentiles. There were usually groups of interested Gentiles who sometimes attended synagogue worship, curious about the God of the Jews, but who did not want to become Jews themselves. Christianity obviously appealed to them.

Paul had been an enthusiastic Jew from Tarsus. In Philippians 3:5–6 he says that he was born a Jew (his Jewish name was Saul) and was a Pharisee. He persecuted the Church, but never says why. Perhaps he thought that the Christians were too lax in following some of the Jewish laws, such as offering sacrifices, and the food laws, but his main reason was probably that some of them had spoken out against the Jewish Temple, saying that it was no longer important to God. Jews treated it as a holy place, and hence the offence. He was afraid that the Christians were leading the people astray with their new teachings.

He was converted after seeing a vision of the risen Christ on the road to Damascus. He might have been thinking things over for some time prior to this, though. He may have been deeply moved by the death of a Christian, Stephen, who died forgiving his enemies. Paul was present at his stoning (see Acts 7:54–8:1).

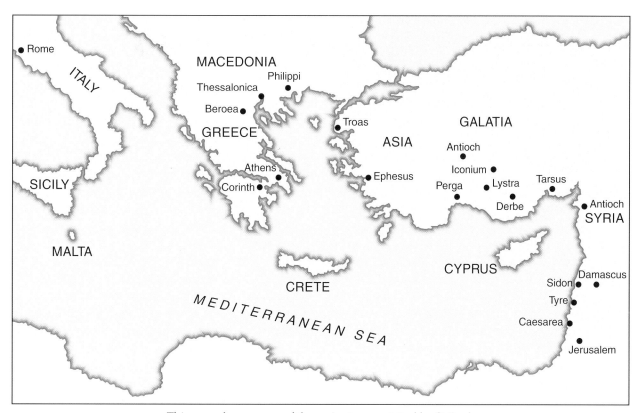

This map shows some of the major towns visited by St Paul.

A sixteenth century painting showing the martyrdom of St Paul. Why would he have been beheaded and not crucified? Notice that he is being offered a martyr's crown and a palm of victory.

Paul's main teaching was that the Law of Moses was only a guide; it had no power to make anyone good. No one was perfect, and no one could keep all the laws of God, and hence you would feel a failure and feel guilty. However, in Jesus, God had shown that he was a forgiving, loving God, who would help a person by his grace (undeserved favour). You did not have to earn God's favour, but to admit your need of it and stop being proud. Then God would come to your aid. This doctrine is called **justification by faith**.

Acts says that Paul made three missionary journeys, and they were not always easy going. For example, in Acts 16:16–24 there is an account of Paul and a companion's visit to Philippi in Greece. They had converted a slave girl and stopped her telling fortunes. Her owner complained to the authorities and charged them with anti-roman activities:

> Then the officials tore the clothes off Paul and Silas and ordered them to be whipped. After a severe beating, they were thrown into jail, and the jailer was ordered to lock them up tight.

Church tradition says that Paul was eventually executed in Rome by command of Emperor Nero.

Why did the Jews and Christians Separate?

There was tension between Jews who believed that Jesus was the Messiah, and Jews who did not, early on. Some Jewish Christians felt that the Temple in Jerusalem was obsolete: God was not to dwell in people's hearts as his temples. This was offensive to other Jews. (Other Jewish Christians did not share this view of the Temple, however, and carried on worshipping in it.)

Then, as more and more Gentiles became Christians, there were soon more Gentile than Jewish Christians. They did not understand Jewish customs and were not used to following the Law of Moses.

The real split came after 70 CE. The Romans and Jews had been at war from 66 and the Christians in Jerusalem had refused to take part. They had fled the city. Jerusalem fell to the Romans in 70 and the leaders of the surviving Jews did not look favourably upon their Christian members. They were expelled from the synagogues in some places, or allowed to attend but not lead the worship in others.

The fall of Jerusalem also meant that Rome became the headquarters of the Christian movement, and when the apostles died, Christianity became a Gentile religion in the main.

Activities

Key Elements

1 Which book in the New Testament describes how the Church grew after the death of Jesus?
2 What were the stages by which the faith spread to the West, and where did the faith end up?
3 Where did the faith spread in the East? What fact suggests that the Apostle Thomas went east?
4 Give four reasons why the Church spread more quickly in the West than in the East.
5 Did the first Christians in the Holy Land regard themselves as members of a new faith? What did they hope to do?
6 Why did it cause problems when Gentile converts joined the Church?
7 Outline the career of St Paul briefly, and state his main teaching.
8 Give three reasons why the Jews and the Christians separated into two religions.

Part of the catacombs, the ancient burial chambers in Rome where some of the early Christians met in secret, and where they were later buried.

The split became so complete that sadly, in the past, some Christians even taught that the Jews were to blame for killing Jesus, forgetting that he was a Jew himself, as were the 12 disciples. It was the Romans, and some of the Jewish leaders, who had Jesus put to death, and not the ordinary Jewish people.

Christians in the Roman Empire

Christians were often suspected of being criminals after the fire of Rome in 64 CE. Nero wrongly blamed it on the Christians and had many put to death. The emperors were worshipped as gods and a citizen's loyalty might be tested by making him offer incense to the emperor and say, 'Caesar is Lord.' Many Christians refused to do this and suffered the death penalty. Some emperors and area governors did not bother with the Christians and let them worship in peace. But others were ruthless in trying to wipe the religion out. Usually a person would be reported to the authorities for being a Christian – perhaps their friends or their friends' slaves had been converted through them – and then they were put to the test: would they sacrifice to the emperor or not?

The story of one Christian martyr has survived from these times. He was Polycarp, an old man who had known some of the apostles in his youth. He was put to death in about 155 CE. When he was asked to sacrifice to the emperor and deny Christ, he replied:

'Eight and six years have I served him, and he has done me no wrong. How then can I blaspheme my King and Saviour?' When he was threatened with being burned alive he replied:

'The fire you threaten me with cannot go on burning for very long; after a while it goes out. But what you are unaware of are the flames of future judgement ... which are in store for the ungodly. Why do you go on wasting your time?'

Activity

- Write a play about the martyrdom of Polycarp. (The full story can be found in *Early Christian Writings*, translated by M. Staniforth, published by Penguin.)

Despite these persecutions, the Church continued to grow. Christians had to meet in secret, in each other's houses, or in the underground burial chambers called the catacombs. They used secret signs to communicate with other suspected Christians, like the alpha and the fish sign.

It seems that many people misunderstood the Christians because of the story of the crucifixion. Many Romans suspected Christians of following a criminal, because crucifixion was a criminal's punishment. Also, many could not understand how a crucified man could be the Son of God, or God incarnate. Crucifixion to them was a sign of failure and weakness.

The turning-point came with the conversion of an emperor – Constantine. His soldiers proclaimed him Emperor at York in 306. He was ready to march on Rome to make good his claim six years later. He was a sun worshipper, as most Romans in the army were, and there is a legend that when he prayed for victory before the midday sun he saw a vision of a cross of light in the sky, and the words: IN HOC SIGNO VINCES ('In this sign, you shall conquer'). He did, and by the

This is an ancient Roman graffito mocking the Christians. It says, 'Alexamienos worships his god.' Jesus is given an ass's head.

Edict of Milan in 313 Christianity was legalised. Constantine adopted the **chi-rho** symbol (see p. 36) as his military standard, and he also made Byzantium not Rome the capital, renaming it Constantinople (now called Istanbul).

The old religions still carried on, and were tolerated, but all kinds of incentives were offered to people to become Christians. Christians had their taxes reduced, and did not have to serve on local councils – a task many found tedious. Many people changed religions, but the change was skin deep. By the year 380, the new emperor, Theodosius, made Christianity the official religion of the Empire. While the old gods were still worshipped by some, this was discouraged and technically illegal. His Imperial letter on the subject said this of non-Christian groups: 'The rest, however, we adjudge to be demented and insane.'

In the early days of the Church it was not safe to be a Christian; now, it was only safe if you were a Christian. Something quite ridiculous had happened. The religion that was a personal faith had become enforced on people by the State. (Jews were exempted from this, but were often suspected of being disloyal.)

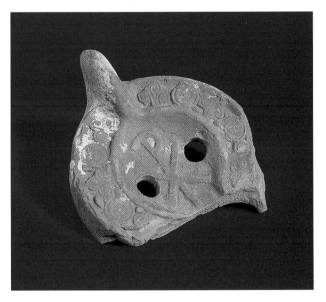

How can you tell that this oil lamp was made by a Christian?

Christendom – Curse or Blessing?

The Church now had freedom, but it was made to serve the State. The emperor saw himself as Christ's deputy on earth, and even called himself 'the visible God'. The design of church buildings in the eastern part of the Empire was altered. The dome of the church represented Heaven, and a stern portrait of Jesus looked down on the worshippers below like a cosmic emperor. His appearance was regal and terrifying. This was a long way from the humble preacher from Nazareth and his message of a loving Father.

The Church structure survived the fall of the Roman Empire in the West in 410, and the Pope, the Bishop of Rome, became more powerful after the last emperor gave up his power in 476 (though there were emperors in the East until 1453). In the Middle Ages he was a political leader and owned large areas of land in Italy, and the kings of the nations of Europe had to serve him as an overlord. This vast political system was known as **Christendom**. It kept the Church going, in a way, but it also manipulated people and forced them to believe.

Activities

Key Elements

1　Why did Christians not want to offer incense before a statue of the emperor?

2　What reply did Polycarp give when he was asked to deny Christ? (Put it into your own words.)

3　Where did Roman Christians hold their secret meetings, and how did they communicate with other suspected believers?

4　Why do you think the person who drew the mocking graffito of Jesus, gave him an ass's head?

5　a)　Which emperor legalised Christianity?

　　b)　Draw a chi-rho sign and beneath it explain briefly his conversion experience.

6　Which emperor made Christianity the state religion of the Roman Empire? What effects did this have on the Church?

The Middle Ages

A mystery play being acted out in Jerusalem. What event is depicted here?

The Church in the Middle Ages affected every aspect of life. There was a lighter side – ordinary people acted out Bible stories each Easter in the **Mystery Plays**. People found help to cope with the hardships of life through prayer and the hope of life after death. But there was a darker side, too. The Church tended to scare people into attending by its stories of Hell. Pictures of the torments of Hell were in many churches; they were like the horror films of the day, but people believed in them: if they were not careful this could be their fate.

Also, many of the bishops were political leaders and were not very spiritual. They cared for money and fine clothes more than for the ordinary people.

There were exceptions of course. St Francis of Assisi, in Italy, lived between 1181–1226. He had wanted to be a knight as a young man, but he felt the call of God. He rebuilt a ruined church at St Damiano in Italy with the help of a few friends, and gave up all his wealth. His little group wore simple robes and worked among the poor. He introduced the Christmas crib, to bring home the meaning of Christmas to the uneducated workers of the time. He received permission from the Pope to found an order of friars (travelling preachers), the Franciscans, in 1210, and he went to Egypt to try to convert the Muslims peacefully in 1219. (The main crusades had been fought by then and there was much ill feeling between Christians and Muslims.)

The monasteries and convents also gave much help to the poor; they provided hospital treatment, taught people to read and write, and gave handouts of food when people were hungry. Monasteries began when some Christians went out alone into the desert in Egypt to pray and study. They gradually grouped together to help one another, and this way of life spread throughout the Christian world. An early rule of life for monks was written by St Benedict in about 540.

A Franciscan friar.

Women did not really play a part in the leadership of society or the Church, but many nuns contributed a great deal and won a measure of independence. They lived in their own communities where they could read or write. Mother Julian of Norwich wrote a classic book – the first known book by a woman in the English language – *The Revelations of Divine Love*. During an illness in 1373 she felt God speaking to her through a series of visions that lasted for over five hours. They were all about the love and mercy of God, and the hope that 'all shall be well, and all shall be well, and all manner of thing shall be well' for everyone, in the end. This was a marked contrast to the usual talk about the punishments of Hell.

Activities

Key Elements

1 What benefits did the ordinary people feel from the Church?
2 The medieval Church had a darker side – explain what this was.
3 How did monasteries and convents begin?
4 How did they help the poor in the Middle Ages?
5 In what way did St Francis and Mother Julian stand out as exceptions in the Church at this time?

The Church Breaks Apart

Roman Catholic from Orthodox

In the fifth and sixth centuries, some Churches in the East separated over their understanding of Jesus. The next major split was in 1054. The Eastern Orthodox Church did not agree that the Pope had total authority over them and he excommunicated its members (declared them to be outside the Church). The patriarchs excommunicated the Pope in return. These excommunications have only been lifted in recent years, and the two Churches are friendly again, though still not united for they disagree on some matters.

The main reason for the split was the understanding of authority. The Orthodox Church was prepared to respect the Pope as a fellow Patriarch. They would even grant that he was like an elder bishop, whose wisdom on matters would be especially welcomed, but they would not accept that he was the sole leader of the Church on earth.

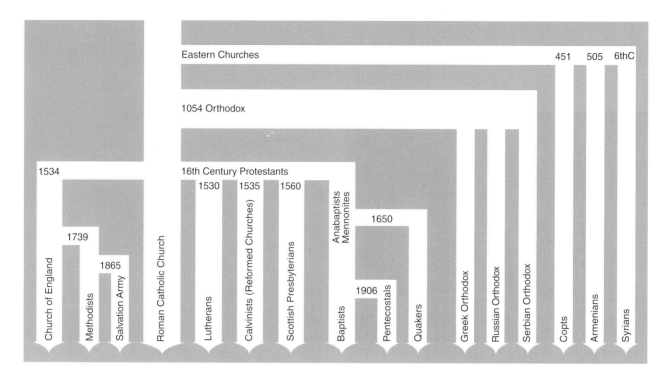

A further disagreement was over a technical understanding of the Holy Spirit. The Western Church had inserted a phrase in the Nicene Creed: **filioque** ('and from the Son'). The Creed says, '... the Holy Spirit, who proceeds from the Father and the Son ...'. They believed that the Spirit came not only from the Father, but from the Son as well. The Eastern Church felt that this made the Spirit inferior and the Son too superior. In their view, the Son and the Spirit were sent from the Father to do his work in the world, like his right hand and left hand. This technical difficulty has still not been resolved between the Churches, though the Western Church is saying that they never intended to make the Son superior. The Spirit came from the Father uniquely, but through the Son. East and West had developed differently in many ways.

The East allowed priests to be married and allowed divorce and remarriage.

Protestant from Roman Catholic

The Western Church was divided about 500 years later. Many of its members felt that

things needed changing, or reforming, for the better, and so the split is known as the Reformation. Many of the Church's leaders were political figures who the reformers thought should be more spiritual, and also many priests were uneducated and careless. They did not take their jobs seriously enough.

Furthermore, pardoners were going round selling relics to people, and assuring them that this would cancel out their sins. They claimed that the relics were holy objects, such as bits of saints' bones. Most of them were forgeries, though. It has been said that there were enough pieces of wood from the 'true cross' to build a galleon, and phials of the 'blood of Christ' were often just the blood of an unlucky farmyard goat. Some people even claimed to have feathers from the wings of the archangel Gabriel!

There was also a tendency for some to teach that a sinner had to go and do various good works to earn forgiveness from Christ. This was the very reversal of the Gospel message (in which God's grace would meet sinners where they were, and forgive them, with good works following on from this).

Martin Luther

Things came to a head when Johann Tetzel, a Dominican pardoner, arrived in Wittenberg in Germany to collect money for the rebuilding of St Peter's in Rome. He sold indulgences to do this. An indulgence was a document signed by the Pope that granted forgiveness for sins and release from Purgatory (the inbetween state between Heaven and Hell). He even had a sales jingle, 'As soon as the coin in the coffer rings, the soul from Purgatory springs'! Poor, uneducated people parted with their money thinking that this would release dead relatives from Purgatory. A monk called Martin Luther was horrified. He was a professor of the Bible at the university and he had been thinking of how the Church needed reforming for some time. He had been plagued by guilt and fear of Hell, and was overzealous in saying prayers and fasting.

Then he rediscovered Paul's teaching about the grace of God that does not have to be earned and he felt a powerful release from guilt by the inner sense of the forgiveness of God. In 1517 he nailed a document to the cathedral door in Wittenberg that contained 95 theses, or points, for discussion. Among them the sale of indulgences was attacked.

This was intended for local discussion among his students, but the printing press had been invented by then, and his ideas were spread all over Europe. Luther was suspected of **heresy** (going against the teaching of the Church) and summoned to see the Holy Roman Emperor, Charles V, at Worms in 1521. He was ordered to renounce his teachings but refused. He was outlawed but was protected by the German princes who wanted to be independent of their emperor. Luther rejected the Pope as Head of the Church, and believed that only the Bible should be given such authority to guide Christians.

Luther had started far more than he realised. Other people spread similar ideas and these people became known as Protestants, 'protesters against the Pope'.

John Calvin was another important Reformer at this time, who wrote many commentaries on the books of the Bible. He settled in Geneva in Switzerland, and the whole town was controlled as a religious state.

The Reformers had pointed out the need for change in the Church, to remove superstition and to rediscover the message of the unconditional love of God that did not have to be earned; but they were intolerant themselves of those who differed from their point of view. Many Roman Catholics agree that their Church did need a reformation, but not the way it happened. They feel that Luther went too far in rejecting the Pope. People were not as ready to listen, though, in those days. The Pope branded Luther as an anti-Christ, and Luther returned the compliment.

> *Activity*
> - Write a paragraph giving arguments for and against the Reformation.

Reform from Within

At the time, there were many Roman Catholics, such as Ignatius Loyola, who were determined to reform their Church from within. He was a soldier who had to rest for a while in 1521 because of a leg wound. All he could find to read were a Bible and some saints' lives. He was converted to a more committed faith, and devised a set of spiritual exercises upon his recovery. These were a series of disciplined meditations on the life of Christ and on his own personal failings. He gathered some followers, and founded the Society of Jesus (the Jesuits) in 1540. Such people led a movement in the Roman Church known as the **Counter Reformation** – to stop the spread of Protestant ideas by improving the Roman Catholic Church from within.

The Inquisition

Many terrible things happened between different groups of Christians at this time. Protestants were tortured and killed by Catholics for having a different faith; Protestants tortured and killed Catholics when they got the chance. The Roman Catholic Church had set up in the thirteenth century the **Inquisition**, which was a special court to judge heresy, but not only heretical actions but also intentions. Officials would arrive in an area and preach against heresy. They would offer a period of grace, when heretics could come forward and freely repent. After this, trial would begin of suspects, and they would be punished.

Two witnesses were required to press charges, and the interviews were held in private. No defence lawyers were allowed, and most people confessed straight away to avoid being tortured and having to spend a long time in prison while their trial was carried out. (Children and old people were given fairly light tortures, and only pregnant women were exempted.) For heresy that was not serious, or committed out of ignorance, there was a light punishment, such as a **penance** of saying so many prayers or fasting for a period. Serious heretics would have to wear special clothes marking them out and

have to pay large fines. They might even lose all their lands. Unrepentant heretics were burned at the stake.

The Inquisition was especially powerful in Spain from the late fifteenth century, where there were large numbers of non-Christians, such as Jews and Muslims, who were suspected of turning people away from the Church by their teachings.

The Protestant Splits

The Protestant movement itself split into various factions. The Baptists wanted the right to baptise adults by full immersion in water, irrespective of whether they had been baptised as infants or not. The Presbyterians and Independents wanted no bishops and preferred locally elected ministers.

John Wesley's Methodists wanted to preach in the open air, and they had lay-preachers who were not properly ordained ministers. The Church of England would not allow this to carry on, and so Wesley's movement had to become a separate Church, much against his wishes.

Much later the Pentecostals wanted freedom to worship in their own way, using the gifts of the Spirit that they believed God had given them.

New Churches are the latest split, when people become unhappy with traditional church life and want to start something new.

The Anglican Church regards itself as Catholic *and* Reformed. It opened itself up to some of the ideas of the Reformers, but it continued many Catholic practices. (Henry VIII removed the Pope's authority from England so he could divorce his first wife.) The Church of England is a mixture of Catholic and Protestant, though some people in it are more Catholic or Protestant than others. The Anglican Church is a 'bridge church', a 'middle way'.

Activities

Key Elements

1. State two reasons why the Orthodox Church and the Roman Catholic Church separated in 1054.
2. State four ways in which the Western Church was corrupt in the Middle Ages.
3. What made Luther nail up the 95 theses?
4. Why did Luther's teachings spread so quickly?
5. Why were the Reformers called Protestants?
6. How did Luther and Calvin show that they could be intolerant of others who did not share their views?

7. Explain what the Counter Reformation was and outline the achievements of Ignatius Loyola.
8. What was the Inquisition, and how did it operate?
9. Why did Christians torture and kill each other?
10. a) Why did the Baptists separate?
    b) Why did the Presbyterians opt out of the Church of England?
    c) Why were the Methodists forced to leave the Church of England?
    d) Why did the Pentecostals have to form their own Church?

The Church Today

Getting Together

The twentieth century has seen the Churches moving closer together after their bitter disputes in the past. They are remembering that they are all followers of the man from Nazareth, and that they worship the same God. The only way to overcome the arguments of the past is to meet together, to talk and to pray. This does not mean that everyone has to agree with everyone else in every way; people can find where they agree and then respect each other's differences.

In 1925, 37 countries sent Church representatives to a meeting in Stockholm; but it was the aftermath of the Second World War that made more people feel the need to come together. The World Council of Churches (WCC) was set up in 1948, with its headquarters in Geneva. It has over 300 member Churches from over 100 different countries. Its theme is 'All one in Christ'. It had six international assemblies by 1991. These have been in Amsterdam, Holland, in 1948; Evanston, USA, in 1954; New Delhi, India, in 1961; Uppsala, Sweden, in 1968; Nairobi, Kenya, in 1975; Vancouver, Canada, in 1983; and Canberra, Australia, in 1991.

The movement to draw all the Churches closer is called the **ecumenical** movement. The word 'ecumenical' comes from the Greek, *oikoumene*, which means, 'one world', or 'sharing one world'.

The symbol of the World Council of Churches. Why does this symbol show a cross in a boat?

Vatican II

The Roman Catholic Church was shaken up in the 1960s. Pope John XXIII was elected as a 'caretaker' Pope, for he was already an old man. People did not expect him to do anything new. But he did! In 1962 he opened the Second Vatican Council where many new ideas could be discussed. (The First Vatican Council was in 1869–70.) John XXIII wanted a breath of fresh air to enter the Church, and he hoped for a 'new Pentecost', a new freshness of Christian-living in the church. He died before the Council closed in 1965, but the effects have been far reaching:

- A willingness to work with other Christian groups.
- Changing the services from Latin to the language of the country concerned.
- Commitment to social action in the world.
- Openness to members of other faiths.

One of the fruits of this change was the visit of Pope John Paul II to Britain in 1982. This would have been unthinkable just a generation before.

Daily Mirror

A LAST SAD BULLETIN:

"The Supreme Pontiff, John XXIII, is dead. The Pope of Goodness expired religiously and serenely at 7.49 p.m."

3d. Tuesday, June 4, 1963   No. 18,492

THE POPE DIES
Peaceful end as 100,000 pray near Vatican

The announcement of Pope John XXIII's death takes up the whole of the front page of an English newspaper.

The Lima Document

The World Council of Churches organised a committee of one hundred theologians in 1982, representing most of the denominations. They worked on a document, compiled at Lima, in Peru, on the subjects of baptism, Eucharist and ministry. A wide measure of agreement was reached in all three areas, and this document has been called an ecumenical milestone. The basic conclusions were:

- There should be a mutual recognition of each other's baptism as baptism into the one body of Christ, no matter which Church carried it out.
- All Churches should celebrate the Eucharist at least on every Sunday, and members of different Churches should be able to hold joint celebrations of it.
- All Christians should have a share in ministry – it should not all be left to the ordained person. Women should have more roles in Christian ministry. There is a need for officials like bishops to oversee the Church, and to link it with the faith of the apostles, even in the Free Churches.

It might be some time before all or most of these suggestions are carried out, but modern Christians are far more open to one another than they have possibly ever been in the past.

The Porvoo Declaration

Anglicans and the Baltic Lutherans entered into a new relationship in the 1990s. These Lutheran Churches are accepted as equal to the Anglicans, and priests and pastors recognise each other's ministries as valid and equal. This followed years of dialogue and joint study. Other Lutheran Churches are carrying on dialogue and working closely with Anglicans.

Activity

- Design a World Council of Churches poster.

Activities

Key Elements

1 What two basic things unite all Christians?

2 a) What is the ecumenical movement?
   b) Does it want all Christians to believe exactly the same thing?

3 a) Why did Pope John call a council in 1962?
   b) What have been the effects of this council in the Roman Catholic Church?

4 a) What three areas of Christianity did the Lima Document discuss?
   b) What three points of agreement were reached?
   c) Which Churches do you think would be most affected by celebrating the Eucharist every Sunday?

5 What did the Porvoo Declaration establish?

Renewal in the Spirit

The twentieth century has seen the rise of the charismatic movement. This wants to see the free and joyful worship of Pentecostal Christians in the mainline Churches. Charismatics stress the work of the Holy Spirit, and say that sharing the Spirit is the real basis of unity. Other differences would then fall into the background.

The charismatic movement has influenced the Anglican and Roman Catholic Churches, and most of the Free Churches to a lesser extent.

Charismatics believe in a personal renewal experience where people become conscious of the Holy Spirit within them. This feels like a deep joy welling up from within, recalling the words of Jesus about the Spirit in John 4:14:

'The water that I will give him will become in him a spring which will provide him with life-giving water and give him eternal life.'

It might also be accompanied by one of the gifts of the Spirit that Paul mentions (see p. 136).

This movement has introduced simple, modern songs into services, as well as the use of instruments like guitars and flutes. It has also stressed the need to feel God's presence

Joyful worship in a charismatic gathering. Why have some people raised their arms?

within, and for more joy in church life so it is not all serious and dull. It has also helped to bring many different Christians together – Catholic and Protestant, Anglican and Methodist – in joint prayer groups in people's houses or in large worship meetings in hired halls or churches.

Some Christians are wary of the movement, though, for a number of reasons:

- Some charismatics treat other Christians as second-class believers because they have not had the renewal experience. This obviously creates ill-feeling in churches.
- There can be a great deal of emotionalism in charismatic worship, which might carry people away with themselves. Crowd emotion can be dangerous.
- Great pressure might be put upon some people to sing out loud, to jump up and down or wave their arms in the air, when that is not their personality. They are quiet and reserved and like to worship in that way.

So not all Christians are happy about the charismatic movement. Yet, despite its extremes and the faults of some of its members, it has made a lasting contribution to

Activities

Key Elements

1 Which Churches have been most affected by the charismatic movement?
2 What do charismatics believe in?
3 a) How has the charismatic movement affected worship in churches?
  b) What have been its effects on Church unity?
4 What problems do other Christians think the movement can cause?

church life in the twentieth century. Charismatic and Pentecostal Churches are the fastest growing Christian movements.

Activity

- Organise a debate: 'The charismatic movement is dangerous and it should stay within the Pentecostal Church.'

Spreading the Word

Christianity is a missionary religion. Jesus told his disciples to go and make disciples of all nations. Christians believe that they have good news to share, and so they send missionaries out. The word literally means 'someone who is sent out'.

The first Christians spread their faith through the Roman Empire. They did this by preaching. The Christian proclamation was, 'Jesus has died for our sins, but God has raised him from the dead. Turn from your sins, be baptised, and you will receive the Holy Spirit.' The Christian message is a challenge to embrace a new way of life.

Irish monks spread the message round the north of Britain, and a party of monks was sent by the Pope to the south of England in Saxon times.

As more and more countries were discovered, more missionaries were sent out to spread the Gospel. Their motives were not always for the best, however. The Roman Catholic Church wanted the riches of the New World that Columbus had discovered, and the natives were often forced to convert on pain of death.

In the British Empire, missionaries helped to spread British culture to conquered lands, teaching the English language, and singing hymns in old English words that sometimes people struggled to understand. The danger also was that Christianity was seen to be on the side of the powerful, and to be a 'white-man's religion'.

David Livingstone

David Livingstone (1813–73) was the most famous and outstanding of the nineteenth-century British missionaries. He studied medicine in Glasgow and London hospitals, and served as a missionary with the London Missionary Society from 1841 to 1856.

A contemporary drawing of Dr Livingstone, the African missionary and explorer.

He was a great explorer, crossing from the west to the east of Africa. He believed that this was God's will, as he was opening up routes through the continent that other missionaries could follow in order to teach and convert the African people. He was also concerned about the slave trade in Africa. The Arabs organised it, and he felt that if their routes were discovered, it could be stopped by the British. He led a British government expedition in 1858 to explore the River Zambezi, but the expedition failed and he returned to Britain. He was soon back, exploring in East Africa until his death.

Livingstone was a man of his time: he believed in the supremacy of British culture and its ability to improve the life of the Africans (at least he felt this for the first part of his missionary career). He also felt that a missionary should not only preach, but should work to relieve suffering as best he or she could. In his case, he helped the sick as a doctor. This was a part of the Gospel message, of caring for one's fellow humans.

Modern missionary movements have been careful to extract Livingstone's positive vision of preaching, and helping people practically, from his belief in a form of white supremacy. While it is true that white rule did improve some social conditions, what it gave with one hand it took with another. It kept the native populations subservient and dependent. Livingstone's views have therefore been criticised as being too 'paternalistic' (i.e. 'fatherly' – well meaning but treating the native people as inferior).

This has led to a twofold stress in modern missionary work:

1 Sending missionaries to help the local community to organise its own church life, and then to appoint its own local leaders. This is called **church planting**. It is so that the local people can run their own worship in their own style.
2 Sending out practical help as well – doctors, nurses, teachers, agricultural specialists and engineers. The engineers and agricultural experts help to train the local people in farming techniques and appropriate new technology, so that they can improve their own lifestyles later on. These methods can help to stop the spread of famine, for example.

There is no more attempt to impose one nation's language and style upon another (by most missions at least), and no attempt to compel people to believe in the Gospel. It is a free choice. Physical aid is not dependent on people becoming Christians first. Modern Christian charities like Christian Aid or CAFOD (The Catholic Fund for Overseas Development) distribute financial aid and send experts to all kinds of people, Christian and non-Christian.

Missionary work is not just about people who travel overseas to spread the Gospel. In this photograph a priest visits someone who is sick and being cared for in a hospice. In what way could this be seen as missionary work?

Christianity and Other Religions

In the past, the Christian attitude to other religions was that they were misguided and perhaps even the work of evil: there might be a glimmer of truth in them, but they were full of nonsense and people should be converted from them. Many Christians felt that a person could only be saved if they became a Christian, and this was one of the motives behind all the energy put into missionary work in the last few centuries.

This was because the scriptures of the other faiths were not known in the West; they had not been translated. Also, when explorers saw strange and different rituals, they often misunderstood them. But since the last century, many more people in the West have become familiar with the holy books of other faiths and their rituals and beliefs have been carefully studied. Many Christians now feel that there is much that is good and true in other faiths, that they are worshipping and seeking the same God in different ways. People are much more aware of the need for tolerance now, and to 'live and let live'.

Some Christians are against any missionary work that is concerned with preaching the Gospel because they feel that all religions are ways to God. Most, however, feel that Jesus was unique and that he shows most clearly what God was like, and they want to share these insights with people of other faiths. They have a right to preach the Gospel, they believe, just as other faiths have a right to preach their beliefs.

In this new climate, people are converted and join the Church, but what also happens is that the influence of Jesus' teaching sometimes makes changes in a society, or reminds people of forgotten parts of their own faith that are about love of neighbour. The presence of Christian missionaries might make people better Hindus or better Muslims. The great Indian leader, Gandhi, read the Gospels, and, although he remained a convinced Hindu, the teaching of Jesus greatly influenced his endeavours to bring different groups in India together in peace.

Evangelism

Preaching the Word ('evangelism') is still the main way of trying to spread the Gospel. Some Churches send out **evangelists** (preachers) to hold large meetings. The most famous of these is the American, Billy Graham, who has pulled huge crowds in the States since the 1950s, and has paid several visits to Britain.

Billy Graham preaching. In America today, evangelists often use television to put their message across. What would be your reaction if evangelists were allowed to do this in Britain?

Samaritan. Here, a man is beaten up and left on a train. A social worker and a vicar decide they are too busy to get involved, and it is a Punk who pulls the communication cord and brings help.

Some American Evangelists use mass advertising and media tactics to pull in the crowds. They video their rallies and televise services for the satellite and cable TV networks. Some of these preachers are criticised for being too emotional, and for making impassioned appeals for money. They often claim that their meetings are full of miracles, but these 'miracles' are not always genuine and often cannot be checked. The controversial preacher, Morris Cerullo, ran a series of 'Mission to London' meetings in the 1990s at Earls Court before the Evangelical Alliance, a Free Church organisation, barred him from their membership over his extravagant claims and appeals for money.

After a few songs have been sung, he will preach the Gospel to the crowds, and then challenge them to make a decision. If they want to commit their lives to Christ, then they step out to the front of the hall or arena. There, someone will talk to them and pray for them, and give them a Gospel and some booklets to read.

Preachers like Graham are very popular, and many people do join the Church as a result of his tours, but some are wary of his style. It is easy for emotions to run high in a crowd, and some making decisions for Christ might do so on the spur of the moment and change their minds later.

Other forms of evangelism are more local. A church might hold a mission, putting on special services and events to invite people in. Youth clubs and coffee bars will be run to interest young people. One popular way of evangelism today is street theatre. A short parable of Jesus will be acted out in modern style, or a symbolic story might be made up. These will be quick and entertaining, like those performed by the Riding Lights Theatre Group based in York. One of their popular items is the 'Parable of the Good Punk Rocker', which retells the parable of the Good

Alpha

The Alpha course is a far cry from the big business of the TV evangelists and mass rallies. This started at the Anglican parish of Holy Trinity, Brompton, in London in the early 1990s. It was the work of the curate, Nicky Gumbel. The idea is to run an introductory course to Christian belief over about ten weeks, meeting for a meal, in a relaxed atmosphere. There is an 'away day' or weekend, where people experience the laying on of hands and prayer for the coming of the Holy Spirit. The course became immensely popular in the late 1990s, with many denominations running it, including the Roman Catholic Church. The books and video material that are used for its teaching are slick, easy to follow and intelligent. Newcomers are encouraged to ask questions and to discuss doubts, forming friendships in their Alpha groups.

Similar courses have been produced, which some church groups prefer to use, as these are less evangelical in their style. These encourage small groups meeting in relaxed surroundings, and try to explore people's own feelings and questions. Courses such as 'Emmaus' and 'Credo' have proved popular.

Activities

- Do some more research on David Livingstone and write an essay on him: (i) give an outline of his career; (ii) explain why he thought it important to explore different parts of Africa and (iii) describe the ways in which he tried to work for social justice as well as preaching. (iv) Conclude with what you think his achievements were and what you think he could be criticised for.
- Organise a debate: 'It is always wrong to try to convert people who belong to another faith.'
- Write your own updated Gospel parable on the lines of the 'Good Punk Rocker'.

Activities

Key Elements

1 What is a missionary?
2 What is the basic message of the Church?
3 What problems have been caused by missions in the past?
4 What is meant by 'church planting'? How does it try to overcome past problems?

Think About It

5 How do Christians react to different faiths today? Do you think the world faiths are all seeking the same God though in different ways? Have a class discussion.

Liberation

Jesus of Nazareth was a humble preacher of love – of God and of humanity. He told his followers that they were not to lord it over people and boss them around:

'You know that the men who are considered rulers of the heathen have power over them, and the leaders have complete authority. This, however, is not the way it is among you. If one of you wants to be great, he must be the servant of the rest; and if one of you wants to be first, he must be the slave of all.'
(Mark 10:42–4)

Jesus stood up and proclaimed this passage from the Old Testament in the synagogue in Nazareth:

'The Spirit of the Lord is upon me,
because he has chosen me to bring good news
*   to the poor.*

*He has sent me to proclaim liberty to the captives
and recovery of sight to the blind;
to set free the oppressed
and announce that the time has come
when the Lord will save his people.'*

(Luke 4:18–19)

All of this seems a far cry from the Church of Christendom with its powerful, rich prince–bishops, and its attempts to force people into believing. It seems a far cry from a Church that sides with the government of the day and does not think anything should be done to change the conditions of the poor except for giving them handouts.

A new movement has begun in the world-wide Church this century, called **Liberation Theology**. It seeks to apply the Gospel message to the society that people live in, and liberationists believe not only in the power of Christ to change people within, but also in his power to challenge unjust structures and systems in society.

The movement began in Third World countries because of the poverty of many of its people. This poverty is not a result of their idleness, but of government and international corruption. Loans are made to the poor countries so long as they will produce certain crops for export, and that often means that there is not enough farmland left to produce sufficient food for the people. Many of the rich landowners pay very low wages to their workers, too. Many Christians in these countries are campaigning for social change, and they do not think that the Gospel is just about personal salvation, i.e. about where you go when you die. Jesus is seen as their brother, as a man sharing their oppression and struggling with them for change.

The Pentecostal Church has grown from strength to strength in these areas, with four million members in Brazil, and one person in every seven being a Pentecostal in Chile, for example. Their simple and joyful worship, where everyone can take part, appeals to the poor.

The most active political groups, however, are in the Roman Catholic Church. The Church has thousands of base communities all over South America. A **base community** (also known as a 'grass-roots community') means a friendly gathering of Christians, with or without a priest, in someone's home, or in a local hall. They pray, worship, study the Bible together, and work out how to help each other practically. They also organise protests against their local councils and the government.

A base Christian community in Panama. What help do you think poor people find from this sort of meeting?

Activity

- Hold a classroom debate: 'Christian leaders should stick to morals and keep out of politics.'

What does Dom Camara think the Church should be doing? Why do some people find this threatening?

Some liberationists mix their Christianity with Marxism, thinking this will help them to change society. Some are also prepared to use violence, and become guerrilla fighters. These groups will pray and study, and then take up their rifles.

Many, however, are non-violent, and a champion of this type of liberation is Helder Camara, the Roman Catholic Archbishop of Olinda and Recife in Brazil. This is the poorest region of Brazil, and Camara's views changed when he went to work there. He used to side with the rich and with the government, but now he speaks out for the poor. He has been involved in various types of non-violent protest. He denies that he is a Marxist and speaks out against violence. He feels, though, that the violence of the revolutionaries can be justified more than that of the rich against the poor. He has criticised both the USA and the USSR for being too 'enclosed and imprisoned in their egoism', meaning that they put themselves first.

Liberation theologians want to see a Church that is:

- A more loving community, with no differences between rich and poor members.
- Less authoritarian, with the people helping to make decisions along with the priests and bishops, and taking part in services.
- Committed to social action as well as preaching about personal conversion.

Question

a) Put into your own words what Jesus said about power and how his followers should behave in Mark 10:42–4.

b) How has the Church departed from that teaching?

Britain

Liberation Theology has had its impact on Churches in the developed countries as well. In Britain the Church of England published a report in 1986 on conditions in the inner cities – *Faith in the City* – which recommended many changes both in the Church and in society, often criticising government policies on issues like unemployment.

A former Anglican Bishop of Liverpool, David Sheppard, wrote an influential book in the 1980s, *Bias to the Poor*, which urged Christians to be involved in social change. This book came from his experiences in an area of Britain where there has been high unemployment for some time.

Some church groups set up special centres in needy areas. Halls and shops give cheap or free food, offer second hand children's clothes and offer advice. Others run shelters for the homeless. The Methodist Church in Sheffield bought up terraced houses and shops, selling cheap clothes, Third World products, and holding worship meetings in the rooms upstairs. This brought the Church to the local community in a very relaxed manner.

Activities

Think About It

1 Referring to what Jesus proclaimed in Luke 4:18–19, is the Gospel only about getting to heaven?

2 How is Liberation Theology affecting Christians in Britain?

Assignments

1 Does the Church of England see itself as Protestant or Catholic? Try to find Anglican clergy who have different views on this, and record their answers.

2 Do a project on the World Council of Churches, giving an account of its work and aims.

3 Write to a relief organisation and find out what their missionary workers are doing: such as Christian Aid (PO Box 100, London SE1 7RT), CAFOD (2 Romero Close, Stockwell Road, London SW9 9TY) and TEAR Fund (11 Station Road, Teddington, Middlesex TW11 9AA).

4 Do a project on the work of one missionary, or group of missionaries (such as the Jesuits in South America), in the past or today, and make a classroom display.

5 Imagine you are part of a base community. Write a journal for a typical week, showing what activities go on.

6 Do some research on one country in the third world, such as Brazil, where Liberation Theology is in action. What has caused the poverty and oppression in this country and what are Christians trying to do about it?

Word List

absolution pronouncement by a priest of forgiveness of sins

Advent 'coming'; four weeks before Christmas observed by Christians as a time of preparation

agape A Greek word for 'love' in the New Testament; a strong love that is prepared to suffer for someone else; also a term used for the common meal of Christians

alb a long, white robe worn by Christian priests at the Eucharist. It symbolises purity.

altar a table made of wood or stone where the bread and wine is prayed over and offered to God as the body and blood of Christ in churches; also called Lord's Table

Anglican Churches in full communion with the see of Canterbury, such as the Church of England

Annunciation the time when the angel announced to Mary that she would give birth to the Messiah, even though she was still a virgin; celebrated on 25 March (Lady Day)

apocalyptic 'revelation'; a style of literature that described the end of the world and the coming of the Kingdom of God, which used vivid symbols and earth-shaking metaphors

Apocrypha 'hidden'; non-canonical books of the Old Testament

apostle one of the 12 disciples of Jesus who were sent out to preach the Gospel after the resurrection. The word means 'to be sent out', 'a missionary'.

apostolic following the teachings of the apostles

Apostolic Tradition the teachings and practices of the apostles, which were handed down in the early churches

Ascension the last appearance of Jesus as he 'ascended into heaven'; celebrated on the fortieth day after Easter (Ascension Day)

Ash Wednesday the first day of Lent

atonement reconciliation between God and human beings, restoring a relationship broken by sin

baptism sprinkling with, or immersing in, water in the name of the Father, the Son and the Holy Spirit. The sign of entry into the Church.

baptistry a building or a specially built pool in churches that have believers' baptism rather than infant baptism

base communities a grass-roots movement in Latin America of ordinary people, priests, monks and nuns. They meet for study and worship and plan social action. Also known as grass-roots communities.

Beatitude one of the nine sayings of Jesus in Matthew 5:1–12, which begin, 'Happy are . . .'

Bible the holy book of Christians; it comes from a Greek word, *biblia*, meaning 'books'

bishop an overseer of churches in an area called a diocese. Bishops claim to have succeeded other bishops, going back to the apostles themselves.

Breaking of the Bread a name for Holy Communion

canon a Greek word meaning 'measure', 'measuring rod'; it came to mean the rules of a trade or a list. In Christianity it means the list of books in the Bible regarded as genuine.

canonisation the process of making someone a saint in the Roman Catholic and Orthodox Churches – to enter into the 'list' of saints

cantor a trained singer in the Orthodox Church who sings part of the service

cardinal a senior member of the Roman Catholic Church (usually a bishop) who advises the Pope and can vote in the election of a new pope

cathedral the main church in a town where the bishop resides

catholic 'universal'; *see* Roman Catholic

chalice a special cup that contains the wine at Holy Communion

chapel a small church, usually built into a large building, such as a school or college; or a place for private worship in a church. Some small Free churches are called chapels, too.

charismatic a modern movement within the Church, emphasising spiritual gifts, such as healing or speaking with tongues

chasuble a colourful robe with decorations that the priest wears during the Eucharist

chi-rho the first two letters of Christ in Greek, used as a symbol for Christ

Christ a Greek word meaning 'Anointed One' or 'Chosen One', God's deliverer. *Messiah* is the Hebrew translation.

Christendom the countries with Christianity as their official religion. In the late Roman Empire and the Middle Ages it referred to the area controlled by the Pope along with the emperor or kings.

Christmas the festival that celebrates the birth of Christ

Church *a* Church is a denomination (e.g. the Roman Catholic Church); *the* Church is the whole, worldwide Christian community – the 'Body of Christ'

church a group of Christians and/or the building where they meet for worship

church planting the process of sending a foreign missionary out to help local people to set up their own church and to use their local talent

circuit a district that a Methodist minister or lay preacher operates in

confession confessing sins to a priest and asking him for forgiveness in Christ's name

confirmation the ceremony where a bishop lays his hands upon a candidate's head and asks that he or she is blessed with the gift of the Holy Spirit. This is an opportunity to confess the Christian faith for those baptised as infants.

consecration the act of making something holy; especially the act of praying over the bread and wine so that it becomes the body and blood of Christ during the Holy Communion service

consubstantiation the belief that Christ is spiritually present in the bread and wine, but no change occurs within them

contemplation a silent form of prayer or meditation; repeating phrases slowly to oneself, or pondering upon a passage of scripture, or just sitting quietly trying to feel the presence of God

contrition a form of interior repentance of being sorry for sinning

Counter Reformation the revival of the Roman Catholic Church in Europe in the sixteenth and seventeenth centuries, which was stimulated by the Protestant Reformation. The Jesuits were at the forefront of the revival.

creed a statement of religious beliefs, often recited in worship; the best known ones in Christianity are the Nicene Creed, the Apostles' Creed and the Athanasian Creed

crown of thorns the crown made from thorn branches by a Roman guard and placed on Jesus' head after his arrest. He was mocked by his guards as 'the King of the Jews'.

crucifix a cross with a figure of the crucified Jesus upon it

deacon/deaconess deacons are assistants to priests, helping with pastoral work and during the services. They cannot hear confessions or celebrate the Eucharist. In the Church of England all male deacons become priests after a year; the first female deacons were ordained in 1987 but they cannot become priests. In the Roman Catholic and Orthodox Churches men can remain deacons all their lives. The Anglican Church ordains women as deacons.

dedication prayer of thanksgiving said for the birth of a child if the parents do not believe in infant baptism

denomination 'name'; a group of churches that follow a particular body of teaching, have certain leaders and certain styles of worship

disciple a person who follows and learns from someone else, especially the followers of Jesus, and in particular the 12 apostles

Easter the central Christian festival in memory of the resurrection of Jesus from the dead

ecumenism a movement to bring all the different Churches together; *ecumenical* means 'worldwide'

elder in the early Church, elders were the priests (*presbyters* in the Greek). Some Free Churches have elders as well as a minister; they are senior members of the church who help to run it.

Epiphany a festival held on 6 January that, in the Western Churches, commemorates the showing of Jesus to the Magi. In the Eastern Churches it chiefly commemorates the baptism of Jesus. The word means 'manifestation'.

epistle a letter written by one of the apostles or their disciples in the New Testament

eschatology teaching of the last things – the end of the world, the return of Christ, the Last Judgement and the afterlife

Essenes a sect at the time of Jesus waiting for the Kingdom of God. Some of them withdrew from society and lived in their own communities.

Eucharist 'thanksgiving'; the thanksgiving meal of the Christian Church, using bread and wine as the body and blood of Christ; also known as the Breaking of the Bread, Holy Communion, the Lord's Supper and Mass

evangelist a writer of a Gospel; also a preacher of the Gospel

excommunication forbidding someone from receiving the sacraments of the Church

faith an inward attitude of trust, hope and belief

Fall, the the sinful condition of humanity; human imperfection and inclination to do wrong. 'The Fall' refers to the story of Adam and Eve as the first humans who committed the first sin.

filioque a Latin word that means 'and from the Son'. This was added to the Nicene Creed in the West and was one of the reasons for the Eastern (Orthodox) Churches to separate from the Western Church in Rome.

font the container in a church for holy water which is used for baptism of infants

Free Churches non-conformist denominations which are free from state control

genuflection going down on the right knee as one enters a church, to show respect for God in the reserved sacrament at the altar

Good Friday the day when the death of Jesus is remembered

Gospels the four books in the New Testament – Matthew, Mark, Luke and John – which tell the story of Jesus; it comes from an old English word for 'good news'. The *Synoptic Gospels* refer to the first three Gospels.

grace love in action freely giving of itself to serve and to save

heresy an opinion contrary to the accepted doctrine of the Christian Church

Holy Communion the central liturgical act of the Church – the service where bread and wine are consecrated following Jesus at the Last Supper

Holy Spirit the third person of the Trinity, active as divine energy in Church and world

Holy Week the week before Easter, when Christians recall the last week of Jesus' life on earth

host the individual wafers or pieces of bread used in the Eucharist

icon a special painting of Jesus or a saint which is an aid to worship and devotion, mainly for Orthodox Christians; the word means 'image'

iconostasis the decorated screen in front of the altar in an Orthodox church – it separates the sanctuary from the nave

Incarnation 'in a body'; the Christian belief that God became man in Jesus

Inquisition the persecution of heresy by special church courts in the Roman Catholic

Church. It began in the thirteenth century. The Spanish Inquisition was established in 1479 and ended in 1820.

justification by faith a Protestant doctrine of God's gift to individual Christians of unmerited forgiveness

Kingdom of God the central theme of the New Testament. Jesus spoke of it as both a future event on earth and as actually present but hidden.

lay/laity a term used to denote the people in a religious tradition by contrast with official leaders in that community

lectern the stand where the Bible rests in a church, often in the shape of an eagle

Lent the season of forty days before Easter when Christians take stock of their lives; it commemorates the time Jesus spent in the desert

Liberation Theology a movement which began this century in Third World countries but which has spread worldwide. It seeks to apply the Gospel message to the society that people live in.

Liturgy divine service according to a prescribed ritual, such as Evensong or Eucharist

Lord's Prayer the 'Our Father' – the prayer that Jesus taught his disciples when they asked him how they should pray

Lord's Supper term used by St Paul when referring to the Eucharist

Lord's Table a table for the bread and wine, usually covered with a white cloth

Mass the Roman Catholic name for the Eucharist

Maundy Thursday the Thursday before Easter; named after Jesus' 'command' (Latin *mandatum*) that the disciples should love one another. The service on this day remembers the time when Jesus washed the feet of his disciples.

meditation thinking about something deeply, often in the light of an ultimate reference point and thus 'prayerful reflection'

Messiah *see* Christ

minister the person in charge of a Free Church. He or she will not call themselves priests because they do not believe that they are any different from other members of the congregation, except for their training and calling to serve the church.

missal a book containing words and ceremonial directions for saying Mass in the Roman Catholic Church

moderator one of the 12 overseers of the United Reformed Church

Mystery Plays also known as Miracle Plays. Religious dramas of the Middle Ages that were usually performed out of doors. The most important were the Passion Plays.

myth a short story form representing one or more basic insights into life, death and the universe. Not just a fictitious tale.

non-conformist Protestant denominations rejecting the doctrine and discipline of the Church of England

ordination the ceremony in which a bishop or church elder lays their hands upon a person who has offered himself or herself for service. In the Free Churches you can be ordained as a minister. In the Roman Catholic, Anglican and Orthodox Churches you can be ordained as a bishop, priest or deacon.

Orthodox Eastern Churches, comprising five major patriarchates.

Palm Sunday the Sunday before Holy Week when the entry of Jesus into Jerusalem is remembered

parable a story with a moral

Paraclete a Greek word meaning 'Helper' or 'Comforter'. It refers to the Holy Spirit.

parish in England, an area under the care of a church minister or priest

Parousia a Greek word meaning the return or presence of Christ – the Second Coming

Paschal Candle a special candle which is lit at the Vigil Service on the night before Easter

Passion, the the term used for Jesus' suffering during his last days, especially for the Crucifixion

pastor from an old English word meaning

'shepherd', hence 'one who looks after a flock'. Some Free Church ministers are called pastors.

paten   a small, silver plate that the hosts are placed on during the Eucharist

patriarch   'great father'; title of the leaders of the Orthodox Church

penance   doing something to show sorrow for sin, whether saying a set of prayers or doing a good deed; one of the seven traditional sacraments

penitence   being sorry for sin

Pentecost   also known as Whitsun. The day when early Christians received the gift of the Holy Spirit. It comes 50 days after Easter.

Pharisee   a member of a Jewish sect at the time of Jesus. They believed in following the Law strictly and in the resurrection of the dead.

pilgrimage   a journey to a holy place from a motive of devotion

Pope   'father'; the title given to the Bishop of Rome, though all bishops used to be called this as the spiritual fathers of their churches. Roman Catholics believe that the Pope is the successor of St Peter and the rightful leader of the whole Christian Church.

presbyter   a Greek word meaning 'elder'. All priests used to be called this in the early Church.

priest   an ordained minister in the Roman Catholic, Anglican, or one of the Eastern Churches. These ministers feel that they are called to specially represent Christ to their churches, offering Jesus' sacrifice in the Eucharist.

prophet   a person believed to speak the words of God

Protestant   a major division of the Church protesting against Roman Catholic belief and practice, as distinct from Orthodox and Roman Catholic Churches

psalm   a poem or hymn in the Old Testament

pulpit   an elevated stand from where the priest or minister stands to give the sermon

Purgatory   in the Roman Catholic Church, a state between Heaven and Hell where people are prepared for final glory

real presence   the belief that Christ is spiritually present in the bread and wine

redeem   to save or set free

redeemer   a saviour or liberator; for Christians, Christ is the Redeemer

redemption   reconciliation (by purchase and liberation) of slaves to their masters – and so, metaphorically, of salvation through the death of Jesus

Reformation   a sixteenth-century reform movement which led to the formation of the Protestant Churches

Resurrection   the rising from the dead of Jesus on the third day after the crucifixion; also the rising from the dead of believers at the Last Day

rites of passage   ceremonies associated with major moments of transition in the life cycle: birth, puberty, mating, death

ritual   physical gestures and/or body language and/or actions using objects that carry deep meanings

Roman Catholic   a major division of the Church owing loyalty to Rome, as distinct from Orthodox and Protestant Churches

rosary   a set of prayers honouring the Virgin Mary, using a string of five decades of beads. There is a special meditation on a part of the life of Christ in each decade.

sacrament   an action that is believed to channel the blessing and presence of God. The outward action has an inner, invisible meaning. In the Catholic and Orthodox Churches there are seven: baptism, confirmation, the Eucharist, penance, extreme unction, ordination and marriage.

sacrifice   something of value offered up to God

Sadducee   a member of a Jewish sect at the time of Jesus. They held political power over the Temple in Jerusalem and were very conservative. They rejected belief in resurrection.

saint   a 'holy one'. In one sense all Christians are saints since they are called to follow Jesus, but the term is usually given to outstanding people whom the Church declares are in Heaven. The *communion of saints* is the spiritual union between every Christian whether in Heaven, Purgatory or on earth.

salvation the healing of a broken relationship between people and God, which brings new life and peace

sanctification the process of being made holy

sanctifier the one who makes holy, the Holy Spirit

scripture revered texts formally recognised by a faith community as the authoritative basis of its faith, often their origins are claimed to have a special illumination from God to humans. In Christianity – the Old and New Testaments. (References in the New Testament to 'scripture' mean the Old Testament.)

sermon the message preached during a service by the priest or minister

Shrove Tuesday the day immediately before Ash Wednesday and thus the day before the start of Lent, named after the 'shriving' (confession) of the faithful on that day. It is also known as 'Pancake Tuesday' because various leftover foods were eaten before the start of fasting at Lent.

sin going against what a person feels to be right, and against what he or she feels is God's will; a break in the relationship between people and God. The Greek word usually translated in the New Testament as 'sin' is *hamartia*, which means 'to miss the mark'.

Stations of the Cross a series of 14 images or pictures in a Roman Catholic church, representing events in 'Jesus' Passion and resurrection, before which people will pray

stole a scarf worn by a priest over the alb at the Eucharist

supplication praying for help

surplice a loose, white tunic that is worn over a cassock usually by clergy and choristers in an Anglican service

symbol that which represents or stands for something more than its immediate form

testament a special agreement. In the Bible a promise between God and humanity; in the Old Testament to the Jews, in the New Testament to all humanity. Also called a *covenant*.

transignification a modern Roman Catholic way of explaining how the bread and wine become the body and blood of Christ. The bread and wine are seen to change their significance, or inner meaning for the worshippers.

transubstantiation the traditional Roman Catholic belief that the inner substance of the bread and wine becomes the body and blood of Christ, while it is still bread and wine on the surface

Trinity the threefoldness of God as Father, Son and Holy Spirit. Three ways of being God.

vicar another name for a parish priest in the Church of England

vigil a service of prayer in preparation or expectation of a greater service the following day

worship valuing truth, beauty and goodness in life; honouring God as Lord and Creator – being thankful for the gift of life

Zealots Jews at the time of Jesus who were committed to violent revolution against the Romans

Index

Numbers in italics refer to illustrations